Boom Kids

Studies in
Childhood and Family
in Canada

A broad-ranging series that publishes scholarship from
various disciplines, approaches and perspectives relevant to the
concepts and relations of childhood and family in Canada. Our
interests also include, but are not limited to, interdisciplinary
approaches and theoretical investigations of gender, race, sexuality,
geography, language, and culture within these categories
of experience, historical and contemporary.

We welcome proposals and manuscripts from Canadian authors.
For further information, please contact the Series Editor:

Professor Cynthia Comacchio
History Department
Wilfrid Laurier University
75 University Avenue West
Waterloo, ON N2L 3C5, Canada
Phone: (519) 884–0710 ext. 3422
Email: ccomacchio@wlu.ca

Boom Kids

Growing Up in the
Calgary Suburbs, 1950-1970

◇◇

JAMES A. ONUSKO

WILFRID LAURIER
UNIVERSITY PRESS

LAURIER
Inspiring Lives.

This book has been published with the help of a grant from the Canadian Federation for the Humanities and Social Sciences, through the Awards to Scholarly Publications Program, using funds provided by the Social Sciences and Humanities Research Council of Canada. Wilfrid Laurier University Press acknowledges the support of the Canada Council for the Arts for our publishing program. We acknowledge the financial support of the Government of Canada. Funding provided by the Government of Ontario and the Ontario Arts Council. This work was supported by the Research Support Fund.

Library and Archives Canada Cataloguing in Publication

Title: Boom kids : growing up in the Calgary suburbs, 1950-1970 / James A. Onusko.

Names: Onusko, James A., 1972- author.

Series: Studies in childhood and family in Canada.

Description: Series statement: Studies in childhood and family in Canada | Includes bibliographical references and index.

Identifiers: Canadiana (print) 20200414801 | Canadiana (ebook) 20200414828 | ISBN 9781771124980

(hardcover) | ISBN 9781771125000 (EPUB) | ISBN 9781771125017 (PDF)

Subjects: LCSH: Suburban life—Alberta—Calgary—History—20th century. | LCSH: Baby boom generation—

Alberta—Calgary—History—20th century. | LCSH: Calgary (Alta.)—Social life and customs—20th century.

Classification: LCC HT352.C32 C35 2021 | DDC 307.76097123/38—dc23

Cover design by Lara Minja.
Text design by Janette Thompson (Jansom).

© 2021 Wilfrid Laurier University Press
Waterloo, Ontario, Canada
www.wlupress.wlu.ca

This book is printed on FSC ® certified paper. It contains recycled materials and other controlled sources, is processed chlorine free, and is manufactured using biogas energy.

Printed in Canada

TABLE OF CONTENTS

ACKNOWLEDGEMENTS

I owe a debt of gratitude to Trent University and in particular the Frost Centre for Canadian Studies and Indigenous Studies, which provided me crucial, ongoing financial and intellectual support. Joan Sangster served as mentor and confidante; she provided more support than anyone could ask. We do not agree on everything; however, she has always encouraged me to experiment and be creative intellectually. Her inherent goodness, scholarship, and activism serve as inspiration, and her encouragement, advice, and feedback on this book proved invaluable.

Many students, faculty, and administrative staff provided support in my time at Trent. Meaghan Beaton, Winnie Janzen, and Jim Struthers were there from the beginning. They made a challenging transition to a new institution, city, and province so much easier with their advice, kindness, and willingness to listen. Dimitry Anastakis, Chris Dummitt, Bryan Palmer, and Keith Walden provided priceless insights into doing good scholarly work. Julia Harrison was a first-rate Frost Centre director—her enthusiasm was infectious. Jeannine Crowe and Cathy Schoel were exceptional sounding boards and always supportive. Kristi Alain, Jodi Aoki, Sean Carleton, Caitlin Gordon-Walker, Adam Guzkowski, Matt Hayes, John Marris, Ted McCoy, Sarah McDougall, Casey Ready, Pamela Rickey, Julia Smith, Amy Twomey, and others were all associated with the Trent Canadian Studies program during my PhD studies—I count them all as friends and colleagues. A new group of colleagues at Northern Lakes College in Alberta also supported the final steps to publication.

The staff at the Glenbow Archives in Calgary treated me like family as I conducted my primary research. Doug Cass must be singled out for his generosity, wisdom, and support. His voice is included as an interviewee in this book. Other oral history participants were vital in making this book what it is. You remain ever youthful to me. Other staff members at several archival sites and schools in Calgary and Ottawa were instrumental in locating primary sources.

Keith Walden, Dominique Marshall, and Margaret Steffler provided much-needed support. Their critical engagement with early research and writing was outstanding. Cynthia Comacchio went above and beyond on so many counts. She has provided guidance and become a dear friend. As the series editor for Studies in Childhood and Family in Canada for

Wilfrid Laurier University Press, she shepherded me through the peaks and valleys of publishing. I would not have completed this book without her guidance. The anonymous readers of the manuscript were invaluable resources and offered important recommendations in shaping this study. Siobhan McMenemy, senior editor at the press, believed in this project— her no-nonsense approach coupled with understanding and kindness was much appreciated.

My extended family and friends outside of academe have been life-lines. I now have lifelong friends in both Alberta and Ontario. I'm not sure that everyone agreed with, or completely understood, what I was doing as I pursued the research and writing of this book, but they never discouraged me from any of it. My sister and her family have been supportive and encouraging. My mother-in-law, father-in-law, and sister-in-law aided greatly in making my research trips to Calgary successful. Their support was integral in allowing me to have productive and worry-free research trips. Special thanks must be extended to Kevin and Jackie Bates for their hospitality, friendship and openness on several research trips to Calgary.

My father passed away in 2006, but he did see me start out on a path toward a master of arts degree from Athabasca University. He was most pleased by this, and I know he hoped my academic journey would end, as I wanted it to, with a PhD, teaching, and publishing in the years ahead. He nurtured in me the twin gifts of curiosity and a thirst for knowledge. He remains with me every day. My mother instilled in me a sense of justice and loyalty. Her support has been of a type that mothers so often provide— unconditional and filled with love.

Finally, and most importantly, none of this would have been possible without TT, Belle, and my wife and partner, Lesli Michaelis-Onusko. My children inspire me every day. Experiencing their childhood has made me a better scholar, father, and husband. Lesli encouraged me to return to my formal studies after a ten-year absence. I am not sure where I would be without her. I do know that I would not have completed and published *Boom Kids*. Because of her, I know what true love means. I love all three of you with all of my heart. You make me want to do better each and every day. This book is dedicated to all three of you.

Introduction

Boom Kids explores the exhilarations, tragedies, and challenges associated with childhood and adolescent experiences in Calgary's postwar suburbs. For many of us, there remains a belief that it has never been as good for young people and their families in Canada as it was in the 1950s and 1960s. The baby boomer generation and postwar suburbia remain a touchstone. The boomers, as they are known colloquially, are important because their impact on postwar Canadian life is unchallenged; social, cultural, and political changes were made to meet their needs and desires. Although they have aged, and time has passed, this era stands still in time in many ways—viewed as an idyllic period when great hopes and relative prosperity went hand in hand for people of all ages. Many postwar Canadians were proud of the country and its achievements. A 1959 Gallup Poll asked more than six hundred Canadians to assess what country had achieved the most in the world from 1950 to 1959. Canada easily earned the largest proportion of responses at 41 percent. Russia and the United States followed at 28.4 percent and 9.1 percent, respectively.[1]

The boomers are linked to the postwar suburbs and their associated lifestyle, which continue to capture our collective imagination. The era was a family-centric one. Divorce remained relatively uncommon until the late 1960s. Marriage was almost universally praised and upheld as one of, if not the most important, institutions in the nation. Some of our most lasting representations of "traditional" families and suburban childhoods derive from postwar television sitcoms, which viewers continue to consume in endless reruns.[2] Yet these oversimplifications do not capture the nuances and subtleties of these times. Suburbia was "sold" as a space about, and for, families. As both a place and a lifestyle, suburbia has held out promise, hope, and possibility for generations of Canadians, as families settled and built their homes and lives.

The baby boomers have had a lasting influence on society, in part because of their sheer numbers, their association with social activism and 1960s popular culture, and their continuing leadership role today. More than eight million babies were born in Canada between 1946 and 1964 (the baby boom years) and more than one million children arrived as immigrants. These young people experienced the arrival of a dizzying array of new consumer products and impactful innovations—some of which were lauded while others became the objects of scorn and ridicule. By the late 1960s, these new products included ballpoint pens, fast food, TV dinners, shopping malls, freeways, home air conditioning, credit cards, tape recorders, garbage disposals, dishwashers, and portable record players.[3]

Social, political, and cultural change also marked the period. The expansion of the welfare state; the large increase in enrolment in, and access to, postsecondary education; the intensification of consumer and popular culture and their centrality in young people's consciousness; the heightened focus on sex, gender, and sexuality for youth and society; and increasing numbers of women working outside the home meant change in Canada. The rapid development and growing appeal of suburbia was another defining trend. Yet that appeal has never been universal nor was it without controversy.

The suburbs are polarizing spaces. Observers hold varied views on how they look, what they mean, what they symbolize, what lifestyle their denizens assume, and what effect they have on everyday lives. The earliest popular and scholarly literature that focused on Canadian, American, and British postwar suburbs tended to portray them as middle-class, dull, homogeneous, conformist, conservative, and alienating.[4] In recent decades a more varied and nuanced portrait of the diversity of experiences in the suburbs has emerged as people have considered age, gender, "race," ethnicity, and class.[5] This study builds on this alternative view while considering the earlier perspectives of scholars, fiction writers, musicians, visual artists, and the public.[6] This book explores children, youth, and childhood in postwar Canada in a setting that was designed to reflect new ideas about the family and home life, showing suburban living for children and adolescents as rich and complex, resisting stereotypes. Young people exercised their agency in shaping their childhoods, a topic that has not been explored in depth from their perspective. Both consciously and unconsciously, children and adolescents influenced suburbia, just as it shaped them.

Suburban life and childhood intersect in important ways. Suburbia has become the definitive residential choice for millions of Canadians and Americans since the end of the Second World War.[7] Suburbs symbolize a great deal of economic, political, and cultural power in Canada, and much of this power began coalescing in the postwar period. By the late 1950s, the media—especially film and television—had established youthfulness as an overwhelmingly desirable objective and a powerful symbol, with the number of baby boomers contributing greatly to this viewpoint.[8] This perception remains today in the efforts of many adults to dress, think, and act "young" to stave off the inevitable effects of aging. Throughout this book, through the lens of childhood and adolescence, I track and explore the position that adolescence and youthfulness came to define this era in Canada, a position argued ably by historian Doug Owram in his influential book *Born at the Right Time*.[9]

Most historiography related to postwar Canadian suburbs lacks one critical component—an exploration of the significance of age in defining experience. Employing age and age relations as an analytical framework, this book moves beyond some key approaches in the history of childhood— demography, cliometrics, public institutions, the law, child reformers, and child welfare—allowing for a critical discussion of suburban childhoods.[10] Furthermore, postwar Calgary and its burgeoning suburbs have received little attention to date, relative to Vancouver, Toronto, and Montreal.[11] Other studies of the suburbs have focused mainly on the experiences of central Canadians, with limited, if any references to other regions.[12] Calgary experienced rapid expansion in population, urban development, and new businesses and services as it became an influential prairie city. High birth rates and marriage at a younger age, and increased immigration rates were prime population drivers in Calgary, as they were elsewhere. Postwar Calgary was home to an influx of new residents from within Alberta, Canada, and the world. The rapid population growth was unprecedented in Calgary's history.

Calgary is situated on Treaty 7 land (negotiated with Siksikaitsitapi, or the Blackfoot Nation, in 1877). Incorporated as a town in 1884, with a population of about five hundred people, Calgary was settled in 1885 as a North West Mounted Police outpost at the confluence of the Bow and Elbow Rivers in southern Alberta; however, the city did not experience a major population boom until the postwar period. Unlike Winnipeg, a prairie city tagged to become the "Chicago of the North," there were no grand expectations for Calgary. There was some modest commercial and industrial growth in the late nineteenth and early twentieth centuries. In comparison, Toronto had 200,000 residents by the early twentieth century. Calgary did not reach this number until the late 1950s.

Overall, Calgary serves as a fascinating and model city because it metaphorically emerged from childhood, experienced an intense adolescence, and matured into early adulthood by the 1970s along with the boomers. Outside of Toronto, the pace and volume of change in Calgary was exceptional when compared to other large Canadian cities. In addition to population growth, major developments included increased numbers of oil and gas head offices, an explosion of elementary and secondary schools, the founding of the city's own university, expansion of existing postsecondary institutions, increased shopping and cultural opportunities, and important infrastructure developments such as roadways, sidewalks, and parks. By 1970, Calgary had become the largest and, arguably, the most influential prairie city in the country; the population growth rate was consistent and sustained in the postwar period.

Similar to other Canadian cities, most of the postwar suburban communities in Calgary did not break ground until the early 1950s. Most notably, E.P. Taylor's trail-blazing Don Mills suburb, just outside of Toronto, was started in 1952. Therefore, this study begins in 1950.[13] This framing allows for a clearer picture and better understanding of Canadian childhoods. This understanding comes from looking at the interplay of class, ethnicity, race, gender, and culture as they influenced postwar suburban children, adolescents, and families without losing sight of the importance of place to our social experiences.

The book focuses on the northwest community of Banff Trail. In the early 1950s, Banff Trail's vacant lots were purchased directly from the City of Calgary. It was one of the last Calgary communities to do so. The shift away from purchasing directly from municipalities reflected the growing influence of land developers that began in earnest in the late 1940s. Large development companies began to shape suburban growth not only in Calgary but across Canada, and municipalities ceded a degree of control to these private companies in the process. The City of Calgary also changed Banff Trail's boundary over time, but only minimally. Banff Trail is an exemplary case because it was created in the immediate postwar era; grew rapidly; had a mix of residential housing, schools, and small businesses (like nearly all mixed-used suburbs); was situated on the growing city's northwest edge; and was located close to important Calgary landmarks such as the North Hill Shopping Centre, McMahon Stadium, the Southern Alberta Institute of Technology, and the University of Calgary.

Like most children and adolescents in postwar suburban Canada, almost all young people in Calgary, from ages five through eighteen, went to school, played, explored, discovered, and observed in ways that were more similar than dissimilar. Yet, importantly, there was no single defining experience for young people in postwar suburbia. Indeed, in listening carefully to the voices, reminiscences, and memories of siblings who grew up in the same house and who, at times, shared a bedroom for several years, it is clear that their experiences varied.

Chronologically, the 1950s and 1960s fall toward the end of the late modern period, which spans from the late nineteenth century through to the early 1980s.[14] Generally, Canadians in the 1950s and 1960s, like others in the United States and western Europe, focused on the future rather than the past. It was a period defined by increasing urbanization, secularism, commodification, consumerism, and an emphasis on applying technology to "improving" everyday life. It was also a time of widescale belief in the benefits and advantages of a market-based democratic system, despite evidence to the contrary in the form of ever-present boom-and-bust cycles, particularly for impoverished, racialized, and working-class people. Structure, order, efficiency, and control were emphasized in mainstream society. There was a fervent belief in the ability of science, medicine, and technology, as progressive forces in society, to heal and improve lives. Psychological advice literature, written by specialists on the child rearing and social regulation of young people, influenced modern ideas about childhood and adolescence in the postwar years.[15] Popular literature also reflected a growing interest in science, innovation, and technology as science fiction writers such as Isaac Asimov, Ray Bradbury, Arthur C. Clarke, and Robert Heinlein captured the imaginations of millions of fiction readers globally.

The Second World War also impacted the lives of postwar suburban children and adolescents because their parents had lived through the war.[16] Some of the people interviewed for this study grew up in the 1960s and early 1970s, and their experiences, as older adolescents, did not fit neatly into the book's temporal bound. Therefore, some everyday experiences from the early 1970s are included. The book's temporal framework therefore opens at the end of the immediate postwar period and ends during one of the more turbulent eras in Canada's social and political history.[17]

While recognizing that the adult world, and adults themselves, necessarily impacted young peoples' cultures, I concentrate on the narratives, everyday experiences, and perspectives of people under the age of nineteen. The school-age years of kindergarten through high school are the focus. *Children* refers to people aged five through twelve. I use *adolescent* interchangeably with *teenager* to refer to individuals aged thirteen to nineteen.[18] Adolescence is a relatively recent age category in the constructed stages of development. It was not until the beginning of the twentieth century that it first received scholarly treatment in G. Stanley Hall's *Adolescence: Its Psychology and Its Relations to Physiology, Anthropology, Sex, Crime, Religion, and Education,* in which, famously, Hall describes adolescence as a period of "storm and stress." While adolescence (along with childhood) is socially constructed, it has a biological basis. It is a time of awakening sexuality with its associated physical changes. Often it is a time for searching for an identity, and for many it is a time to ally with peers in rejecting, or at the very least questioning, social mores and conventions. The use of the category "juveniles" is based on the legal definition used during this period, namely, those aged twelve through sixteen in Alberta and most of Canada.

Unlike analytical categories such as race, ethnicity, sexuality, gender, and class, age has been less influential as a major category of historical inquiry. Philippe Ariès's *Centuries of Childhood* was the first study to prioritize children as a primary historical category. Key for Ariès was that medieval children lived in an adult world, working, playing, and interacting with adults in unrestricted ways. His greatest contribution was not only his focus on children as historical actors but also his emphasis on childhood as historically and socially constructed—as a category that changed over time.[19]

Working from Ariès's initial positioning, the concept of childhood is more than a biological or demographic classification: it is a sociohistorical construction. Although both children and adolescents experience biological changes, which often prompt changes in their emotions and attitudes and those of the people around them, childhood and adolescence are socially dynamic. Defining childhood is more a matter of human decision-making than a cultural or biological imperative. While there is no universal childhood or child in terms of experience, a form of childhood has marked all human cultures. Cultural anthropology reinforces the conclusion that, throughout human history, children and childhood have been viewed as different than adults and adulthood. Experts conclude that hunter-gatherer peoples, for example, universally viewed childhood as a unique and distinct stage of development.[20]

Since the 1980s, the history of childhood has included the voices, texts, and cultures of young people's everyday experiences, even as studies of child welfare, education, health, and juvenile delinquency continue to be important paths to understanding childhood in the past.[21] Although it is acknowledged that children are critical to gaining a richer understanding of historical developments,[22] locating sources remains an essential challenge for historians. Finding archival materials created by children is difficult and is especially challenging for poor and working-class children whose families may not have had the literacy levels, physical space, or the material resources to create and keep items. Creating written texts, and texts in other forms that can be "read" or interpreted, including photographs, drawings, sketches, paintings, and so forth, often required materials for production that were not readily available to many children. With mandatory schooling barely a century old in much of Canada, official records, when they have been preserved, often have a distinct class, racial, ethnic, and gender bias.

To better understand childhood in this era, knowing that children and adolescents clearly had some power and that they did not express powerlessness or passivity is important. They were active participants in their lives on the personal, educational, community, and municipal levels; they influenced the lives of their peers and adults. Society transmits its values and norms through the socialization of children, and children's experiences, needs, wants, and desires in turn shape adult lives. Children, often very early in their lives, are brought into contact with the broader society and its institutions. These institutions are typically in children's neighbourhoods and larger communities—their impact on childhood and adolescence are important, but there are other influential elements.

In this study, a major consideration is how the lives of children and adolescents in Calgary suburbia fit with Canadian childhoods across time and space. Comparing and contrasting my findings with Neil Sutherland's groundbreaking work has been fruitful. Sutherland charted the movement from economic interdependence, especially among the poor and working class, to a more profound emotional attachment of parents and guardians to their children.[23] This movement was tied to larger processes of urbanization, industrialization, child-saving campaigns, and compulsory education that necessarily made children more vulnerable and less economically vital. Sutherland noted that children came to influence the lives of their peers to a greater degree than ever before over the course of the twentieth century, a finding reinforced here.

Age, particularly youth, became an important identity marker as the twentieth century wore on. Cynthia Comacchio argues that, by the 1950s, parents and other authorities had more active and interventionist roles. Former "flaming youth" became the parents of adolescents as the latter's schooling and dependency lengthened and as postwar reconstruction and relative stability became key national objectives after decades of upheaval.[24] Evidence of this is reflected throughout this book, although responses and resistance to this trend were always bubbling just below the surface and at times boiled over.

Women's contributions, especially to family and community life, are central to the history of postwar suburbia. Veronica Strong-Boag's foundational study contextualized the themes of identity, alienation, and belonging that emerged in the archival record and in the oral histories. Her stance that women, and especially mothers, shaped the everyday experiences of suburban children is borne out.[25] Life in postwar Banff Trail highlights the important roles that women played, roles that often blurred the lines between public and private in their everyday activities as caregivers, teachers, administrators, organizers, and volunteers.

Although children contributed to the construction of their individual and shared childhoods, discourses of childhood did impinge on the everyday experiences, values, and practices of children. And modernity was not experienced evenly; children experience it differently depending on their historical, racial, class, spatial, gendered, and familial circumstances.[26] At even the most basic level, this is demonstrated in some of the differences noted among extended family members, neighbours, and community members and between siblings. Ultimately, social class, while at times "invisible" to young people, has the most influence on the lives of children; yet this is not totalizing because children are dynamic and active agents in childhood cultures and associated social developments.[27]

The influence of feminist theory on the historiography of childhood is an important one. Tamara Myers's work emphasizes the material conditions of both women and girls in the period preceding this study. Myers's study of wartime Montreal reveals that it was a critical time for youth in Canada, as urban social policy brought childhood, children, and adolescence into sharper focus for the authorities. The surveillance of their behaviours expanded in the name of the wartime emergency, and parallels can be found in the Cold War ideologies that influenced baby boomer lives.

In this context, both materialist feminist and social regulation theories inform this study. As with scholarship on gender and women, scholarship on the history of childhood is aligned with established agendas demonstrating an unequal and structurally discriminatory society for both women and children, and a social structure that ensures neither category has a universal experience. Furthermore, the postwar period is viewed as one where suburban women were predominantly in the domestic and private sphere rather than the public sphere. Historical evidence further unsettles notions of gendered, and "natural," public and private spheres. As demonstrated by scholars such as Joan Sangster, women were making integral contributions to household incomes in postwar Canada despite the male breadwinner family ideal.[28] In 1950 the rate of married women's participation in the workforce had not yet reached 15 percent. By the early 1970s, more than 40 percent of married women did paid work outside the home.[29]

Materialist feminism does not separate the materiality of meaning, identity, the body, or the state from the gendered division of labour that supports the desire for profit in capitalism.[30] Materialist feminism reinforces the notion that despite performing most of the world's socially necessary labour, women remain far more vulnerable to poverty than men.[31] It emphasizes the importance of social and material conditions in framing the lives of women, children, and adolescents in the suburban environment and offers a critical view of the formative influences of capitalism and patriarchy on women's lives.

Elements of social regulation theory also influence this analysis. Particularly important are the discursive constructs directed at regulating sexuality, specifically the sexuality of adolescents. Aimed primarily at containment in this period, discourse effectively enhanced awareness of sexuality and, in fact, served as one more reason for children, adolescents, and families to talk about, and focus on, adolescent sexuality. Particularly relevant to the discursive construction of childhood is the influence of institutional discipline, which both requires and develops a range of spatial conditions that make possible its successful implementation. This reality is central to Mona Gleason's work on the disciplining and regulation of children's bodies by parents, officials, administrations, and institutional regimes in the early part of the twentieth century and later.[32] Also important are Foucauldian conceptions of power as productive rather than merely oppressive, as things that can bring about behaviours and events with the possibility for resistance by the oppressed—in this instance, children and adolescents.

A close reading of materials located at multiple archival sites in Calgary and Ottawa was foundational to this study. I draw on collections that reflect the views of professionals, educators, and some state-affiliated officials who were concerned with monitoring, aiding, and regulating children and childhood. Archival sources included municipal, provincial, and federal government documents, dozens of archival fonds, contemporary local and national newspapers, and school-based publications such as newspapers, newsletters, art, and yearbooks. In Calgary, archival research was conducted at Branton Junior High School, the City of Calgary, the City of Calgary Police Services, the Glenbow Museum, the Southern Alberta Institute of Technology, the University of Calgary, and William Aberhart High School. In Ottawa, archival research was undertaken at Library and Archives Canada. Archival documentaries, television, and radio shorts from the CBC digital archives and the National Film Board were used. Everyday cultural products such as novels, feature films, and television shows were used to provide context, nuance, and richness.

Although locating examples of young people's culture remains a challenge, rich records exist in small pockets. Artifacts from postwar childhood culture have often been mediated, or in some way influenced, by adults in their production. This is unavoidable. Many children and adolescents understood that what they produced would be, if it were not mediated, viewed, consumed, and potentially edited by adults in positions of influence.

A key research methodology was oral histories. The intent was not to focus on adults who raised children, during but rather the world through adult memories of childhood. I completed eighteen oral history interviews with individuals who grew up in the Calgary suburbs, at varying times, from the early 1950s through the early 1970s. The focus was on depth and breadth rather than merely producing a set number of interviews. More does not mean better when doing qualitative research. Patterns and shared experience emerged from these interviews, and the addition of the interviewees' voices adds an unmistakable richness to this study. I also use dozens of interviews with postwar Banff Trail residents that appear in *From Prairie Grass to Sidewalks,* a book that emerged from a local partnership between students and community members. Memoirs and oral histories from other North American boomers offer additional depth.

With some interviewees, initial contact was made at archival institutions and Banff Trail schools. From there, a snowball technique was used to find further interviewees. This yielded the bulk of my research participants. I used a combination of in-person and telephone interviews. The interviews ranged in time from about twenty minutes to two hours. All interviewees responded to the same thirty-four questions. Some questions were direct, but many were open-ended with an opportunity for participants to shape the dialogue. Open-ended questions allowed for richer responses. They were shared conversations. While it is possible for nostalgia to be productive, I did not want to discuss only the positive aspects of these interviewees' childhoods. I can never know fully—it is not in any way my right to know—what some participants may have blocked out when recalling their childhoods. Yet several interviewees talked openly about the pain in their childhoods, of loss, humiliation, violence, sexism, and other major disappointments.[33] In interviews we touched on many more lives than the participant's own. The experiences of dozens of friends, family members, and other community members emerged from the individual oral histories.

Participants were generous, gracious, and thoughtful during the interview process. Nine of the interviewees requested anonymity; nine did not. Twelve of the interviewees confirmed that they were now living, or had lived, in a suburb as adults; five more had not; and one chose not to divulge. Ten of the participants identified as women, eight as men. Sixteen of the interviewees had siblings; two did not. There was a range of ages: two were born in the 1940s, three were born between 1950 and 1954, four were born between 1955 and 1959, eight were born between 1960 and 1964, and one chose not to disclose her birth year. One of the participants was an adoptee while the remaining seventeen grew up with their biological families in Banff Trail. One of the participants grew up in a one-parent home while the others grew up in two-parent homes. All the participants were white and confirmed that they had European heritage from several different countries. Further information on these interviewees can be found in the Appendices.

These interviews provided a wealth of information. In a few instances, some people initially failed to recall prominent landmarks, dates of significant moves, and names of friends. None of this is uncommon, particularly when many of these events happened forty to sixty years prior to the interview date. Studies show little evidence to suggest that people misremember events, certainly not consciously; overall, most people retain memories over long periods of time with little significant memory loss.[34] Yet memory can be coloured by physical deterioration, cognitive decline, and the influence of nostalgia, by personal biases of the interviewer and interviewee, and by the influence of group and retrospective versions of the past.[35] These concerns are not specific to oral history. The documentary historical record is also selective, incomplete, and contains innumerable untold biases. For the most part, age does not appear to negatively influence the reliability of memory.[36] The value of oral history consists in the fact that "wrong" memories remain psychologically "true" and that this truth can be equally as important as facts.[37]

Oral history practitioners are aware that memories likely contain multiple histories and have been reconstituted on more than one occasion. This does not invalidate them. In fact, when asked about the routines of everyday life, even many decades in the past, people often recall in vivid detail the things they carried out on a regular basis: their walk or bike ride to school, routinized play, or the processes experienced at work—both paid and unpaid.[38] In most instances, people remember what is truly important to them with little difficulty. These memories are organized into two basic categories as scripts. Routinized or daily activities tend to be situational and are often common to several people. Other scripts are personal or may include memories in situational scripts, which most of us use to organize our memories of childhood.[39]

Another way to theorize memory is to categorize remembrances as episodic memory, which includes some events or episodes as a type of time travel, where we remember the event and our place within it.[40] Flashbulb memories can by contained within episodic memory. These memories are vivid, have a photographic or visual quality, and are often personal and emotional.[41]

Historian Alessandro Portelli theorizes that memory assists in facilitating meaning; he argues that inventions, and myths may lead us beyond facts to meanings.[42] Furthermore, it is imperative to recall that orality infuses the texture of the "official" written record.[43] This does not mean that we must question (and, in many instances, reject) much of what we encounter in the historical record. It does reinforce the importance of the historian as interpreter, critical thinker, and aggregator of knowledge.

Participants' individual stories cast light on the collective scripts of other children and adolescents from this period.[44] With inductive reasoning, these scripts allow one to create larger connective webs from individual childhood experiences to other childhoods.[45]

The interview text is infused with the agency of both the interviewer and the participant.[46] There is some debate about how much the oral history method allows for shared authority in the creation of historical writing. While Michael Frisch promotes the idea of shared authority, others argue that shared authority is ultimately unattainable, given that the scholar crafting the narrative has the final interpretive authority.[47]

Oral histories are a vital and essential component to this study. What follows in Chapter 1 is a discussion of space, place, and landscapes and their meanings in childhood and adolescence. Banff Trail experienced profound changes over these twenty years, and by the late 1960s, because of tremendous growth to the north and west, it was transformed spatially. Childhood memory is often linked to place. In exploring the homes, streets, and parks of Banff Trail, as well as nearby sites of the postwar era, it is clear that childhood spaces and places had a significant influence on shaping the consciousness of children and adolescents, both individually and collectively.

Chapter 2 focuses on war, anxieties about "the bomb," and postwar classrooms. Aside from homes, classrooms were spaces where children and adolescents spent more time than anywhere else. Postwar students spent thousands of hours in schools for formal schoolwork, and as they aged, they spent even more time in extracurricular activities such as volunteer work, yearbook duties, art projects, music performances, and sports. This volume of classroom contact meant that the school's influence, both direct and indirect, was profound on the everyday lives of children and adolescents.[48] Both the Cold War and the First and Second World Wars also impacted the everyday lives of some youngsters through stories, images, and representations.

Chapter 3 focuses on race, class, and the work of suburban children and adolescents.[49] Although participants discussed race and ethnicity in oral history interviews, and postwar youngsters wrote about it, Banff Trail, like so many Canadian suburbs in this period, was not racially and ethnically diverse. In terms of social class, Banff Trail did not fit neatly into the categories of middle-class or working-class suburb. Especially in its earliest years, it had a mixture of working-class and middle-class families. The working-class families cannot be characterized as poor. There were few rental properties in Banff Trail, reflecting the dominant pattern of home ownership that marks postwar suburbia.

Chapter 4 analyzes sport, recreation, leisure, and play. Popular culture and leisure activities were geared increasingly to children and adolescents in this period. Modern impulses influenced both structured play and emerging suburban children's cultures. As young citizens were increasingly removed from full-time employment, leisure and "free" time were enjoyed by nearly all of them. Nevertheless, suburban middle-class families did have the means to pay for leisure activities that working-class families could not afford.

Chapter 5 considers gender, sexuality, and general health. Representations of boyhood and girlhood, as well as the individual experiences of boys and girls, remained distinct in many ways throughout this era, reflecting, for the most part, adult gender conventions. Within the context of expert advice, the health and wellness of young people also came into sharper focus and took greater hold in schools and families by the early 1970s, assisted by universal health care in the mid-1960s. Alongside class, gender and sexuality were important in determining general well-being and how childhood and adolescence were experienced.

While young children and adolescents have been influenced by adult practices and discursive constructs throughout time, they have often demonstrated resilience and agency in negotiating these powerful influences. The balance of power did not favour them often, but the young were not merely passive participants in an adult-dominated world. Chapter 6 considers the night, delinquency, crime, resistance, and rebellions. Nighttime often has negative connotations where the young are concerned, particularly from the perspective of adulthood. Darkness signals a time when young people, particularly pre-adolescents, are meant to be both quiet and unseen. But many young people's night activities permitted them relief from adult gazes, which, even if usually well-meaning, were oftentimes disapproving, restrictive, and constraining. For a significant minority, suburban adolescence was marked by crime, delinquency, and violence.

Chapter 1

Mapping Suburbia

Childhood memory is often linked to place, and for most the family home anchors memories related to our earliest years. Neighbourhood playgrounds, individual children's bedrooms, rumpus or recreation rooms dedicated mainly to young people, and public high schools were a new norm by this period.[1] These constituted play spaces were, at least in theory, designed to accommodate play, but in most instances this did not mean they were tied to a specific purpose or goal.[2] Although programming designed specifically for children ramped up and general angst concerning children's free time existed in the postwar years, there were no strict goals associated with most play spaces. Socializing and having fun were a derivative of the increasing leisure time and space that many sought for children.

Homes, schools, and play areas are central to young people's lives. The importance of space was recognized in the late nineteenth century, when public education institutions began physically islanding young people on a large scale; however, with attendance not mandatory in some jurisdictions in these years, the process was experienced unevenly.[3] By the postwar period, mandatory schooling had been normal practice for nearly fifty years. The use of physical spaces is a good measure of a society's attitude toward childhood.[4] The increase in these physical spaces dedicated to children and youth, not only in the postwar period but also throughout the twentieth century, demonstrates the primacy of childhood in Canadian suburbs and elsewhere. Yet the built environment cannot be considered on its own. There is a dynamic relationship between a physical place, its social characteristics, and childhood—idealized or constructed. Space is tangible, social, and a discursive construction, all at the same time.[5]

Most children spend the majority of their time, both waking and sleeping, at home. Typically, our homes in childhood serve as safe spaces;

however, while homes are often cherished, they continue to be the primary sites for domestic violence. They can serve as the most dangerous spaces that children and women experience.[6] In exploring the homes, streets, and parks of Banff Trail, as well as nearby sites in the postwar era, it is clear that childhood spaces and places had a significant influence on shaping the consciousness of children and adolescents, both individually and collectively. For most young people, where they lived was critical to developing a sense of identity; homescapes had a profound effect on them, both at the time and in adulthood. Banff Trail offered much to youngsters, and their suburban childhood was not hollow and monochromatic. Instead, it was a childhood marked by relative freedom, discovery, and, occasionally, danger. In other words, the postwar suburban landscape, particularly in its earliest incarnation, offered much more than serenity.

Canadian Suburbs in the Early Twentieth Century

Suburban spaces were not exclusive to the postwar period, as there is a rich and notable history of Canadian suburbs in the first half of the twentieth century. Furthermore, there is no single definition of *suburb* in either an historical or contemporary context. Suburbs have been defined and interpreted differently by economists, demographers, architects, sociologists, and historians. Each group focuses on different characteristics and offer varied yet interrelated definitions. Economists base their definition on the macroeconomic relationship between the core city and surrounding regions, demographers tend to focus on commuting routes or residential density, architects focus on building types and geographical locales, and sociologists focus on behaviours or the dominant lifestyle of the residents.[7] Historians have considered all of these characteristics, but change over time has been the overriding concern for most.

Canadian suburbs are typically found on the edges of a city, or near to a city or metropolitan area. They are a considerable distance (requiring a form of transportation) from a city's central business district and are less densely populated than other urban residential spaces. Suburbs feature primarily single-family housing, have relatively high levels of homeowner occupation versus renting or co-operative arrangements, and, despite some initial rural qualities, are unmistakably urban in form. Being a singular political space is not an inherent component of the Canadian definition of *suburb*.[8] Because they are under the jurisdiction of the provincial government, municipal districts do not have the same autonomy as many American cities under various state and federal laws and regulations.

The postwar suburban housing form is the most familiar to many; however, diverse suburban forms were common in the early twentieth century. Richard Harris identifies five main ones: the affluent enclave, the industrial suburb, the middle-class suburb, the unplanned suburb, and the mixed-use suburb.[9] These categories are not easily reconciled with our common notions of suburban forms, as the affluent enclave and the middle-class suburb have dominated representations of suburbia since the 1960s. Yet working-class suburbs were common in many cities. Most owner-builders in the suburbs were working people, and men, women, children, and adolescents contributed to home construction in the early twentieth century. In many smaller cities, suburbs remained overwhelmingly slums until well into the twentieth century. In Calgary, groups of cheap dwellings were built on the narrow flats along the Bow River as late as the First World War.[10] At the turn of the century, there were widespread housing concerns across Canada, and escape from crowded, unsanitary homes in the city core became possible on the suburban fringe. Over time, many of these opportunities were eventually closed off to working people by public-health regulations, planning control requirements, and fire codes.[11] Prohibitive suburban housing costs also precluded many working people from purchasing suburban homes as time wore on, especially in cities where housing prices increased at a much greater rate than inflation.

Canadian cities and most suburbs in the late nineteenth century were not considered healthy or particularly safe for Canadians, although the rhetoric may have overridden the realities in many centres.[12] The suburbs were not necessarily healthier than inner-city neighbourhoods in Canada. Most suburbs were not pristine and isolated enclaves; many, particularly those nearest to manufacturing sites, were not often bastions of health, yet in growing cities across the Prairies the primarily residential suburbs seemed to hold a health advantage over all other categories of urban environment.[13] In growing cities across the Prairies, including Calgary, even in the 1920s, barely half of all suburban households had sewers.[14] These suburban spaces were marked by their diversity and by relatively little planning and few municipal regulations, which came to define most postwar suburbs across the country. In this earlier period, class was vitally important to the character of many suburbs, as the working-class suburbs that grew on the fringes of cities removed the sights and smells of poverty from the everyday experiences of wealthier citizens.[15]

The working-class composition of many early twentieth-century suburbs, not only in Canada but also in England and the United States, was a direct result of factories, plants, and offices moving into suburban spaces.[16] With workers continuing the nineteenth-century pattern of walking to work sites, it made sense that working people—oftentimes unable to afford personal transportation, and with streetcar development in Canada not nearly as widespread as it was in most major American cities—would seek housing as close as possible to their workplaces.[17] Unlike later fully developed and packaged suburbs, which came to dominate the suburban landscape by the 1970s, many residents were owner-builders in this era.[18]

These homes became havens for many workers and their families, no matter how modest the house. They were sites in which the every-day pressures of the factory or other workplace could be set aside.[19] As Suzanne Morton has demonstrated in her study of a working-class suburb in Atlantic Canada in the 1920s, the need and desire for good housing at least partially reflected the value that many working-class households placed on domesticity and comfort.[20] Domestic life helped shape the entire class experience, much as the workplace and other working-class institu-tions, such as labour unions, had in the first decades of the twentieth cen-tury.[21] While the family model dominated by the skilled, male breadwinner existed, there were female-headed households and employment oppor-tunities for young women that, along with technological and economic change in Atlantic Canada, made the ideal of a sole male breadwinner in the home impractical and unattainable for many people.[22]

Much of the urban and suburban growth in the first half of the twenti-eth century was unregulated, unplanned, and relatively haphazard, despite nascent efforts to shape housing standards and community development by the three levels of government in Canada. By the mid-1930s, with gov-ernments across North America forced to respond to the Great Depression and its devastating effects on working-class people, the Canadian federal government reluctantly entered the housing industry, and municipal gov-ernments adopted national building standards over the next fifteen years. Provincial governments became involved after the Second World War.[23] All levels of government continued to privilege the market, as co-operative housing and strict rental rate controls were never given anything more than cursory treatment by the state.

Calgary in the Early Twentieth Century

Like most urban development in Canada in the first half of the twenti-eth century, spatial growth in Calgary was not coordinated or planned to any great degree. Like several American cities, but unlike Canadian cities such as Toronto, Calgary's differentiated districts and communities grew in tandem with the street railway system, begun in 1909.[24] These systems appeared in many American cities as early as the late nineteenth century.

For those people fortunate enough to have capital to build homes, it made sense to build along this line unless other options, such as a private automobile, were available; however, automobile ownership was not widespread, and the street railway system was the main artery for Calgary's burgeoning transportation system until the 1940s. While the city's administration and its planning department were relatively small at this time, there were some building regulations and restrictions for both residential and commercial builders. One of Calgary's first affluent enclaves was built during this period. Mount Royal, now an exclusive inner-city community, was built well away from the working-class homes and industrial districts that defined much of the southern part of the city.[25]

The 1950s boom was not the first experienced in the city. Young people, in particular, had moved to urban centres across the country in the first fifteen years of the twentieth century, and this trend was not exclusive to Calgary. Increased opportunities for work, the pursuit of formal education, and an expanded social life were all factors. The oil and gas sector began forming following the Turner Valley discovery in 1911. By this time, Calgary's function as a vital service centre for industries such as meat-packing was well established, and the city had become a major supply, processing, and market centre for a vibrant and important agricultural network.[26]

In the second decade of the twentieth century, most of Calgary's residential development occurred not in the north and the west quadrants of the city, as it would in the 1950s and 1960s, but in the south and east.[27] Most of Calgary's industrial, commercial, and manufacturing growth was concentrated in these spaces, although an anticipated boom based on oil and gas discoveries did not develop in the 1920s, as many hoped. Another reason for this growth pattern was that the Centre Street Bridge—a major thoroughfare linking Calgary's north and south ends—was not completed until 1916, so the housing market to the north side of the Bow River was slower to develop.[28] The Bow River has always been a major geographical dividing line between north and south.

While Calgary's population did grow in the first few decades of the twentieth century, the anticipated land boom collapsed just before the outbreak of the First World War, and there was only limited development until the mid-1940s. Unlike the present-day realities of reduced land availability and comparatively high costs, it is estimated that two-thirds of the land within the city limits had reverted to city control as tax-forfeited property by 1919, reflecting the broader hardship that many residents experienced. These forfeitures were an important factor in postwar growth, as they enabled the city to have direct land-development control by the late 1940s, when pressures to develop new areas increased exponentially.[29]

International observers did travel to Calgary in the early part of the twentieth century to assess the city's urban planning. One of them was highly critical. In 1918, A.S. Chapman of the London, UK, County Council noted that land should have been set aside along the river for large boulevards, "and one cannot but fear in the interests of this progressive community, that the future development and street traffic increasing enormously in rapidity and volume, have not been sufficiently anticipated, nor has the provision of open spaces for objects of beauty, playgrounds and parks for recreation and fresh air been adequately considered."[30] It is difficult to know all of Chapman's motivations, but he failed to note the substantial amount of green space in the city available for public use. Calgary was not without its parks by the end of the Great War, but many open spaces were sport-specific rather than designated for general use. Other spaces were developed for the public's enjoyment. Relevant to many young people, particularly in southern Alberta, the Calgary Zoological Society was organized in October 1928, and dinosaur park construction began during the 1930s. The park featured thirty replica statues from prehistoric times.[31] By the 1930s, parks and recreation development was formalized within the City of Calgary's jurisdiction.[32]

By the late 1940s, Calgary had become one of the largest cities in western Canada and was poised to become one of the fastest-growing cities in North America. As in many other centres, thousands of Calgary residents sought affordable housing, but with limited means and options to do so as young families. By 1950, an agreement between parks and the local school boards brought school playgrounds and yards into the urban-planning mix. These school playgrounds and yards were now available for public play after school hours and on weekends; these joint-use sites became standard practice across the city, including Banff Trail in the 1950s and 1960s.[33]

Postwar Suburban Space

Outside of a few regions, namely, the Far North and most of Atlantic Canada, nearly all parts of Canada were home to the phenomenon of postwar suburban growth. The Banff Trail community experienced profound changes in the years immediately following the Second World War. By the late 1960s, because of tremendous growth to the north and west of Banff Trail, the community was a much different landscape than in 1950. By the early 1970s, Banff Trail and a handful of bordering communities featured thousands of brand-new homes, expanded roadways and sidewalks, a newly built university, shopping centres, and dozens of new businesses.

During the postwar period, suburbs increasingly became one of the most common residential spaces for children and adolescents in Canada.[34] Whereas in the first post-Confederation census in 1871 over 80 percent of children lived in rural households, by 1971, there was a near reversal of this, with over 75 percent living in urban centres.[35] New roads, schools, and parks were built across the city, particularly in the city's suburbs, as a result of this tremendous postwar explosion in population.[36] While there was growth across the province, it is significant that Calgary's percentage of the provincial population rose from 11 percent in 1941 to 25 percent in 1971. Housing availability was an issue for many Calgary families in the 1950s and 1960s, as Calgary's suburban boom began. As early as 1946, more than two thousand Second World War veterans and their growing families were on a waiting list for homes.[37] This was a national phenomenon, as the same pressures were felt in most Canadian cities during these years, especially in Toronto and Vancouver. In high-use suburban spaces around the country, struggles over the meaning of space were important. Young people were a part of this process in that they engaged with suburban spaces— often on their terms. This process played out across the nation state. The entire country, not just Calgary, had become undeniably urban by the early 1960s, with fewer than one-third of Canadians living in rural areas.

Increasingly, schoolyards and parks became available for children through changes to agreements between the city and the Calgary school boards. In the next twenty years, these suburban spaces became important play areas. This was particularly so given the number of new schools built with their associated green spaces, which children and adolescents used during and after regular school hours. In some parts of Banff Trail, especially for those residents nearest to the schools, these spaces were recalled as some of the most important to youngsters unable to leave the suburban home without some supervision and for those with smaller yards. Not all postwar suburban homes had large lots dedicated to childhood play or gardens, which were favoured by some families. Most children spent hours,

TABLE 1.1 Rural Population in Canada	
Year	Population (%)
1941	45.6
1951	43.8
1956	33.5
1961	30.4

Source: Frederick Elkin, *The Family in Canada* (Ottawa: Vanier Institute of the Family, 1964).

on a daily basis, in the common green spaces that were fundamental to suburban children's social lives.[38]

While there were elements of the rural in suburbia, the residential suburban experience was essentially an urban one, particularly once the built environment expanded.[39] Suburban space was varied throughout the city of Calgary, much as it was in other areas on the edges of other growing cities. Even into the late 1950s though, Banff Trail had some lingering rural characteristics. The Haggertys, who moved to Banff Trail in 1957, five years after the first residents had built their homes, recalled: "Morley Trail was not paved when we moved here, only a gravel road. Our sidewalk was in but we had no lawn. The area behind us was undeveloped—just prairie grass."[40] Another early resident, Maxine, recalled: "[We] thought we were out in the country. There was nothing there! Pheasants, rabbits and prairie chickens all came to our door. It was much simpler then."[41] Other communities bore similar characteristics, as a suburbanite in southwest Calgary, Gwen, recalled:

> Our new home faced an open green space with no other homes in front of us. Fifty-Third Street was the main traffic artery immediately west of us ... At this stage, it was a quiet unpaved road with a treed hillside to the west. This became a favorite area for walks, enjoying wildflowers and in season, picking Saskatoon berries (with a little competition from a group of horses pastured there). This western area also became a popular spot for the neighborhood children to climb trees, explore and feed grass to the resident horses.[42]

While these kinds of scenes were often short-lived, they illustrate a different phenomenon than in many urban developments, especially those much nearer to downtown cores. Many proposed suburban sites were not considered prime real estate. Land that had little use served the needs of those seeking housing because they were being crowded out of cityscapes across the country.[43]

The planned development of Don Mills, Ontario, situated just outside the borders of Toronto, roughly six miles from downtown, defined the community-design concept associated with Canadian postwar suburbs.[44] Following the Don Mills model, the suburban lifestyle was expected to centre on the community, with schools, shopping, and leisure activities placed throughout. Ideally, in following this model, there would be an internal walking system throughout the community that would avoid traffic-filled roads and be bordered by trees and parks.[45] Levittown, built on Long Island in New York State, was the American equivalent of Don

Mills.[46] While new Calgary suburbs such as Banff Trail featured attract-ive amenities for residents such as modern homes, the promise of nearby schools and parks, and close proximity to new shopping centres, there were material realities that outweighed these pull factors. Much as in other parts of Canada, such as the rapidly growing suburbs in and around Toronto, where people wanted to live at times had little to do with where houses were built.[47]

Upscale suburbs were built across the country in this period, but in the simplest terms, many families were drawn to the suburbs by the high availability and relative affordability of building lots.[48] In Banff Trail, one of the earliest resident families, the Foxes, recalled spending $100 on lots; once the roof was in place, the city reimbursed them half of that amount.[49] As time went on, other future residents paid more for lots—between $500 and $1,000 in some instances. These lot prices were relatively affordable for many young, working-class families with modest savings and incomes. While children and adolescents were not often consulted, they were often important factors in the decision-making process.[50] Residents of all ages understood the relative affordability of Banff Trail.

This Calgary suburb was different than places such as Don Mills because of Banff Trail's proximity to the city's central business district, where many residents worked. From Banff Trail, with some effort and free time, older children and adolescents could get to the downtown core on their bikes in about twenty minutes, one way.[51] The new Banff Trail community reflected broader changes to residential municipal planning, which included the remarkable growth of suburbia. Mayor Don Mackay sought planning advice from several sources, and much of the urban plan-ning was directed from the top down. When gathering background infor-mation in Dallas, Texas, Mackay was advised by Dallas's mayor to annex the surrounding municipalities so that the city could retain and further establish a single urban identity. By building out, Calgary could avoid the leapfrogging that supposedly created awkward and unseemly gaps in city form.[52] His advice reinforced the links between Texas and Alberta, not only in terms of the migration of oil-industry workers, management, and their families but also at the level of ideas.

Provincial guidelines also influenced Calgary's planning. In 1952 the province revised the Town and Rural Planning Act, which required build-ing developers to set aside at least 10 percent of new subdivision land (nearly exclusively suburban) as municipal reserve.[53] The plan, as it was for most newly developed areas in Canadian suburbs, was to see these reserve lands dedicated to family-centred activities, particularly children's general well-being.

In Calgary, and specifically Banff Trail, the postwar era was a transitional period for neighbourhood design. The gridiron pattern was the defining pattern for the first half of the twentieth century and continued until 1954. It is an interesting hybrid model that bridges two distinct eras of neighbourhood planning. As Banff Trail took shape, significant modifications were made to the basic gridiron pattern as curvilinear street designs, central schools and parks, and new neighbourhood shopping centres were introduced to the overall community design.[54] Banff Trail, and nearby Capitol Hill, were noteworthy in that they were also sites for further innovations in neighbourhood planning from the mid-1950s forward, innovations mandated by new provincial regulations and an internal street system shaped increasingly by the now influential Don Mills model. The goal was to develop safe, attractive communities and to discourage heavy traffic flow directly through suburban communities. The result was well-defined boundaries and adequate park space for Banff Trail.[55] Reports make it clear that children's safety was paramount; however, despite planners' efforts and concerns, vehicles, streets, and children have a long and tragic history of serious injury and death. Archival records in Calgary hold numerous references to child-related deaths and accidents. Throughout this period, entire sections of the annual Calgary Police Force annual

Banff Trail siblings pose in their backyard in 1965 before leaving to enjoy Stampede activities as a family. The bungalows in the background were the most common design in Calgary suburbs in this period. (Reproduced with permission of the family.)

reports were dedicated to detailing them.[56] In these times, car accidents were a part of everyday life for people of all ages in Calgary's suburbs.

There were pragmatic reasons for changes to the gridiron design. With the baby boom well underway, and exploding numbers of school-aged children by the mid-1950s, there was not enough land allocated to accommodate larger schools. The ever-increasing demand for housing lots led to a dearth of park space.[57] In the new suburban areas, these pressures were even more acute because three- or four-children families were common. Banff Trail, while not based on a strict neighbourhood unit design, did feature Garden City suburb principles such as cul-de-sacs and scattered park space.[58] While big developers and much larger subdivisions were normalized by the mid- to late 1960s, the early postwar residential building industry was defined by small contractors who built dozens, rather than hundreds, of units in the communities that sprang up across the city.[59] The move to broad development by a large construction conglomerate, namely, Carma Construction, did not take place until later. It developed hundreds of northwest Calgary homes in communities close to Banff Trail such as Brentwood, Charleswood, Charleswood Heights, and University Heights.[60]

Royal Canadian Mounted Police patrol car accident on Banff Trail in April, 1957. (Photo by Jack De Lorme and reproduced with permission of the University of Calgary Archives and Special Collection, NA-5600-6810A.)

Despite the growing influence of municipal politicians, administrators, and planners, suburban spaces were not designed and shaped solely by these groups. Postwar Calgarians of all ages were important contributors to these processes and their neighbourhoods' identities. Their expectations and needs were important, and community associations served as conduits to communicate them to city planners.[61] From a planning perspective, the situation in Calgary and Edmonton differed from other growing metropolitan areas across Canada in that both cities contained, at least until the mid-1950s, a multitude of vacant lots and substantial land parcels that continued to be primarily agricultural.[62] Concomitant to this planning was the building of Banff Trail's defining feature. This unique space, called Motel Village, was an important retail area, and several of Banff Trail's young people worked in its motels and restaurants. The triangular-shaped geographical space was originally zoned in 1951 for motel use; initially, it was made up of modest one-storey motels and trailer pads.[63]

While the postwar suburbs are often characterized as exclusively residential, many featured restaurants, compact strip malls with a handful of businesses, and much larger shopping centres boasting dozens of stores and huge parking lots for consumers of all ages.[64] The building of large shopping centres began early in the immediate postwar period in the United States

The North Hill Shopping Centre, seen here in 1962, featured anchor stores such as Simpsons-Sears and Woolworths. Other specialty stores like United Cigar Stores were also popular with shoppers. The mall also featured a theatre with seating for more than 800 patrons. (Reproduced with permission of the University of Calgary Archives and Special Collection, NA-4476-354.)

though less so in Canada. Dixie Plaza was the first to open near Toronto in 1955; in northwest Calgary, the North Hill Shopping Centre opened in 1958.[65] It was a fifteen- to twenty-minute walk or an even shorter bike ride from most Banff Trail homes to this popular shopping destination.

In this growing and changing suburban space, Banff Trail children and adolescents grew up and came of age. Physical spaces are where childhood is experienced, as the material world determines how children "use, interpret, shape, and imagine their everyday lives."[66] These sites, vital in childhood, were more than space. As Tim Cresswell argues, it was also a place.[67] The people who grew up there had an emotional attachment to it—both positive and negative. This is a key attribute that turns a space into place. Banff Trail had specific locales where young people met, played, idled their time away, and, at times, worked. There were specific locations for these activities—schoolyards, parks, and the strip mall, which were built in this period as gathering places.[68] Homes, however, were the primary sites of childhood and adolescence.

Children at Home

The postwar suburban home is often represented as sprawling, spacious, and surrounded by a picture-perfect manicured lawn.[69] While most Canadian cities had some suburban enclaves with these features, this was by no means universal, nor was it common. By the late 1950s in Calgary, 80 percent of the new houses were single-storey bungalows, and while the average bungalow grew from about 900 square feet to 1,200 square feet by the 1960s,[70] Banff Trail homes were more representative of the postwar suburban norm across North America. By today's standards, most of these homes were modest and compact. Doug Cass remembered his childhood home much this way in that "it was a typical fifties bungalow ... about 950 square feet, with an unfinished basement, three bedrooms ... The exterior was stucco. Everyone was developing their yards in those days, putting in the grass, planting trees, and building garages. My dad built a garage."[71] Much like other working- and lower-middle-class suburbanites in this time across the continent, many Banff Trail homeowners were skilled workers who brought with them to the suburbs toolkits composed of craft knowledge and home-renovation and maintenance skills.[72] These skills allowed working-class homeowners to make additions and renovations that otherwise would not have happened if they had to be contracted out at a higher cost.

Lesley Hayes noted that her parents' 1,400 square-foot bungalow was built in a slightly later phase of development. Though it was larger than most of the first houses built in Banff Trail in the early 1950s, it had similar characteristics in that the bedrooms were quite small. She remembered that there was some variety in the neighbourhood and that homes "were quite different; a lot of four-level splits on our street. At fifteen I moved to the basement. [My parents] finished the basement when I was probably ten or twelve; [suddenly] we also had a second bathroom. It had everything we needed. It didn't feel like it was a palace, but I never felt ashamed to bring anyone home."[73] These later homes, more varied in design and larger, indicate the rising incomes of middle-class families by the end of the 1950s and into the 1960s.

Brian Rutz recalled that his first bedroom was simple and that he did not have to share it as there were only two children in his family. He didn't have a say in decorating his room as a youngster and didn't recall having any real interest in doing so. There was a shift as an adolescent, as he moved downstairs, where the basement had been partially finished. There was both a pool table and a ping pong table for his and his friends' use.[74] Elizabeth Davidson recalled sharing her upstairs bedroom in her family's modest bungalow with her brother during her early childhood years.[75] Several interviewees mentioned that because their rooms were quite small and other spaces seemed expansive, they did not spend a lot of waking hours in their rooms; quite simply, it was boring to spend extra time in their rooms given the limited space for toys, games, and general play.

Jim Farquharson recalled that through his elementary years he also shared his room, which was not large, with siblings, as part of the home was also rented out to university students who paid for room and board with their family.[76] This indicates a need for some working-class or lower-middle-class families to generate extra income to pay bills. William Wright recalled that he always had his own room and that he was allowed to make some decisions on what was in it; he fondly recalled having a fish tank.[77] Frank Edward remembered that his bedroom was really not anything special: it had a single bed, cabinet, and some personal items on the wall.[78] While most interviewees couldn't recall dimensions exactly, many estimated that their rooms were about ten feet by twelve feet, at most, which aligns with most bungalow floor plans from this period. This was a transitional period, as this modest suburb featured many homes right around the 1,000-square-foot mark. At times, they were even smaller by at least 100 to 200 square feet. Suburban homes by the 1970s were often at least one-and-a-half times larger. The larger home was also an important contributor to separating childhood and adolescence, as teenagers increasingly had their own rooms by the late 1960s.[79] Whereas preteens often shared bedroom spaces, even across gender lines. This switch, particularly when there were two genders, is unsurprising as much of the advice from child-development experts for decades cited the need for older children to have separate bedrooms as a means of developing a healthy view of sex and avoiding potential incestuous relations from developing.[80] This was part of a prevailing North American discourse led by the influential Dr. Spock and his call for a renewal of family life largely centred on child-rearing practices.[81]

Banff Trail's development and design continued broader shifts from previous decades in the sense that community development, while not completely unplanned, was not closely controlled by large development companies. While some homeowners did choose to have larger developers build their homes, particularly as the 1950s shifted to the 1960s, conformity in form was not a feature, particularly from a childhood perspective. As many respondents noted, despite some striking similarities among homes—such as floor designs, yards, and siding types—there were subtle differences, and through the viewfinder of childhood, all suburban homes did not look the same. Many homes were changed and renovated substantially as family needs and wants arose. Unfinished basements were transformed with a few months of home renovations, and the usable living space in homes nearly doubled. This was important to adolescents seeking additional space and solitude as they made the transition to adulthood.

Home renovations by residents were not isolated to Banff Trail. Historians of Levittown, New York, found that even though houses looked similar when they were built, within ten years they were different.[82]

TABLE 2. Percentage of Canadian Homes with Given Facilities and Equipment			
Equipment	1963	1951	1941
Refrigerator	94	48	21
Telephone	87	60	40
Radio	96	93	78
Automobile(s)	73	43	37
Television set	90	NA	NA
Vacuum cleaner	72	42	24
Washing machine	87	74	NA
Phonograph	54	NA	NA
Freezer	18	NA	NA

Source: Frederick Elkin, *The Family in Canada* (Ottawa: Vanier Institute of the Family, 1964).

Homeowners were able to shape their homes and build upon them as their means allowed. These suburban homes featured an increasing number of appliances and features. Participants did say that renovations were, on many occasions, accompanied by some new appliances that were purchased to ease the family workload. Canadian households clearly featured an increasing number of consumer products in the 1950s and 1960s.

Calgary reflected changes taking place in suburban neighbourhoods across North America, changes that saw the 1960s—especially as it closed—bring larger houses and higher income levels for some working-class people and a larger portion of the middle class.[83] In residential developments in the city's northwest quadrant, mainly to the north and west of Banff Trail, larger houses were built. Many were ranch-style and were not only bigger but also built on larger lots to accommodate their larger footprints.[84] The one-level ranch house was significant because it suggested spacious living, and a comparatively easy relationship with the outdoors. Mothers with young children did not have to contend with many stairs.[85] Many homes came to reflect and reinforce the idealization of the nuclear family and its most precious resource, young people. Banff Trail in the earlier 1950s was representative of the postwar Canadian suburb landscape. The community space was modest, and residents recall that "there was absolutely nothing north or west of us except for the dairy farm on the hill ... There was a farm fence at the end of our property on the other side of which were a few cows. A young neighbour boy four doors east of us would go by each evening swinging his milk pail."[86]

The homescape was particularly important, as it was the main place for childhood play, alone, with family members, or with neighbourhood friends. As a form of expression, play is unmatched in children's lives. The sites for suburban children's play activities served as building blocks for creating and asserting their own childhood cultures.[87] While there were multiple settings for children's and adolescents' play, particularly when it was unstructured, suburban homes and backyards served as the primary sites for free play.

Beyond children's homescapes, outside the fluid childhood boundaries of Banff Trail, the nearby natural environment, public spaces such as streets and school playgrounds, and the nearby University of Calgary campus also served as significant play sites. Youngsters shaped their play while being inspired by larger events on both a national and international scale. Some people were keen to discuss the many kinds of supervised and unsupervised everyday activities they engaged in, as they were an important part of their younger identities, and many of them believed that unsupervised activities were more prevalent than they are today. This is noteworthy because in many ways there was a mythical landscape created by children, a space that created a kind of parallel universe that reflected the physical space but also designated it as being impervious to temporal and spatial shifts that were transforming the real world, as defined by adults.[88]

Transforming space for play is a universal childhood experience. In reference to Montreal during this period, a young boomer recalled: "We'd play hide and seek and there were a lot of places to hide. People built coverings for their stairs in the back of their houses. They used planks and we called these places 'the sheds.' Sometimes they would be three stories high. They always seemed very spooky to us on the inside."[89]

Suburban homes often had backyard spaces that were either novel to the youngest children or much larger than what they had played in at other homes. Some yards were large enough to accommodate elaborate play areas

Three members of a local Banff Trail "gang" of local kids on their trikes in a typical neighbourhood backyard in 1965. (Reproduced with permission of the family.)

that reflected broader events from the late 1950s and early 1960s. As Bruce Wilson, an only child, remembered, the omnipresent rockets of the Space Age were, in so many ways, key to his playmates' outdoor activities. The play area they created "was a rocket launching set of three or four launchers. We dug in the backyard, and we would make missile silos like Americans had in Montana. We buried these things down, practised launching them, and it was a huge thing during playtime in our lives, the boys especially."[90] There was a gendered component to some of this play, although siblings, both boys and girls, often played at home with one another and neighbourhood friends. Brothers and sisters were often the default choice as primary playmates. Gender was often not a factor in some instances, as playmate choices were often limited, especially for pre-adolescents.

Cass recalled how gender shaped his childhood play in the immediate space around his home. In his pre-adolescence, his play area was confined to two or three blocks from his home. What he encountered was predominantly female neighbourhood children, and he "thought that was very odd at the time. Almost all of the families in our neighbourhood on the two or three streets around us were almost all girls, and I had three sisters ... So finding a boy to play with was a challenge [*chuckles*]."[91] He didn't express any regret over this or that it had been problematic. It was a simple matter of fact that his neighbourhood space was dominated, at least in numbers, by girls. This imbalance did not seem to influence his play activities.

Contrary to persistent stereotypes, it was not always the case that childhood play was outside and that all children, especially boys,[92] embraced unstructured and casually supervised outdoor play. Despite some of the nostalgia about this postwar era and its associated childhoods (that children were constantly outside), some children did not enjoy spending time outside their homes and were relatively uncomfortable with the suburban landscape and with what it offered them.[93] Allan Matthews's experience was different from many. He recalled rejecting playing outside, at times, and preferred to stay inside many days. He said that he'd "look out over the park [easily visible from a window in his bedroom], as I was an indoor guy, not an outdoor guy, so I would watch the kids play but didn't do a lot of it myself."[94] This experience, supported by others who expressed similar sentiments, contradicts a long-standing trope of gendered childhood play that universalizes boys' play as active and outdoors and girls' playtime as relatively passive and often indoors. Matthews also remembered that he "found being a child incredibly boring, so [he] was just glad when it was over ... [He] couldn't wait to grow up."[95] A statement like this undermines the ongoing romanticization of contemporary childhoods. Not everyone shares in this view, and in this case, Matthews's recollections link him to the adults, particularly some women, who expressed boredom and disillusionment with postwar suburbia.

Siblings shared many of their best moments with one another at home, and in most instances participants said that their siblings were good friends. While some of these relationships were marked on occasion by tension and conflict, nearly all interviewees said they had positive relationships with their brothers and sisters. Mary Baker recalled being "very close to [her] younger brother" and "adoring him" despite a difference of fourteen years in age.[96] Wendy Glidden said that in childhood, she and her siblings were "best friends," and within her large family, these bonds were clearly important throughout childhood and later.[97] Siblings were there to help with household chores, assist with homework, or, most importantly, serve as playmates for sports, board games, cards, and playing outdoors. The larger neighbourhood and surrounding area were important spaces.

If the geography of childhood's cultural landscape is conceptualized as personalized and made up of expanding circles, with the child's family home at the centre and the northwest quadrant of Calgary as the outer ring, the diversity of experiences is reinforced.[98] Some suburban children were quite attached to their inner circle, centred on the family home, especially given the increasing domestication of children's lives.[99] The home was central for most, yet streets were key sites of activities.

The Streets

During the 1950s and 1960s, playing on sidewalks and streets was not discouraged as it is in some North American neighbourhoods today, where noise, safety concerns, and activity by-laws have put greater restrictions on children and adolescents. In some instances, these by-laws outlawed noise derived from basketball play or, in other situations, they seek to lessen the potential threat of property damage from street hockey play.[100] Streets were a vital part of the social lives of urban children, particularly teenagers, in North America for well over a century, until they became increasingly off limits with the establishment of drinking and driving-age restrictions, bans on adolescent smoking, and stricter enforcement of laws governing sexuality. Collectively, these rules led to spatial islanding and the isolation of many young people.[101]

The terrain of streetscapes changed over time. In the 1950s, many of the early suburban streets were little more than dirt roads. Banff Trail was no exception. Jim Farquharson remembered that "when Canmore Road and Morley Trail were still dirt roads, a friend and I were playing near a badger's hole [right next to one of these streets]. The badger started to come out ... We had a shovel nearby, which I grabbed, and started to fight with it. The badger became very ferocious. I started to hit it with the shovel. Adrenalin pumping, I continued to bash the badger until it died. I was maybe four or five years old."[102] Suburban children constantly experienced the built and natural environments coming together. Many interviewees said that games such as tag, kick the can, riding bikes, and various other sports often took place in the streets, especially before new parks and schoolyards were built.

In addition, suburban streets held dangers that led to experiences that children may or may not have shared with adolescent siblings or adults. Parents and guardians were not as present in children's everyday lives to the same degree as they are in many twenty-first-century middle- and upper-class childhoods. For working-class families, it was not a matter of choice, as parents were away from home, working. Increasingly, city streets were sites for young people clashing with the growing car culture of the 1950s and 1960s. Car culture, and all that came with it, began to mark the lives of children and adolescents, particularly in city streets. Statistics and accident reports contain details relating to children and adolescents as increasing vehicular traffic, not only in Banff Trail but across Calgary, negatively affected people's lives. In 1942, for instance, there were 936 accidents with 18 deaths and $82,926.64 in property damage; only ten years later, in 1952, there were 2,567 accidents, 523 injuries, 13 deaths, and $657,656.66 in property damage.[103] While North American automobiles were equipped with more safety features by the 1950s, more people owned and drove cars, and vehicles became much more expensive and important to owners.

By the early 1960s, Banff Trail teenagers discussed the streets, the effects of traffic, and, notably, implicated parents and teachers in traffic accident occurrences. One 1962 *Aberhart Advocate* student article explained that people did not see cars as potential killers and that people were careless, expecting cars to avoid them—often unavoidably. The article stated that "by law, the responsibility for this accident lies on the motorist, but in actuality it lies on parents and teachers who failed to instill in the child a knowledge of basic traffic safety."[104] Experts and teenagers alike scapegoated parents and teachers.

The streets also served as a battleground between local residents and students. Ironically, it was often community members, people with families and friends with children, who lodged some of the loudest complaints about children, especially adolescents, in the streets. An *Aberhart Advocate* article related that the Calgary police had visited William Aberhart High School in recent months to address the students' growing reputation as poor drivers with bad driving records, much of it based on local community reporting. Police threatened to issue tickets to negligent and careless drivers. The author exhorted student drivers to "buck up and give our school the excellent reputation that it deserves."[105]

To better promote traffic awareness in the early 1960s, the Calgary Police Force began regular visits to all schools, with various safety campaigns. The trend in this period to have police positioned as "friends" rather than disciplinarians has been noted in other cities in Canada such as Montreal.[106] Police were joined by important groups such as the Amalgamated Transit Union Local 58, and from the early 1960s through the 1980s over 100,000 Calgary children were taught vehicle and bicycle safety by transit operators.[107] In the Calgary chief of police's 1960 report, a "Traffic Safety and Education" report appears for the first time. Highlights in the one-page report include "Lectured to 95 Elementary Schools, 34 Junior High Schools and 6 Senior High Schools at 135 school assemblies. Panel discussions on traffic safety conducted at all Junior and Senior High Schools [Branton Jr. High and William Aberhart High School in Banff Trail]. Active Participation: Teen-age Rodeos, Pedal Pusher Clubs, Motor Scooter Club, High School Safety Campaign."[108] By 1962, different statistics were kept regarding traffic accidents, and some of the changes were striking. The annual report recorded that there had been 11,468 accidents, 1,315 injuries, and 20 fatalities in the city. By this time, with the changing focus of reporting, the reports contained the ages of the persons injured: 106 of them were under the age of six, and 220 of the persons injured in traffic accidents were between the ages of six and sixteen.[109] In 1970, the statistical categories related to traffic accidents were the same as they had been in 1952, Banff Trail's first year of existence. In that year, there were 14,134 traffic accidents, 1,563 persons injured, 36 deaths, and $7,638,623.00 in property damage. Eighty-nine of the persons injured were under the age of six, 291 were between the ages of six and sixteen.[110] Calgary's streets, suburban or not, posed real dangers for both children and adolescents. The suburban adolescent experience, in this instance, meshed with that of their fellow urban schoolmates during these years.

Heightened awareness of the dangers of Calgary streets was part of a larger construct focused on youth, safety, and well-being. The discursive construction that juvenile delinquency and generalized rule-breaking and lawlessness were on the rise across Calgary and, indeed, the continent, helped to fuel much of this hyper focus. This process had begun in the 1940s in Calgary. In municipal government documents, references to efforts to stem rising delinquency patterns are referred to as "a modern miracle if they did succeed where parents, teachers, church leaders, police, probation officers and other interested individuals all have tried and failed."[111] Despite attempts to monitor them to a greater degree, streets remained an important site for children and adolescents to live parts of their everyday lives. While Banff Trail's streets were busy with childhood activities, it was the parks and unsupervised spaces within the community that captivated many children and adolescents.

Parks and Unsupervised Spaces

While homes and streets were important for many children, it was time away from the watchful eyes of adults and older siblings that young people relished. Yet parents reported that although they were not watching children's activities directly, they did know where they were. A 1956 Gallup Poll of more than a thousand Canadian parents asked whether knew where all their children were at that time; 89.6 percent of the anonymous respondents said that they did.[112] Among youngsters, much unsupervised time was spent in parks within the community, just outside of the community, and, particularly in the 1950s and early 1960s, in larger areas of the city's expanding northwest quadrant, including the corridor toward Cochrane. In many ways, children made large parts of these areas, at certain times of the day, their own. This was not unprecedented, as playgrounds have been available for appropriation by children across time.[113] Bike rides that covered more than fifteen or twenty miles in one day were common for many young baby boomers who visited nearby towns such as Cochrane or headed to other parts of the growing city. The ability to roam and enjoy the space that the edges of the city offered held a strong pull for some children. Jim Farquharson recalled that even prior to his teenage years, he'd "get up every morning before breakfast ... go for a bike ride, come home, and have my breakfast [before heading off to school or to weekend activities]. My mother used to get concerned, and then she got used to my habits ... I never left a note or anything."[114] With their nearby open spaces, the suburbs offered opportunities for young people to get away from their homes in minutes, particularly on bikes. Most, if not all, interviewees said their parents usually knew their general whereabouts but rarely shadowed them, especially once they were of school age.

Children have always been resourceful with their uses of space, and it was no different with the sites near Banff Trail. Madeline Gablehaus recalled a small area of parkland that children explored while enjoying time together. On "some summer nights the fathers would put up an old tent we had, and the neighbourhood kids and our own would spend the night sleeping out under the stars. In the morning they would all troop to our house ... [for] a nice pancake breakfast."[115]

Children spent time in community parks and green spaces with adults and other young people from a wide range of ages.[116] Young people, sometimes on their own but often with others, used, shared, or reconstituted spaces for their activities. At times, and in certain Canadian cities, the era was marked by a contest over the use of space in urban landscapes. Cities were increasingly crowded, and while playgrounds were designated as children's spaces, youngsters challenged adults for both use and control of territories that had not yet been claimed; space that could have multiple uses had several claimants. While Calgary may not have been as crowded as some other cities such as Toronto or Vancouver, rapid expansion meant that space was both contested and coveted as the postwar era wore on.[117]

School parks were sites for children's after-school activities. Branton Junior High, Banff Trail Elementary, and William Aberhart High School were the three main schools within the community boundaries. William Aberhart High School served students aged six to twelve in its first two years of existence (1958–60), and then it became a dedicated high school, as space for elementary students was at a premium while a new high school cohort was just forming. It was Calgary's fifth-largest high school: it sprawled over ten acres and featured thirty-three rooms.[118] All three schoolyards served as play sites for Banff Trail children, and much of the early evening play was unsupervised and spontaneous. Schoolyard green spaces are sometimes overlooked as park areas, but they were ideal for play, particularly when there were trees on the borders, for play and shade, or, in the case of William Aberhart High School, when there were large fields. This was not unique to Banff Trail, as schools, along with churches, often provided the only nonresidential land use throughout many parts of Canadian suburbs; in most developments, they were in central locations so that children could reach them easily on foot.[119]

Postwar childhood was marked by localized mobility, and suburban children relished opportunities to explore and discover their neighbourhoods and nearby expansive spaces. In the early 1950s, there had been limited urban development to the north of Banff Trail. The Lawrences noted that "[present-day] Confederation Park was a wide open area with prairie grass and a creek running through it. It was a wonderful place to roam through and great for wiener roasts."[120] Boomer parents remembered the importance of space as well. Access to this space was open for most children from the northernmost edges—near Nose Hill—of the Banff Trail suburb, which was still dotted with old farm houses and horses put out to pasture. Roy Farquharson recalled that "by walking north some 100 feet and climbing over an original barbed wire fence one would find themselves right out in the country ... Our children ... had a happy childhood there and enjoyed the wide open spaces, the crocuses, the buffalo beans, the birds and the horses."[121] This recollection necessarily draws on tropes of a romanticized, carefree, agrarian-based childhood that some enjoyed but that exists as much in the mind as it did in everyday life.

Following its first phase of construction in 1960, the University of Alberta at Calgary—renamed the University of Calgary in 1966—was located within walking distance of Banff Trail, just across present-day Crowchild Trail. Many Banff Trail residents considered the new university and its modern facilities to be part of their larger community landscape. By the mid-1960s, young people thought of it as an extension of their space to explore, long before many of them had made their way to the university as students. William Wright, along with several others, recalled that by the time he had reached adolescence in the late 1960s and early 1970s, the university was essentially a playground for him and his friends, who used to "hang around and fool around on the elevators ... I just loved the campus ... It was very modern and futuristic; and the buildings, the design, the architecture was just amazing. I spent a lot of my time hanging around the campus at night. It was my hiding place."[122] These experiences with his friends link Wright temporally to other young people in other eras. Historian Howard Chudacoff notes that urban children in the early twentieth century were resourceful: urban kids appropriated and transformed streets, sidewalks, vacant lots, dumps, rooftops, and buildings for their shared amusement.[123]

Nonetheless, cityscapes, even in developing suburban areas (possibly even more so, given the large number of construction sites), held potential dangers for children and adolescents. For some young people, peril and tragedy coloured their childhoods in Banff Trail. Regardless of whether children live in urban or rural settings, past or present, accidents will be a part of their lives.[124] Children have never been immune to grave danger. Despite greater surveillance of young people, and the increased monitoring of children over the past half century, elements of chance or risk will never be removed completely. In postwar Montreal, death and childhood were intertwined. A baby boomer recalled that his neighbourhood "had its share of tragedies over the years. One that stands out was the boy who was tunneling into a snow bank on the side of the street to build a fort. As he was tunneling into the huge snow bank, a city snowblower went right through the snow bank and killed him."[125] Banff Trail was not immune.

Jim Farquharson discussed how a young boy from Banff Trail died and another boy narrowly escaped with his young life while playing in one of the unsupervised spaces. He discussed in detail how some of the neigh-bourhood kids had dug some tunnels in the sand hills and were playing in them, before lunch, just west of the Banff Trail Elementary school. He wanted to go back after lunch, yet

> my father forbade me to go; he had just recently been in Toronto at a con-ference, [where] some boys had been killed while playing in sand hills. At that moment, Barry MacDonald's dog came barking at full tilt, followed by some of the boys who were hollering that the tunnels had caved in. Barry and Bobby Johnson were unaccounted for. We grabbed some shov-els and ran to where I had been ... A pair of legs was exposed from the waist down ... My dad started digging the boy out ... It was Barry, who lived directly behind us, and he survived ... Bobby was found by a fireman using a shovel to dig. The shovel scraped Bobby's spine, and that's how they found him. He had been buried too long to survive.[126]

Given the near-frenzied pace and volume of land development in postwar suburbs, it was almost inevitable that these tragedies, stemming from nothing more than childhood play, could and did happen. Others men-tioned the number of construction sites that existed well into the mid-1960s and that it was surprising that other, more serious, accidents had not happened, given the number of children and the amount of time they spent unsupervised.

Children and adolescents have never lived their everyday lives in com-plete isolation from tragedy. Childhood accidents are inescapable, and the postwar suburban landscape was no exception, despite efforts by nearly all adults to ensure that children and friends came to no harm; however, chil-dren and youth were safer in these less densely populated parts of Calgary than they were in downtown areas.[127] At its heart, though, the suburban landscape offered children and adolescents opportunities for spontaneity, creativity, and countless hours of activities. These childhood landscapes existed both materially and in the imaginations of those who lived in them.

Imagined Suburban Spaces

Postwar suburban space has been imagined and reimagined count-less times over the past decades by residents, visitors, casual observers, and critics. It has served as a site of promises (realized and unfulfilled), dreams, and, for some, fantasies.[128] At times, representations have come to define these suburban spaces. Historian Brian Osborne posits that land-scapes are culture before they are nature; once a certain representation of landscape, or a myth, establishes itself in a real place, it has a strange way of mixing categories, of making the metaphorical more tangible than their referents and of being part of the scenery.[129] There are times when the imagined has reflected what many early residents found in the postwar suburbs. Margaret Atwood presents a literary representation in her novel *Cat's Eye,* which focuses on Toronto's postwar suburbs. Comments by her main character, Elaine Risley, suggest that the realities of her suburban childhood did not meet expectations. When moving in, she says that the "road in front is muddy too, unpaved, potholed. Dust is on everything: the windows, the window ledges, the fixtures, the floor."[130]

Atwood's protagonist later adds that the process of developing and modernizing her suburban community was taking much longer than her childhood patience allowed and that the collective experience in these patchwork suburbs was a "far cry from picket fences and white curtains, here in our lagoon of postwar mud."[131] Atwood's depiction parallels images recalled by Banff Trail's earliest residents, who experienced similar landscapes.

Many participants also expressed the sense of security and warmth they felt in their younger years.[132] Even contemporary critics of the suburbs such as Peter Wyden acknowledge that there was widespread agreement that suburban spaces gave kids the undeniable feeling of security, possibly because they liked the suburban environment so well.[133] Economic security and its effects on young people's psyches should be considered. Comfort is oftentimes associated with place for young people. Because home often serves as the site for meeting the basic needs for shelter and food, depictions of stable and secure housing in narratives for children can be read as an adult commitment, or promise, that the world is a place where young people cannot merely survive but flourish.[134]

For former childhood residents with positive associations, imaginings of suburbia continue to influence them, as many have chosen to live in other suburban neighbourhoods or, in some cases, in Banff Trail itself. For some of these people, the search for a familiar and comfortable childhood home was also a search for a sense of the childhood security that they may have experienced, but in many ways, by the time they reached adulthood, this childhood was an imagined one.[135]

Regardless of whether they are nostalgic, more recent positive suburban portrayals have not often come from academics but appear in the letters, interviews, and books by the children of postwar suburbia.[136] For these children, a sense of community, while imagined in some ways now, was much more rooted in place in the postwar era. *Community* in that period referred to children and families, defined geographically and spatially by where they lived, worked, and played.[137]

This should not be surprising because people's first spatial and environmental relationships are with their homes and the communities in which they grow up. These places are marked in our imaginations as given, perhaps even natural.[138] One of the most common imagined features of suburbia is that it is a place well away from the urban centre; however, contrary to this familiar representation, postwar suburban development did not routinely take place in isolated fields, far from the city core. Much as in Banff Trail, new housing developments were integrated into existing centres (even if right at the edges). At a community level, there was a good chance that there was already a "place" in these new places.[139]

Conclusion

Space has always mattered to young people. As with things such as time and distance, it can be perceived, and experienced, in different ways by children. One American boomer remembered of the 1950s: "It's hard for people now to remember just how enormous the world was back then ... and how far away even fairly nearby places were. When we called my grandparents long distance on the telephone ... it sounded as if they were speaking to us from a distant star ... Everywhere was far from every-where."[140] Banff Trail was representative of Canadian postwar suburban neighbourhoods in that working-class families were undoubtedly pressured by rising home costs,[141] especially by the mid-1960s, which witnessed the ever-increasing privatization of housing developments, not only in the sub-urbs but also in cities across Canada. Public housing never took firm hold outside of a few pockets in Canada. In this period, Toronto's Regent Park was the most notable attempt to house thousands of low-income, working people.[142] The majority of postwar suburb developments did not do the same. While working people, their families, and children found modest, and at times, affordable homes there, this development occurred within a system that encouraged relatively large mortgages and private home ownership. Affordability and accessibility decreased steadily throughout the 1950s and 1960s. People seeking alternative models, such as public or co-operative arrangements, would not find them in the typical sub-urb, such as Banff Trail. Critics across the continent feared that public housing, much like Medicare, public education, and government pensions, would be deemed a right and that the majority of citizens would demand its implementation.[143] While these discussions did not often include young people, their lives were impacted on several levels by the programs that were implemented and by those that never came to light.

Bombs, Boom, and the Classroom

In 1969, a student editorial appeared in the *Aberhart Advocate* that discussed appropriate and inappropriate school outfits for young women. It's surprising that it was written in 1969 because nostalgia often causes us to view the 1950s as the more likely decade to find evidence of sexism and discussions of teenage clothing. The article also indicates, in a meaningful way, that adolescent girls had challenges to meet in the era's suburban classroom that adolescent boys did not. While trivial to some, the inability to wear slacks or long pants to school suggests just a slice of the larger pie of rules and regulations that children and adolescents faced in the context of the Cold War. Gender roles, conformity, and control created tensions surrounding "freedoms," democracy, and the choice that all Canadians were promised as benefits of Western democracy in a polarized and politicized world:

> We've been living under School Board Regulations for so long that we no longer even hope for the enlightened reform. This accounts for the shock of last Friday's announcement concerning the relaxing of clothing regulations ... On Monday morning, though, the Bubble of Hope was cruelly burst. For some reason the interdict on trousers for girls was slapped back on ... We doubt that the sight of a girl in a pair of pants will corrupt anybody's morals. The regulation is no doubt founded in the society of ten years ago when pants were for casual affairs only.[1]

Aside from home, children and adolescents spent more time in the school classroom than anywhere else. Since the mid-nineteenth century, no formal institution in Canada has had a greater effect on the lives of children and adolescents than schools.[2] Postwar students spent thousands of hours in schools for formal schoolwork and extracurricular activities, including volunteering, yearbook duties, performing arts, fine arts, and sports.[3] In certain instances, some young people spent more of their waking hours in school than in their family homes. This much classroom contact meant that the school's influence, both direct and indirect, was profound on children's lives.[4] Yet these schools did not exist in isolation. The classroom experience for young people reflected and refracted the broader adult threats of the 1950s and 1960s, particularly the Cold War with its omnipresent chill. While nostalgia, some contemporary accounts,[5] and, at times, popular discourse indicate that young children were protected from Cold War machinations and associated fears, print material from schools, combined with compelling oral histories from people who grew up in the postwar suburbs, suggests otherwise. Mothers also aided in the defence from these Cold War forces, both real and perceived, across Canada—linking classrooms and homes in yet another way.[6]

Historian Elaine Tyler May argues that suburbia was represented as stable, prosperous, and peaceful to prove the superiority of Western capitalism in the Cold War era.[7] While this relatively benign childhood was a reality for a small minority of suburban children, particularly those growing up in upper-middle-class suburbs, many more suburban children were, in fact, exposed to aggressive imagery, discursive constructs, and focused activities that attempted to discipline them generally, for potential military service, and for ongoing participation in civilian defence. These images, constructs, and practices created a cultural landscape that prepared them to engage with "enemies" who lay both within and outside postwar Canadian suburban spaces.

Nowhere was this more apparent than in school classrooms. Ironically, the very term *postwar* suggests that war and military realities had evaporated from the minds of children, yet this was not the case. In fact, not only the Cold War but also the First and Second World Wars continued to influence the everyday lives of young people through stories, images, and representations. This influence is unsurprising given that almost one in ten Canadians had served in Canada's Army, Navy, or Air Force between 1939 and 1945.[8]

The Cold War, Children, and Adolescents

The 1950s and 1960s, and especially the latter, were years of important social change despite arguments that for many—and especially middle- and upper-middle-class young people—this was a time marked by a comparatively carefree existence.[9] The idea that children and younger adolescents were either shielded or blissfully unaware of the machinations of war and the growth of the North American military-industrial complex during the twenty-five years following the end of the Second World War can be challenged.[10] Increasingly, the overarching societal concerns were the perceived threat of the spread of communism and the threat of nuclear war. Existential or not, peoples' collective angst was real.

Cold War refers to the challenging diplomatic relations that existed between the USSR and its allies and the United States and its allies.[11] Canada's position was based on its historical, political, economic, and cultural ties to both the United States and the United Kingdom, coupled with the state's fundamental opposition to the Soviet regime. The home front was essential to the prosecution of the Cold War because domestic support for the use of taxes and other resources for rearmament and diplomatic and military commitments had to be prioritized and sustained.[12]

H-bomb surface testing on both sides of the Cold War from 1945 through the early 1960s created an atmosphere of an ever-present threat of nuclear devastation for many suburban children and adolescents.[13] It was not only educators and state officials who made anticommunist education part of their social agenda. Anticommunism was realized through intervention in the National Film Board (NFB), labour unions, and many other civil society organizations. NFB filmstrips and films were widely used in Canadian schools and shaped what children could see, hear, and, potentially, think about the Soviet Union. Also, many women's volunteer organizations took up the cause. The Imperial Order Daughters of Empire, which had previously been concerned with immigration and race, turned its primary attention to anticommunist education in the postwar period. So, too, did other women's groups traditionally involved with children's education, and they ranged from social democratic to conservative in their political orientation.[14] A national tour travelled across the country in the mid-1950s to emphasize the dangers of impending nuclear war with the Soviet Union and its allies. Organized by the federal government, it was meant to leave schoolchildren with a sense of their responsibility to defend themselves, if required. Convoy organizers similarly hoped to underline the message that the exhibit had an educational benefit.[15] It is notable that youngsters in the Soviet Union were also experiencing state-sponsored attempts to educate them about the Cold War from the communist perspective.[16]

A 1955 Calgary high school newspaper article illustrates what many young people were experiencing through various media in regard to the Cold War and, more specifically, A-bomb testing in Nevada. The author doesn't state so explicitly, but it is an interpretation of another account of these events, as the writer was not on site for the testing. The article is

largely descriptive, does not offer any sustained analysis of the developments, and, at some points, is flippant in its commentary and terminol-
ogy. It does, however, offer evidence that young people interpreted these
events with some humour and obvious interest in what was going on in the
larger world:

> There were radiomen, reporters, television operators, contingents of the
> Canadian Army and some ordinary public spectators ... Most personnel
> were so overjoyed at being allowed to see an Atomic blast that not one
> complaint was heard ... When the bomb was dropped ... a brilliant flash
> illuminated the area for miles around, followed by a sudden surge of heat.
> When contact was made ... the spectators there were quite disgruntled,
> because after flying dirt and rock, blown into the air by the bomb has
> landed on their helmets, a cloud of dust had surrounded them, so pre-
> venting them from seeing anything.[17]

While there was no evidence of any Banff Trail bomb shelters being
built, childhood fears, in some cases, were recalled vividly. Bruce Wilson
remembered there being widespread recognition that the Soviet Union
was to be feared, and "that was a huge influence ... They were the enemy ...
[and] represented kind of the opposition. You had to be careful about what
you said about them, that kind of thing. Certainly, in the sixties it was us
against them. [We were] right with the Americans all the way."[18]

Suburban youngsters engaged with and used several forms of military
imagery, material culture, disciplining practices, and play within their
bounded space—schools, streets, homes, parks, and unsupervised sites—
throughout the postwar period. Teachers, administrators, and school curriculums reflected the Cold War's influence on the lives of students both
inside and outside the classroom. North American youngsters of all ages
experienced—both formally and informally—the effects of government
policy; however, much of it focused on white middle-class children.[19]

When the topic of the Second World War was broached with participants, a number of them instead remembered hearing stories centred on
the Great War from grandparents, other family members, and friends.
Some of those born in the 1950s recalled that the Second World War had
been important in a few ways. The war had contributed to familial cohesion
for some. Allan Matthews recalled discussions during Sunday dinners that
focused on his father and his uncles and that cast war in a positive light
from his perspective. The stories were likely sanitized for young ears, and
he recalled in the retelling that "there was a marriage that came out of
that, one of my father's cousins. It was really expressed in positive, in

kind of family terms ... I don't think anyone got killed [in the way war was presented]."[20]

An article that appeared in the *Calgary Herald* in 1950 demonstrates that there were concerted efforts to engage Canadians of all ages in everyday Cold War defence practices. Canadians were encouraged to follow the lead of the United States as the Canadian defence department increased efforts to embolden a continental defence system at several levels. A civil air-raid warning system was designed in concert with one in the United States; it would be implemented by the US Air Force and then maintained by civilians.[21] Operation Lifesaver was operational and working successfully in Calgary by the mid-1950s. One operation involved a neighbourhood right next door to Banff Trail. The operation saw hundreds of residents stream northward out of Calgary on Edmonton Trail to various nearby towns, including Rockyford, Trochu, and Innisfail. The City of Calgary oversaw operations with the help of the RCMP and the Calgary Police Force. Calgarians registered with volunteers upon arrival in the receiving centre and enjoyed hot meals made by local citizens as part of the mock drill.

National polling from the time suggests possible ambivalence about the need for these efforts. A 1959 Gallup Poll asked respondents to look ahead

Cars here are leaving Calgary during Operation Lifesaver civil defence exercises as photographed by the *Calgary Herald* in the fall of 1955. (Reproduced with permission of the University of Calgary Archives and Special Collection, NA-2864-974-2.)

twenty years to consider the possibility of atomic war between Russia and the United States. Over 84 percent of Canadians polled answered no.[22]

This air-raid system was implemented in thousands of towns and cities across North America by the late 1950s and early 1960s.[23] By that time, suburban children had a heightened awareness of events associated with the potential armed struggle and practices for dealing with a Soviet invasion or bombing. Larger events such as the failed Bay of Pigs invasion of Cuba and everyday disciplining practices from the early 1960s were recalled in the context of running home while in grade two or three and having the efforts recorded and timed. Bruce Wilson recalled that "we didn't have the air-raid siren. They had one at Capitol Hill School ... [and] you could hear that thing from miles away. It was kind of scary at the time ... It brought back memories for some parents of being in England and the air raids [from the Second World War]."[24] The air-raid sirens prompted him to think of the Soviet Union and the Cold War in a broader context. Clearly, the Cold War affected his young psyche and certainly shaped some childhood actions and language. He also mentioned how these Cold War practices and sounds had merged with the memories of some survivors of the German bombings in England during the Second World War. He also recalled, in vivid detail, the rectangular blue evacuation sign and route from Calgary's northwest suburbs that children were instructed about in the event of a nuclear attack: "Your dad would come home from work with the one car you had. You'd be home already because you'd run home quickly. Your parents would be ready to load the car to leave town, and those [signs] marked the quickest evacuation routes out of the city."[25] There was a matter-of-fact attitude toward these practices. Despite not seeing the sign for over forty years, he was able to recall, correctly, the shape and colour of it. This everyday practice had become so ingrained that it became a "natural" part of his childhood experience in the mid-1960s.

Military-like disciplining of children took several forms. Although the following account of a trip to an international jamboree in Ottawa appeared in a high school newspaper from outside of Banff Trail, many postwar suburban youngsters (including some research participants) took similar trips.[26] In the article, "Boy Scout Jamboree at Canada's Capital, 1953," reference is made to several disciplining practices involving clothing, being well-organized, producing usable items, and so forth; it also focuses on the outdoor skills gained specifically in Boy Scout training:

> We finally got to Connaught Camp which is just outside of Ottawa, and "piled off" the train ... We then put on our "Stetsons" and "jeans," got our chuckwagons out and proceeded to "live-up" the camp ... After causing

a "minor riot" with the new camp's first "Chuckwagon" race down the main street we stopped to cook and "dole out" a few hundred "flapjacks" ... Attending the camp were 3,500 scouts from every province in Canada, from the U.S.A. from Cuba, Mexico, Australia, England, Scotland, Grand Cayman Island, Sweden, Norway, Greece, Italy, [and] France.[27]

These adolescent Boy Scouts reinforced many Calgary stereotypes on this trip, but the article also emphasizes the hard work, basic skills, and testing that were central to scouting. This emphasis reflected the utilitarian focus in school curriculums, which school principals and vice-principals stressed in their essays to students and papers.

Doug Cass recalled the growing importance and popularity of scouting within the Banff Trail community in the late 1950s and early 1960s. As with many other childhood activities, he noted that it was his parents who initiated and fostered his participation: "Scouting was something they [my parents] would have just signed me up for at six or seven. Almost all of my close friends were from that group of boys. At one time, I remember people talking about St. David's having one of the largest scouting programs in all of Canada; four Scout troops with 24 boys in each."[28]

The Cadet program was designed to prepare adolescents directly and fully for military training. Young people may have had individual motives for entering into formal programs and may not have been interested in the goals of adult programming. Bruce Wilson stressed the continuing importance of remembrances of the First and Second World Wars, along with Remembrance Day. He recalled it being the impetus for his joining the Cadets, although he did not necessarily intend to join the Armed Forces in adulthood: "Dad told me a lot of stories about the war ... That shaped our respect for the Armed Forces and the military. It was a positive attitude towards that—it was a positive thing."[29] Countless advertisements for the Armed Forces can be found in high school yearbooks, especially in the 1950s and early 1960s.

Newspapers in the postwar period featured countless reports related to Cold War developments. While the youngest children did not read the newspaper, many school-aged children did, and thousands of children and adolescents across the country delivered these newspapers door to door on their paper routes. In the early 1950s, newspapers such as the *Calgary Herald* blared headlines such as "Chinese Fortress Falls: Allies Mop Up 'Iron Triangle.'" This particular article described advancing forces moving across the central Korean plains and "rubbing out" the Communists' iron triangle.[30]

For some youngsters, the Second World War, and some of the earliest events associated with the Cold War, had important residual effects on their lives. Born in the late 1940s, Mary Baker fondly remembered the huge numbers of kids on Banff Trail's streets due to the postwar baby boom, but she also had more sobering memories associated with the Second World War, including a friend's father whose personality still reflected his haunting combat experiences. She recalled: "I had a friend whose father was quite grim. My understanding was that he had come home from the war that way ... I certainly had the sense that World War II was a just war, which was so interesting, because I immediately knew that Vietnam was not."[31] It is interesting that these two major wars were represented in her memories in very different ways. As an adolescent, she was thinking much more critically about war and its meanings and inferred that her friend's father was likely suffering from undiagnosed posttraumatic stress disorder caused by his duties associated with the Second World War, something she had not considered as a young person.

Bruce Wilson recalled that family stories about the Second World War shaped his childhood understandings of both war and Canada's military. These stories also affected how he felt about the Vietnam War as a junior high student in the mid-1960s. He recalled that there seemed to be general support for the Vietnam War. His memories contrast with several archival documents and with the memories of others, who indicated that this was not the case. Yet this is what he remembered. His account offers a richer and more nuanced understanding of how children and adolescents tried to understand these conflicts: "When the Vietnam War came later, there wasn't that negativity within our group. In the context of Banff Trail, it was pretty promilitary, pro-support of what had happened in the war [Second World War], for those who had veterans or family members who were participating."[32]

Early 1950s newspaper articles, citing Canada-wide public opinion polls, reflected a shift away from the view that Canada's older male teenagers and young adults should serve in the Canadian Armed Forces, regardless of whether they had a desire to do so. A *Calgary Herald* article excerpt titled "Public Tends to Oppose Younger Age for Draft," from 1951, reveals that public opinion was firmly in favour of Canada not having a universal draft. Public opinion was also shifting toward the continued blurring of the teen years with young adulthood. When asked about the draft, if conscription were in place, only 30 percent of Canadians favoured setting the initial age at eighteen instead of twenty-one.[33]

Despite this overwhelming public sentiment, it is striking how many recruiting advertisements were found in Calgary school yearbooks.[34] These advertisements contained action-oriented and aggressive military representations, and they outlined the potential duties and benefits of serving in the Armed Forces. Often, these representations drew on First World War imagery in appealing directly to teenagers.[35] Furthermore, these advertisements appeared in both junior and senior high school yearbooks. One advertisement, from Crescent Heights High School, which was attended by some of the earliest Banff Trail teenagers, is representative of dozens of similar Armed Forces advertisements. It stresses the flexibility available to male recruits and the national importance of enlisting. Training was limited to twenty-eight weeks. Upon receiving a commission, a recruit could choose to serve between three and five years.[36]

Wendy Glidden referred to an uncle who had not wanted to discuss his role in the Second World War. She recalled that she had held some childhood fears related to the Cold War in the 1960s and what could happen because of the ongoing conflict. While she did not think of these events as having a profound effect on her childhood, she implicitly did so through her words and tone when she recalled that the silence surrounding her uncle's participation was important in itself, as he "never wanted to talk about it. Because my dad never served, it was never brought up much ... other than I remember the [school-related] drills, and I remember the Soviet Union was bad ... because they were against the United States. I distinctly remember watching TV and President Kennedy."[37]

Young people were aware of the effects of war on former combatants. Glidden said that she knew even as a child that this topic was not to be broached with her uncle. The fear associated with these disciplining drills was also emphasized when she recalled "being a little scared, I think because we practised these drills. I don't think we understood why we were doing them so much, other than the Soviet Union was a bad place. Maybe they could invade; and communism was bad."[38] These memories reinforce much of what is said in student essays, articles, and editorials: young people, particularly preteens, often felt ill-informed about the reasons why there were told to do some things. This speaks to the marginalization experienced by children when adults assumed they were unable to deal with these issues cognitively and emotionally. The untold, the unspoken, and the unexplained likely heightened fears for some children.

Others recalled incidents directly associated with Cold War events. One remembered expressing some empathy with child victims of the Korean War. Reflecting other people's fears, respondents related that the overarching themes of danger and impending disaster were prominent in their formative years. Mary Baker said that when she was sick and didn't want to eat, she'd suggest sending her food to kids starving in Korea. She also remembered that while the Russians were considered dangerous, it was more the global situation, including the Cuban Missile Crisis, that was feared.

She recalled thinking, "I'm going to be out of class the next day ... What will they let a girl do? ... I can't remember being virulently anticommunist [because at home] there was not a lot of demonizing [of the Soviet Union]. Khrushchev was considered funny and a fool."[39] She also expressed some frustration associated with her gender and not being confident that a young girl would be allowed to do something about the crisis if it were to ever escalate. Imminent danger and the fears associated with it clearly affected adolescents negatively; adolescents were more sophisticated than children in remembering, and critically analyzing these events.

In addition to discussions about the atomic bomb, students continued to discuss the previous wars until the 1960s. In this brief editorial from the *Aberhart Advocate,* a student expresses the importance of the twentieth century's two world wars and the uncertainties of the future in the context of the ongoing Cold War:

"Ideological battles are not won on the poppy sales corner, they're won in the minds of men." But I believe that the horror of two world wars must never be forgotten, if we are to press onwards for peace in our time, and I for one, would not like to leave such ideological battles to the author of the above statement ... We are inheriting a world with a threat of war, hor-rible beyond the realms of imagination. In our hands will the nightmare become reality, and the fiction fact? The future is hours [*sic*] but the past must not have been in vain.[40]

This student seemed to have some sense of the past and that it continued to influence present circumstances.

William Wright recalled the overriding angst that defined the time for many children and adolescents. He also broached the topic of the United States's relationship with Canada and that, from his perspective, the mutual respect between the two countries seemed at a higher level in the late 1960s.[41] While he was nearly twenty years younger than the oldest boomers, the Second World War and its importance still resonated with him. He noted that while not all children were moved by Remembrance Day, he certainly had been during a time when, at least to his mind, it was more relevant than today. He recalled "a sense of American history being perva-sive. Big Brother was watching over us from the States. I remember it being much more respectful of the United States ... and feeling the effects of the Cold War ... People were still nervous about where the world was going."[42]

In this case, from the perspective of childhood, "Big Brother" was not viewed in an Orwellian sense. Wright was someone who had been comforted by having the United States as an ally and who understood how the relationship benefitted Canada in a global context. A review of Alberta textbooks from the period also reveals an emphasis on positive United States–Canada relations, especially in the context of broader geopolitical happenings.[43]

For others, the Cold War did not affect their childhoods to the same degree. Surprisingly, despite it having ended decades earlier, echoes from the Great War continued to be heard, and some young people continued to experience that war vicariously. For some, the earlier war had greater resonances than the Second World War. Anecdotes relating to the world wars were passed down from older family members, including former combatants. Sharon Johnstone remembered her dad recalling that "on the radio they were listening to how Hitler had hid out in the bunkers and it was victory for the English ... Dad's father had a wonderful story that got written up in *Reader's Digest* about the First World War, swapping buttons at the Front and, on Christmas Eve, going out with a football and playing with the enemy."[44] This story, despite first appearing in *Reader's Digest* and being told from the perspective of adulthood, was almost child-like in its recollection, making combat acceptable for a wide readership. It humanized the war effort for this baby boomer and shifted focus away from the violence, drudgery, and brutality that marked trench warfare in the Great War.

The Cold War also inspired poetry and other creative writing from several young people, particularly once they were in suburban high schools. This writing also demonstrated a clear line between childhood and adolescence. Some of it was powerfully written and suggests active and engaged minds. The following poem's language is both haunting and angst-filled. In other words, it does not read as being created by a worry-free teenager, unaware of the world outside insular suburban life:

I am a citizen of a silent world.
Grey and stark against a crimson sky
Stand the ruins of an age gone by.
And I.
Rubble and stone have chalked the crying ground.
Torn and scarred, this a dying land.
Destruction wrought by one misguided hand,
Un-planned.
I alone, am left to rule a world,
Alone, beneath a hungry waiting eye,
I could live. But for what reason:
Why?
I die.[45]

As time passed and the Cold War's effect on young suburbanites changed, a different tone pervaded children's and adolescents' literature. While there was no question that the sense of foreboding remained with many, some essays expressed hope for a better future. While children have been mobilized and continue to be used as sources of inspiration for the future, at times they also cast themselves in this role.[46] Many adolescents did not look through rose-coloured glasses, and they were able to understand at least some of the complexities of the international geopolitics that seemed to make less and less sense to some young people over time. While some were prone to hyperbole, a piece that appeared in the *Aberhart Advocate* in 1963 emphasized that many young people were frightened to turn on the "idiot box" for fear that war had broken out with an enemy who "he doesn't know." The writer argues that kids were the ones that had to speak out in the absence of leadership from elders, parents, and other leaders. He writes, "[It] would be a long hard struggle, probably longer and harder than most of us can imagine. But, it would mean that our children, and their children's children would grow up in a green, peaceful world."[47]

In this proposed scenario, young people would lead their parents and there would be a sense of collective consciousness. For the writer, individuals could do little, but together, as part of society, they could achieve great things. This idea resists much of the discourse in this period that stressed individuality, resourcefulness, and gaining competitive advantages rather than working with others toward a collective goal.

In another article in the *Aberhart Advocate* titled "Space Law," a teenaged writer explores one of the most significant Cold War issues from the early 1960s: negotiating and managing governance and law in outer space. The potential for outer space becoming a theatre for war is discussed, along with some of the similarities between outer space and the high seas. The issues of sovereignty, control, and the consequences of war are central: "The most feasonable [*sic*] solution to the problem of space vehicle control would be to apply the rules of the high seas ... This is no assurance that space could not, like the high seas, be turned into a theatre of war if a vehicle was stationed there for the purpose of conducting war-like activities."[48] The fact that some students had concerns about the spread of conflict into space demonstrates again how aggression, war, and angst influenced their thinking.

Individual differentiation in childhood experiences is, nonetheless, important. For some children and adolescents of the late 1960s, the Cold War was not front and centre. While the Soviets remained the enemy, some young people believed that military confrontation might not mean total destruction for the major powers and that Canada was safely on the periphery in some ways. Lesley Hayes, one of the younger boomers, remembered that by the early 1970s the Soviets had been firmly established as the bad guys. It was communism (bad) versus capitalism (good), with the latter being represented by Canada. She said it was clearly black and white and that "Canada was a little bit [separate from the United States] ... It was kind of something we watched as opposed to [engaging in it ourselves]; I always felt pretty safe ... I thought there might be bombs overhead ... but I never felt they could land here and my dad would go to war."[49] Oftentimes, to varying degrees, children and adolescents did grapple with broader issues derived from the adult world. As in all eras, some children and a larger portion of adolescents reacted to a complex world.[50]

An editorial that appeared in *The Albertan,* clearly the more conservative of the two Calgary dailies in 1969, offered some sweeping generalities not reflected by young people's writings or participants' memories. While the editorial grants that there were serious conflicts around the globe, it does not ascribe many, if any, positive qualities to children and youth. It dismisses many in the group as privileged, incapable of working hard, and essentially immoral. It calls for sympathy given the "savage, barbarous age" and contends that young people, along with being spoiled, lacked discipline and rules. The author continues: "Children today have been brought up in the atmosphere of war and rebellion. Many believe there is nothing wrong with stealing; it's being caught that's the sin ... They see the lies about Vietnam ... about disarmament talks and nuclear bomb testing."[51]

Contrary to much of what was postulated in this editorial, adolescents produced satirical pieces that played with words and concepts in a sophisticated manner. In "Musical News Report," which appeared in the *Aberhart Advocate,* the writer matches the Cold War's Cuban Missile Crisis to contemporary music:

> Khruchev [sic] has been trying to maintain his friendship with Fidel Castro of Cuba to strengthen the ties between their two countries (Let's Get Together). Castro said that his country would always be one of Russia's most valuable allies (This Land is Your Land). On October 22 President Kennedy announced to the public that he had discovered that missiles and missile bases were being shipped from Russia to Cuba (Johnny Get Angry). Khruchev denied that this was true (Rumoured). Kennedy, however, said that he had had pictures taken and could prove that they were being built. He was very shocked at Khruchev's denial (Your Nose is Gonna Grow). When Khruchev finally admitted the truth Kennedy said that a quarantine would be put on all ships going to Cuba until the missiles were shipped back to Russia (Return To Sender) ... Kennedy's

quick action on this matter will undoubtedly make Communists more cautious of him in their plot to spread their idea (Big Bad John) ... At a U.N. meeting early this year Khruchev in a heated argument found it necessary to pound the table to emphasize his words (If I Had a Hammer). Unfortunately he didn't so he used his shoe."[52]

Teenage writers, such as this one, were attuned to the broader world and had a clear sense of ethics, at least in their minds. It is another reminder that some young people have had, and continue to have, meaningful and thoughtful intellectual engagement with current events.

Young people also wrote jokes associated with the Cold War. This one, from a 1950s high school yearbook, was written shortly after the Russian launch of one of the Sputnik satellites:

JOE: Did you hear what Sputnik got for Christmas?

JIM: No, what?

JOE: A guided mistletoe?[53]

In a similar vein, Allan Matthews recalled being somewhat irreverent regarding some of the disciplining practices of the time, including religious teachings and sermons that broached the issue of the Cold War and its potential for ending the world. His words also reinforce that, much like adults, some adolescents coped with important issues in other ways. He made light of some of the practices that young people were asked to perform in reaction to a potential bombing by the enemy. He also found some humour in what these disciplining practices meant in a broader Cold War context, in terms of basic logistics related to the comparatively harsh winters in Calgary: "Putting our heads under our desks during 1962 and 1963 ... the only thing was that you got to get home from school early ... It was a bit of an adventure. We had all these hot bikes, so we could get home in two minutes. You just hoped they didn't drop an atomic bomb in January, and you'd have to put your snowsuit on."[54]

Classroom Lives

By the postwar era, young people had been going to school for more than a hundred years, dating back to the pre-Confederation colonies.[55] All children attended school in some form. The importance of formal education in the lives of children and adolescents, by the early 1950s, was well established. Schools, and all they offered, mattered on many levels.

Classroom experiences reflected both continuity and change throughout the period. Wendy Glidden recalled that her elementary school had separate entrances for boys and girls—something that would fade from school practices following this period. She recalled the newness of schools—the shiny linoleum floors, for instance.[56] Windows were also more common in new buildings, and the introduction of fluorescent lighting meant that school spaces had more light.[57] Several students remembered that green chalkboards replaced blackboards, adding to the classrooms' brightness. Doug Cass recalled that the influx of kids was large but that the infrastructure was not in place. For him, this meant having to spend a year of elementary school in a wing of the newly built William Aberhart High School.[58] New school construction could not keep up with housing construction and the burgeoning cohort of kids, especially in the late 1950s and early 1960s, when numbers peaked. The youngest students mingled with much older students in the new high school for part of the day, prior to moving into a brand-new elementary school.[59] Regardless of where school was, most participants were excited to head to it.

While the individual experiences of students varied, by the 1950s school classrooms provided an opportunity for young people to explore other sides of their personalities, attempt new activities, build new friendships, and, quite simply, spend time away from parents and guardians,

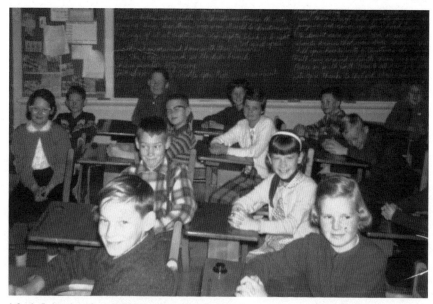

A Grade 5 class from Capital Hill Elementary School in Calgary from January of 1962. Banff Trail was one of the main feeder communities for this school. (Reproduced with permission of the family.)

all while learning about and navigating the postwar world. School was an important setting where the personal qualities and characteristics of young students could be acknowledged and developed.[60] By these years, the central institution of adolescence was, unquestionably, the high school.[61] Socioeconomic change meant that adolescents identified and were associated with school, recreation, and leisure more than with paid labour.[62]

This period saw recovery from the Great Depression and the effects of the Second World War and tremendous growth for public education in Alberta. Increasingly, teachers specialized at specific grade levels rather than teaching in multigrade classrooms. More and more students completed high school across Alberta, as they did across the country. Throughout the 1950s, Alberta had the highest per capita spending on education in Canada[63] within the context of economic growth and increased provincial government spending. Growth in Calgary's school population was constant and tremendous (reflected in a lack of schools, in some instances). A 1962 *Calgary Herald* article titled "School Population Up by 5,000" provides a good snapshot of the year over year changes that happened across the expanding city, especially in the expanding suburbs: "There are a total of 58,848 pupils behind desks this year, as compared with 53,786 last year. The Calgary Public School Board counts 48,279 students in its classrooms, while at the same time last season there were 45,119. There are 10,569 pupils attending separate schools in the city. Last year there were 8,667."[64]

By the end of the 1960s, little had changed in that new school infrastructure was badly needed across Calgary. While there had been need for expansion as early as the late 1940s, these needs did not stop with the end of the baby boom in 1964. As the 1960s closed, the following newspaper article detailed existing school construction and anticipated needs in the city:

> Calgary's ever-growing public school population is forcing school board officials to provide within three years a record $33,000,000 worth of new schools and additions—13 times as much school construction as they needed just 12 years ago. With more than 3,200 additional students entering the Grade 1 classes each year, the Public School Board is faced with providing 13 new schools and 8 additions as soon as possible ... The new schools required are in addition to the nine new schools, 14 portable classrooms and 20 additions to existing schools the Public School Board currently has under various stages of construction.[65]

Even though the baby boom came to an end in 1964, its reverberations continued to be felt in the everyday realities of children: the youngest boomers did not enter kindergarten and grade one until 1969 and 1970.

Throughout the period, influential policy-makers had specific concepts about and made recommendations on how young pupils should be educated. Alberta educationists such as University of Alberta's Professor William Hardy argued that education for democracy did not mean that all children should experience the same schooling or the same courses. He recommended the establishment of special classes for the gifted that would use more traditional methods of instruction and a more rigorous academic curriculum.[66] The school curriculum, while always written by an elite academic or professional, at times imposed ideas about citizenship on schools and at other times attempted to respond to people's concerns in the province.[67] These concerns ranged from programming content, to the quality of instruction, to streaming and "special" classes. It was not uncommon for students to be administered intelligence and achievement tests to determine special programming or materials. These issues were not unique to this era by any means.[68]

The Alberta government established the Cameron Commission in 1957 to assess and recommend changes to the province's approach to education. The final report, released in 1959, contained more than 250 recommendations for the development and improvement of education and school curriculums in Alberta. The recommendations focused on concerns as diverse as the pedagogy and merits of progressive education, the beginnings of the Space Age, the frustration of business with the supposed unsatisfactory skills of graduates, and the dissatisfaction of university groups with the alleged inadequacy of high school programs.[69] Reflecting many influences, the commission's report recommended core subjects, highly specialized curriculums, standardized testing, direct-teaching methods, and citizenship training. Some aspects of the report were in line with the broadest outlines of progressive education, but it is too simplistic to characterize it as either progressive or antiprogressive. It had elements of both. Alberta was not alone in Canada in undertaking a major study of its education system. Between 1960 and 1970, every province in the country examined its systems of elementary, secondary, and postsecondary education.[70] Alberta classrooms reflected both progressive and antiprogressive (traditional) elements in the 1950s and 1960s.[71] Ultimately, the Alberta example demonstrates that, despite efforts to train teachers, education in progressive pedagogical techniques failed because it really did not help teachers fully understand and internalize theory and praxis.[72]

The media was a part of this discussion, particularly from the earliest years of the postwar period. It reflected healthy skepticism about the possibility of implementing progressive education tenets in Calgary classrooms, arguing that "if Junior is courteous to the school janitor and isn't shy, he will get a good mark on his report card. And Calgary school officials consider such characteristics as important as high marks in arithmetic, spelling, and the other school subjects."[73] Traditional practices seemed much more entrenched than the proposed progressivism touted by some allowed.

Corporal punishment was decried in progressive education theory, but it remained in many suburban classrooms until the 1970s—and beyond. A 1969 Gallup Poll asked participants if the discipline in their local public schools was too strict or not strict enough. Fifty-three percent felt it was not strict enough, and 44 percent believed it was "about right." Only 2.5 percent believed it was too strict.[74] A decade earlier, national polling revealed that 93 percent of respondents believed that discipline in schools was not severe enough.[75] Bruce Wilson remembered his disciplining in school and that the "strap was in vogue ... I never got it [as] I was one of those kids that avoided that kind of thing ... By the time we got to junior high, a little more open ... I was in the Matriculation Program of Honours group, so we were pretty tight [as a cohort]."[76] A 1959 national poll asked Canadians if teachers should have the right to "paddle" students in grade school as a form of punishment. Fifty-two percent of respondents said they should, indicating that there was support for some forms of corporal punishment in these years.[77]

Wilson also mentioned tensions between progressive and more traditional education practices, with the latter still focusing on discipline, corporal punishment, and pervasive everyday regulation. He also stressed that social divisions were evident by high school, not necessarily along class lines but between those students who were university-bound and those who were not.[78] At least in his recollections, students who were not university-bound tended to be more involved in the drug culture of the mid-1960s. If conformity and regulation gained favour with some teachers in suburban classrooms, it must be stressed that everyday practices did not necessarily change, despite recommendations from educational theorists. Along with an expanding cadre of administrators and professionals such as physicians, psychologists, and social workers, there were new tools at the disposal of school leaders. By the 1960s, high school guidance counsellors were probing adolescent personalities—along with intelligence—in schools across Canada and the United States, and the findings were recorded in closed, permanent records.[79] As in other modern institutions involved in heightened surveillance, such as prisons and hospitals, elementary, junior high, and secondary schools were places where young children and adolescents were observed and classified, required to obey rules, measured in terms of their relationship to specific standards, and directed to modify behaviours and their physical appearance.[80] Interviewees said that the elementary school and junior high years were marked by order and discipline. Seating was in rows, often by alphabetical order; at times it related to performance. Teachers did much of the talking, copying from the board was a constant, and rote memorization was encouraged and fostered.

Some people recalled with fondness their walks to school, of varying distances, and the sidewalks being filled with young people either on foot or on bikes. Frank Edward said that he could hear the bell ring from his house and still make it to school on time.[81] First days were not as intimidating as they might have been otherwise. While some students recalled being apprehensive about meeting teachers and learning the new rules, most recalled that older siblings and friends of older siblings helped make the transition to school much smoother than it would have been otherwise.

Many recalled that the schoolgrounds often filled before the bell rang. Arriving early allowed for additional socializing at lunch hour or after school. Routine marked the school day, as most recalled easily. While the routines were not the same each and every year, most days started with the recitation of the Lord's Prayer and singing "God Save the Queen" (some younger participants recalled the national anthem by the late 1960s), with an acknowledgement of the Canadian Red Ensign or, later, the flag featuring the Maple Leaf, which was prominent in most, if not all, classrooms.

For others, the routines and rhythms of learning were not especially notable. It was school activities outside the classroom that they found most memorable. Sharon Johnstone recalled choir as an appreciated outlet for music and that she was also involved in band.[82] Art classes were also memorable and welcomed. William Wright also recalled that drama and film clubs were important, both for the work they encouraged and for feeding a young ego that relished the opportunity to perform and be creative.[83]

Various female interviewees recalled that school provided a much-needed outlet for physical activity among younger girls. Organized sports and teams were unavailable to many girls, even in the 1960s. Tammy Simpson remembered that participating in track and field and volleyball at school were especially noteworthy. Elizabeth Davidson recalled volleyball as enjoyable and emphasized that the opportunity to be in an all-girls shop class was relished. Michelle Macdonald recalled that it was fun to participate in all sports, but gymnastics and track and field were highlights. Donna McLaren said she played every sport at school that she could and that it was her main focus—it was a defining feature of her school experience. Competition was not cited as being especially important for most participants, although for some it was fun to compete; for the large majority, it was participation and being physically active that mattered more than anything else.[84]

The arts, which could take many forms, were also a large part of student life. Choir, band, and music in general mattered to several participants. Jim Farquharson recollected playing in the band was a good experience in his junior high years.[85] Tammy Simpson said that choral singing was important and that a memorable music teacher helped to foster her interest.[86] Elizabeth Davidson mentioned with fondness both choir and acting, activities she joined once she was in junior high. Sharon Johnstone also remembered that spending time with friends and singing in the choir was fun. She described art class was "pretty good" and viewed playing in the school band as a positive experience. The new options offered after elementary school in junior high were appreciated.[87]

Some participants recalled that classroom seating (at least by the high school years in the late 1960s and early 1970s) was changed by some teachers and that group work featuring lively discussion was encouraged by some teachers in some courses. University-bound students were encouraged to engage in these sorts of discussions. Despite these changes, it was the school principals and vice-principals who remained influential in shaping representations that came to define the era in many ways. Their messages were placed prominently in yearbooks, and at times principals and vice-principals wrote short essays directed at students that defended some of the core values of traditional education. Many of these principals, exclusively male in Calgary suburban and nonsuburban schools, had been involved in the Canadian, British, or American school systems for several decades so there were more traditional exhortations to work hard and persevere in these messages. In most settings, principals were now being asked to oversee hundreds of students and dozens of teachers while implementing more complex systems and curriculums than there had been in the interwar period, when many of their teaching careers had begun. The following yearbook message, from 1957, directed at a wider audience than just students, was the first principal's message from the newly built Branton Junior High School in Banff Trail. The qualities stressed by E.M. Borgal in this message, and emphasized by many others, were grounded in traditional teaching, including being prepared to contribute positively (both economically and socially) as citizens.[88] He focused on personal development in the form of good habits in the hopes of creating better citizens who would be "industrious, cooperative, and enthusiastic." Schoolwork and extracurricular activities would "set up standards that will establish precedents for future years. I wish to congratulate you upon your private effort toward the progress of the school ... Individually, your success in school can be measured to a large degree by the attitudes and habits you have established."[89] Clearly, the goal of schooling, at least for this principal, was above all else to produce dependable, conscientious students for the capitalist workplace. There was an emphasis on the individual as opposed to anything that could be construed as "collective."

In this same yearbook, the school's namesake, W.A. Branton, echoed much of what Principal Borgal expressed, but he emphasized that these school years were the most important of young students' lives. This message reinforces narratives that emerge in both the archival record and

Yearbook advertisements for post-secondary scholarships, this one sponsored by the City of Calgary, often featured words and phrases like "leadership," "serious-minded," and "hopes for tomorrow." In ads like these, high school students were exhorted to do their best in order to succeed. (Crescent Heights High School yearbook, 1950–51 and reproduced from the author's personal collection.)

interviews that counter the idea of a carefree, young suburban life without significant responsibilities and pressures or consequences for actions. In these narratives, appeals to individual achievement are prominent, with hard work and discipline at the core of the message.[90]

In Alberta, and across Canada, curriculums in the 1950s and 1960s focused on imparting the values of utility and hard work; the public, politicians, and educators continued to discuss creating "good" future citizens.[91] The other virtues that educators mentioned, such as responsibility, freedom, persistence, and reliability, were, at most turns, associated with "successful" and "pertinent" employment. Classroom teaching was important, but supervised extracurriculars such as student newsletters, annual yearbooks, and clubs were designed to instill values such as responsibility, dedication, and good citizenship. Several participants, such as Frank Edward, mentioned that they were not joiners.[92] Yet others, such as Michelle Macdonald, recalled joining clubs such as the Library Club and its importance to her school experience.[93] Mary Baker remembered being a member in a drama club; writing for the school newspaper, the *Aberhart Advocate*; and serving as the yearbook editor in high school.[94] Contributing to school projects, measured creativity, and being productive were mentioned often by participants.

These memories indicated that at least some students were able to exercise some decision-making and had creative outlet for their interests, even though many educators overlooked qualities such as creativity, personal initiative, and independent thought.[95] It was within the context of the Cold War that these qualities were emphasized and then deployed. Education in Canada had to be seen in all ways as superior, since it was both perceived and believed to be one of Canada's "national resources" and a critical investment in the competitive and ideologically volatile postwar world.[96] It reinforced the larger "battles" between East and West, capitalism and communism, and, for many, right and wrong.

This emphasis on values such as responsibility, utility, and hard work applied easily to physical activity and sport. Not all young people, however, accepted this emphasis wholeheartedly and actively. Sharon Johnstone recalled that much of her learning did not seem designed to stimulate. She remembered classroom work as contrived, over planned, and flat in many ways.[97] Young people questioned the curriculum's content and its pedagogical focus, as argued by an William Aberhart high school student in the *Aberhart Advocate*:

> There are many factors ... which indicate that the mind is fast losing in
> the battle of brawn versus brains ... Mind Over Matter is a statement
> which is becoming quite difficult to believe as far as the acceptance of

the diligent student against the outstanding athlete is concerned ... The duty of any school is to exercise and train the mind, rather than to train and exercise the body ... One can learn physical fitness at home where it should be taught.[98]

This questioning can be read as antiactivity statements, but it also reflects a genuine resistance to the pedagogy of the times, which reinforced the school's central role in educating students holistically or, as some might see it, worked to regulate both body and mind.

In a 1964 piece titled "Is School Spirit Necessary?," resistance to being considered a "bad patriot" and "lacking national spirit" for not participating in or supporting school sports events is paramount.[99] At the time, school-based sports and recreation activities were often cast as crucial ways to maintain healthy bodies and self-discipline in the increasingly competitive Cold War world. The article also discusses democratic principles, citizenship, and patriotism. The author points out that many high school students would be entering adulthood the following year and that many of these activities were foolish for those standing on the edge of being adults, regardless of their actions. The editorial ends with a declaration that young people need to be treated as individuals, as emerging adults with complex interests and qualities:

Most of us come here to be educated, not to be bellowed at for our lack of school spirit ... The school is run on democratic principles and ... that being so, is a citizen of that state called a bad patriot and lacking national spirit because he does not attend football games, join the curling league or bowl with the bowling team? ... We are now "young adults" and many have interests in things other than school clubs ... We are individuals with varied interests and should NOT be massed together as a group having stereotyped avocations.[100]

There are some age-old arguments being made here about teenagers on the cusp of adulthood seeing themselves as much more than children, as individuals engaging in adult activities such as doing paid work and driving cars. Possibly more important is the author's questioning of the truism that interest and ability in sports is a measure of school spirit or its adult form, proper citizenship. This conception of citizenship fits well with the idea that both educators and industry leaders wanted the postwar high school to meet the needs of all young Canadians by catering to their interests, keeping them in school, and preparing them to be productive as workers and, just as importantly, consumers upon high school graduation.[101]

In the early 1970s, adolescents continued to seek answers to questions regarding education and its meanings. In an article that appeared in *Lead Balloon* in 1970, Laura Fowler expressed reservations about an education system, and its adherents, focused more on results (often the right job and material gains) than on pursuit of knowledge for knowledge's sake. She employs some of the sexist language that was still in wide use; men, for instance, are assumed to be the future leaders. She argues that most people view education not as the search for knowledge but as a way to obtain more material items. The article states that teachers often say, "'Oh! You don't have to bother with that, they never ask about it in the finals.' When teachers of today take that attitude, what can you expect of the leading men of tomorrow?"[102] But by the early 1970s, other shifts were viewed positively. Elizabeth Davidson recalled that her early elementary years were defined by nurturing teachers and that creative outlets such as creative writing were encouraged and fostered in the classroom.[103]

By the end of the 1960s, young suburbanites were offering sophisticated critiques and analyses of their Cold War classroom experiences. While not endorsing some of these new practices outright, they were obviously curious about the new practices used in the classroom. Some lobbied for a learning experience that would operate outside the bounds of the classroom in the form of a "free school" that would be a place with a great deal of freedom and few regulations and restrictions. These schools would foster curiosity and lead students to the "slums, to the zoo, to the courthouse, to the slaughterhouse, any place where they can probe deeply into matters of great interest ... Admittedly, in a society smitten by the Protestant work ethic, the idea that learning can and should be fun is a bit hard to take."[104] This final point took a swipe at the age-old Protestant work ethic and its ongoing impact on pedagogy in classrooms. Sharon Johnstone said that when it came to teaching and consistency, "there was no consensus on many things."[105]

There is a general impression that the education system, as a whole, was constantly expanding and more inclusive than ever during the postwar era, but this was not the case for all age groups. Like their counterparts in other provinces, for many years in this period young suburbanites in Banff Trail were not able to attend kindergarten in a public school because there was no appropriate funding from the provincial government, as outlined in a *Calgary Herald* article. It noted that the Calgary Public School Board, making a decision based on surveys, questionnaires, and recommendations from across North America, and beginning in 1956, would no longer fund "immature" children for kindergarten and that "Calgary, up to the fall of 1954, was the only centre in Alberta where kindergartens were operated as part of the system."[106] Other school systems, even outside of Canada, could and did influence decisions made in the Calgary, although this did not mean that certain communities, such as Banff Trail, could not take direct action when it came to community, neighbourhood or local works.

Kindergarten schooling did not stop with the end of direct provincial funding; communities, as they are often forced to do when the state cuts social programming, cobbled together programs to help educate young students. Many believed that this early childhood education was critical to preparing youngsters for more formal education. Provincial funding for kindergartens did return in the early 1970s, and Banff Trail was one of the communities that implemented a program in the interim. A former teacher remembered that she had twenty-five to thirty students and that the community supplied equipment. She taught from 1963 to 1971, and the community kindergarten closed in the early 1970s, when the province decided to offer kindergarten across the province.[107]

As understood by some in the 1950s and 1960s, progressive education (as opposed to traditional education) was amoral because it was irreligious

In this *Calgary Herald* photo, youths cram in to Campus Life Crusade "Club Tub" at William Aberhart High School in 1966 as part of evangelical outreach. (Photo by Ken Sakomoto, reproduced with permission of the University of Calgary Archives and Special Collection, NA-2864-892B.)

and rejected the notion that the aim of education was to walk with God.[108] While some Canadians, of all ages, remained fervent in their religious beliefs and practices, ties to formal church institutions grew weaker for many young people across the country—especially by the late 1960s and early 1970s.[109] Yet discussions of faith(s), religion, and education were prominent in the province in the postwar era. Alberta had maintained an element of religion in everyday life and politics while the Social Credit Party was in power from 1935 through 1971. It was important to at least some Albertans. Although a relatively diverse group of people was involved in Social Credit, its founder, William "Bible Bill" Aberhart, had a tremendous influence on the party and the province as a whole.[110] In this context, and with the increasing secularization of curriculums and classroom practices, some parents came to resent this new education. Elements of a generational schism are evident in a 1968 letter to the editor of the *Calgary Herald*. In the letter, the mother of a William Aberhart High School student addresses other parents directly and expresses grave concerns about late 1960s pedagogy; the powerful influence of the secularizing, progressive suburban classroom; and extracurricular activities (namely, the play *Inherit the Wind*) of the time:

> Are you aware of how the teachers have made going to church and believing the Bible as foolish sentiment? ... Is this what you want your boy or girl to learn at school? I don't. We spend hours teaching our children to obey God, live by the precepts of the Bible, obey parents. Our school spend [sic] days breaking down our efforts, destroying the faith they have in God and our Savior, the Lord Jesus and the truth of the Bible because they have that 35 hours a week to indoctrinate their un-godly theories.[111]

Students placed themselves into this larger conversation. A student newspaper editorial on religious teachings in schools that appeared a few years prior to the above letter reflected elements of the progressive teachings of the time. In it, students once again demanded to be considered as individuals with distinct and complex needs. A "one size fits all approach" to religion and religious training was rejected on several levels. Teaching religion in the schools was expressly rejected, with the writer arguing, "We say no! Religious training is a highly personal matter, a matter which is the business of the individual ... To teach religion in school is wrong, both morally and legally."[112]

Other postwar oral histories emphasize that while church membership remained high in some areas, it did not necessarily translate to a heightened spirituality or religious commitment.[113] Humorous memories of irreligious and indifferent fathers highlighted many oral histories; taken together, these memories hint at the male religious apathy of the post-war period. In other words, regular church attendance was not evidence of regular prayer at home, and in a number of these suburban homes, fathers did not participate in church services and activities consistently. In many homes, women led the way in attendance and guiding their children to church. Some of these realities were echoed by participants in memories of fathers who did not attend church services regularly. Protestant church leaders in Calgary were certainly aggressive in seeking new suburban churchgoers and in appealing to members who were increasingly influenced by modern ideas.[114]

These memories reflect a general societal trend away from churches and religion by the late 1960s. Not only in Calgary's suburbs but across the country there were challenges to Canada being defined as a Christian nation. By this time, experts note, "the historic privileging of Christianity in Canadian national public life began very visibly to crumble."[115] National polling numbers reflect this. In Canada's 1961 census, only 0.5 percent responded with "none" to the question "What is your religion?" when the response category "No religion" was not provided; however, in 1971, when it was given, 4.4 percent of the country responded with "none."[116]

Conclusion

Previous academic studies, nostalgia, and popular discourse suggest that children and adolescents were relatively protected from the machinations of war in a world that wanted to move beyond the devastating realities of the Depression and the Second World War. Young people's writing, contemporary magazines and newspapers, and oral histories indicate an alternative narrative.[117] There were myriad representations of the military that reflected something other than a movement away from war and its concomitant horrors; rather, the war remained a significant part of many young suburban lives. As seen throughout this chapter, from the perspective of childhood, the era was "postwar" in name only for many suburban young people.

Banff Trail offered families a unique choice for much of the late 1950s and 1960s in that students could attend elementary through postsecondary institutions within walking distance of their homes. One resident remembered "moving into the Banff Trail Community... March 3rd, 1960... our children all attended Capitol Hill Elementary, Branton, William Aberhart and the University of Calgary."[118] Another recalled that being in close proximity to the nascent University of Alberta at Calgary campus, well within walking distance of their new home, had drawn his parents to the Banff Trail community in the early 1960s.[119] Interviewees said attending a postsecondary institution and earning a degree was expected. This was reflected in the statements of other young suburbanites in Canada. One said: "I never seriously questioned whether or not I would go to university. I always took it for granted that I would. In fact, I hardly even thought about a college education until I was in Grade XIII. I just knew that I would go and that was all."[120] This was the new normal in Canada for older teenagers. The school, as institution, was central in the lives of families, adolescents, and children.

Chapter 3

Diversity Deficit and Working Days

Banff Trail was not racially and ethnically diverse in this period, but this does not mean that young people were unaware of racial or ethnic markers. Children and adolescents did consider racism and ethnocentrism, even if it seemed removed from their everyday lives. This chapter focuses on race, class, and the work of suburban children and adolescents.[1] The postwar suburbs are often represented as racially homogeneous: racial covenants ended in Canada in 1951 with a Supreme Court decision.[2] This did not, however, lead to a sudden influx of visible minorities, or marginalized ethnic groups, into the suburbs.[3] The practices of citizens do not necessarily follow new regulations, laws, and legislation. Although adults discussed how they understood race and ethnicity as youngsters in oral history interviews, and although some adolescents wrote about their views, Banff Trail, like most Canadian suburbs in this period, was predominantly a white and English-speaking enclave.[4] The whiteness that defined this postwar suburb fits into a larger national identity that has been both mythologized and reinforced as a norm of purity for many.[5]

In terms of social class, Banff Trail did not fit neatly into the categories of middle-class or working-class suburb. Especially in its earliest years, Banff Trail had a mixture of working-class and middle-class families. With increasing incomes, working-class family life continued to become more like that of the middle class. The family-centred activities (rather than class-based community activities) that marked middle-class domesticity, a prewar trend, became increasingly common.[6] Despite a shift to the nuclear family unit, Banff Trail did have vibrant community-based programs that children and adolescents enjoyed by the late 1950s.

Because of the increasing importance of public schools in the lives of young people and the homogenizing effects of these schools, cultures of childhood were not as divergent as they once had been, particularly along class lines. By adolescence, youngsters seemed to have gained a deeper understanding of class, especially young people from working-class or lower-middle-class backgrounds. According to interviewees, class was not a prominent topic among adolescent suburbanites, and there was limited discussion of class in the literature and art created by students. Despite this apparent lack of awareness, children and social class were topics of discussion in contemporary public discourses.[7] Class remains a key determinant in the everyday lives of both children and adolescents. While race, gender, and ethnicity are important influences, class is invariably linked to health and health care, family status, education, and work and leisure activities in childhood and adolescence across all periods.[8] There was a degree of homogeneity that led to some of these young people not recognizing class, but class lines were also blurred culturally in that middle- and working-class young people attended the same schools, played the same sports, engaged in similar activities, and had comparatively similar homes in Banff Trail. Certainly, some middle-class children had "extras," such as memberships in clubs, nicer clothes, or more travel opportunities, but the suburbs seemed to mute class differences in many ways. Banff Trail's schools played a part in this. By the late 1960s, a prevailing discourse saw prominent professionals advocating for education as a vital means to ease class, race, and religious differences.[9] This did make Banff Trail different than some model Canadian suburbs. Suburbs such as Thorncrest Village in Etobicoke, Ontario, reflected order and stability while securing upper-middle-class residents' financial investments and their social status.[10]

In both working-class and middle-class homes,[11] many suburban children and adolescents worked during this period—often retaining their personal incomes. Nevertheless, even if children's wages were not absolutely necessary to the pooled family economy, suburban children were working a great deal, in one instance doing heavy manual labour before the age of ten.[12] Interviewees gave many reasons for working, and they diverged on whether the impetus for paid and unpaid work came from themselves or their parents. While some were indifferent to the paid and unpaid work they did in their households and outside of them, many of them discussed how their work contributed to their changing and growing sense of identity.

Race and Ethnicity in the Suburbs

Hostile Indians all over our plains,
Now there're houses and fields of grains;
Just a covered wagon, with a driver named Joe.

Now speeding cars and buses we know;
All around there are Indian teepees.
Now beautiful houses with rows of sweet peas.
Calgary's seventy-fifth birthday! Oh, boy!
Everyone's filled with loads of joy.[13]

From a 1950 school yearbook, this poem, titled "Excitement," touches on several important themes relating to childhood and adolescence in this period, including progress, modernization, growth, and explorations of race.[14] The reference to "hostile Indians" is notable for its racism. The long-standing underrepresentation of Indigenous Peoples in the suburbs is well known to demographers, sociologists, and urban studies scholars. Banff Trail in these years was no different. For most who grew up in postwar Banff Trail, or in the nearby community of Charleswood, Indigenous Peoples were imagined and essentially exotic. The annual Calgary Stampede, occasional trips into the nearby foothills, and a growing presence in media provided most of their childhood contacts and subsequent conceptions of Indigenous Peoples.[15] The city was certainly beginning to shift ethnically and racially. By 1961, Calgary was home to a quarter of a million people, but Asians, Russians, Ukrainians, Poles, Jews, and "others" accounted for fewer than 45,000 people, just over 20 percent of the total population. In terms of appearance, most children were white and did not appear as "others" to children and adolescents at this time.[16]

Race is at once an important analytical category and a social construct. Human differences are real; however, the ways in which researchers choose to organize differences between human populations are methodological ones. These differences cannot be hierarchized or ranked—the process of racism—as has been done in the past by countless anthropologists and evolutionary biologists.[17] Contemporary racial differences cannot be conceptualized as absolute and unchanging. Genetic variation is continuous and has several influences.[18]

Postwar children gained their understandings of race from their families, who had similar experiences of it growing up in white Canada. Yet "others," and the racism surrounding them, have a long history in this country. Since the late nineteenth century and the building of the Canadian Pacific Railway line through Calgary, people from China have lived in and around Calgary. A space resembling the Chinatown of the 1950s had already formed in the downtown area by the early 1920s. It contained its own school, a Freemason association, and Chinese family associations, or tongs; over time, it would be the social and cultural heart of Calgary's Chinese community.[19] For Banff Trail's young people in the 1950s and

1960s, Calgary's Chinatown was one of the few racialized spaces in the city. Allan Matthews remembered suburban "diversity" in the era:

> [*Long pause*] There were Catholics [*laughs*]. You know, I don't think so [there being much ethnic diversity]. I mean a couple of [Chinese families]. You went to Chinatown and had Chinese food. There wasn't really pizza so ... we didn't know about the Italians [*laughs*]. There was a Chinese family that lived behind us, and they lived beside the Catholic family, so that was the really "bad" side of the alley [*chuckles*] ... Natives, we saw them in the Stampede Parade and then the Indian Village ... I didn't really see the disadvantaged side of the Native side. I just saw the kids wearing feathers and leather on the Stampede grounds."[20]

Indigenous Peoples were not part of his everyday experiences. Despite his claim that he held no racial stereotypes, he clearly did; Indigenous Peoples were seen at the Stampede, part of a pageant, a past, not the present. In several interviews, the lack of diversity, not only in Banff Trail but across the entire city, particularly in the first two decades following the Second World War, was clear. This is supported by demographic data from the period. In 1951, only 32,033 Calgarians, or 24.6 percent, were foreign-born. Nearly 27,000 of that number were from Great Britain, the United States, Scandinavia, Germany, and Italy. In other words, given the ethnic and racial composition in those countries at the time, they were not visible minorities.[21] Just over 4,000 Calgarians were Asian, "Others," or "Unspecified." Although the raw numbers increased, the proportion of foreign-born Calgarians actually decreased to 22.7 percent by the early 1950s.[22] By the early 1960s, Canada was no more ethnically diverse (by percentage at least), as the following table demonstrates. This was mirrored in Calgary, both anecdotally and statistically.

In terms of religion, the United Church was the dominant denomination in the city by 1961; with the influx of people from Eastern Europe, the Catholic Church was the second largest denomination, followed by the Anglicans.[23] Doug Cass recalled little diversity. He did not remember it being a popular topic of discussion. He said that "up until the mid-seventies, there wasn't any type of significant non-WASP populations in Calgary. In school, there were a few Chinese boys and in our Scout troop. There was no change whatsoever [in the broader city]."[24]

This lack of diversity was not isolated. Others recalled a lack of diversity, outside of a small number of Banff Trail families in the 1960s. Wendy Glidden recalled that the community was predominantly white and middle-class: "We did have a couple of Chinese students ... I was looking at my grade three picture, and it was pretty white ... Within the city, there might have been the occasional person [of colour] but ... it doesn't spring to mind that there were kids of other minorities."[25]

Bruce Wilson also remembered the whiteness that marked the city, the suburb, and his classrooms in elementary and junior high. Again, as it had been for other young Calgarians, it was at the Stampede that he came into contact with Indigenous peoples from the area. He remembered only a single Indigenous classmate from his elementary school years. This was borne out by the numbers: only 335 individuals were identified as "Native" in Calgary in the 1961 Census.[26] When asked about diversity in Banff Trail, he said, "No. We had maybe two Oriental families ... There was one girl, Emily, the first Native person I had ever met ... It was very, very white-oriented. I don't remember any Black children at all until high school [in the 1970s]. It was pretty much Caucasian-oriented in Calgary [more generally]."[27] Yearbook photographs from this period reflected this reality.

TABLE 3.1. Population Distribution by Ethnic Group, 1961	
Ethnic Origin	Percentage
British Isles	43.8
French	30.4
German	5.8
Ukrainian	2.6
Italian	2.5
Netherlands	2.4
Scandinavian	2.1
Polish	1.8
Jewish	1.0
Russian	0.7
Other European	3.9
Chinese	0.3
Japanese	0.2
Other Asiatic	0.2
Native Indian and Eskimo	1.2
Other and not stated	1.3

Source: Frederick Elkin, The Family in Canada (Ottawa: Vanier Institute of the Family, 1964).

While most interviewees remembered at least a few Chinese Canadian families in the Banff Trail community in the 1960s, Lesley Hayes recalled that there was one memorable family from another part of the northern hemisphere: "There wasn't any [nonwhite kids] in my [classes]. But there was a kid from Iceland. That was exotic, and his brother was called Thor. I think it was junior high [the 1970s, in her case] before I saw kids from Jamaica, Africa, or that kind of thing."[28] Like most, she did not recall there being any visible African Canadians or young people from Caribbean nations until the 1970s. These childhood memories reflected Canadian immigration policy, which did not lift restrictions on the entry of Caribbean people until the 1960s. Calgary suburbs were not the only spaces to reflect whiteness. These recollections from childhood demonstrate the inherent lack of diversity and exclusion that have been an element in Canada's immigration policies for more than a century.[29]

Despite the lack of diversity, or possibly because of it, many people did not recall many racist acts or words by schoolmates.[30] Doug Cass recalled that in the context of what was happening in the United States in the mid-1960s, race relations seemed much more positive in suburban Calgary, and in Canada as a whole.[31] This perception was not uncommon at this time,[32] despite some very real conflicts across the country. Ontario had some very real human rights issues centred on towns such as Dresden, Ontario; Quebec was rife with conflict regarding a number of social issues; and Indigenous Canadians, as part of a larger Red Power movement (some of it centred in Alberta), continued to demand increased rights across the country throughout this era, with varying degrees of success.[33] Sharon Johnstone revealed that as a child, she might very well have been unaware of any overt racism that was happening. She did not recall racist behaviours and believed the neighbourhood was not racist:

> That was one of the things I was proudest of about Canada. I enjoyed being a friend of triplets [three Black children] that were just around my age ... I had some friends at my church, and they were lovely. I remember that skin scars differently, and I noticed and was interested in the colour of their scars. I noticed how a scar for a Black person looked really shiny and mine just looked ugly and red.[34]

This fits also with some of the antiracist political discourses that circulated in this period. The idea of raceless children was a powerful trope in postwar Canada.[35]

Not all memories regarding race in childhood and adolescence were positive, a finding that fits with child development theories that posit that children begin to learn difference based on ethnic, racial, or religious grounds from a young age.[36] Brent Harris recalled racism being part of his childhood landscape; some Indigenous children were teased and taunted at his elementary school:

> [My] earliest recollection of the existence of different ethnic [and racial] groups was probably in ... grade three. I knew that there were Asian Canadians because you had the Chinese grocery store, and some of those kids were in your class. But we had a couple of kids come to the school that were First Nations kids, and I remember those kids getting a hard time with some hurtful adjectives and descriptors, and that was the first time I was aware of an ethnicity, race, and racism. [There was] an understanding at school and in the community that there were people different from me ... It wasn't until junior high that I recognized different races and cultures. So people from Asia ... Indian and Pakistan and that sort of thing [early and mid-1970s] ... Banff Trail was fairly homogenous ... I couldn't tell you when I saw my first Black person [across the entire city], which is probably a pretty narrow view.[37]

From an adult perspective, he thought of this view as narrow—something that was not unique to him as an interviewee. Despite this concern, it did not change what he recalled. Outside of western European peoples, there were relatively few other groups represented in Calgary. This was reflected in Canada more broadly, as the proportion of foreign-born people among the general Canadian population was below 16 percent until the early 1980s.[38]

Most interviewees did not recall a great deal of formal discussion about race, racism, and ethnicity in their classrooms. Many recalled discussions increasing by their later adolescence and early adulthood, which for some was the early 1970s. Doug Cass noted that the expanding mediascape of the 1960s provided a virtual forum, although by the late 1960s some discussion had begun in certain suburban classrooms as well. When it was broached, we "talked about it in school or [watched discussion] on television; pretty arm's length, academic kind of environment. [The discussions were] very much pro, in favour for civil rights and equality."[39] Again, as others had mentioned and what many students' creative writing suggests, there was a much greater focus on the United States, race relations, and the civil rights movement, rather than a focus on invisible Canadian social issues related to race.

People did not remember discussing race, racism, and ethnicity to any great degree with friends and family. William Wright remembered feeling that as a child he was missing out on a more cosmopolitan world in his particular suburb. Exposure to diverse ethnicities and races was experienced more vicariously for him until he reached adulthood. Although it was discussed in school and at home to a degree, it was not the same as having the opportunity to befriend and spend time with people from other ethnic or racial backgrounds. He remembered that in the late 1960s and early 1970s there were youngsters from Asia, but "absolutely zero Black people." He said that everyone in elementary school was white but recalled thinking, "I wish there were more Black people." That did change in junior high when he met a "really nice guy" who was the "only Black guy I had seen in school. I remember thinking it wasn't giving me much life experience ... I remember learning very early on about the taboo of racism, of being very tolerant of other people ... It seemed very textbook-like, because we didn't have any real-life examples."[40] Whiteness truly defined the ethnic and racial landscape for most of these suburban children growing up in these years, and hierarchies within the concept of whiteness were not mentioned or explored in the school literature. They also had little exposure, or at least no memory of exposure, to the Africville protests in Halifax, Nova Scotia; Indigenous revolts, conditions on nearby reserves, and so on.

Calgary's racial mix changed by the late 1960s, and a more pronounced racialization of space was established by the late 1970s. These changes reflected larger Canadian immigration patterns that saw many visible minorities coming to Calgary from East Africa, the Caribbean, Southeast Asia, and so forth. As noted by researchers in the City of Calgary's Social Service Department in 1963: "Any scheme recommended for urban renewal in Calgary is not complicated by large racial segments."[41] The use of the term *complicated* is revealing in that it reflects the ease with which whiteness defined the Calgary landscape.

The situation was summed up in the recollection of Frank Edward, who grew up in the Banff Trail in the 1960s: "Any sort of ethnic diversity; it's pretty thin in Banff Trail. In the larger city, I recall when northeast Calgary really began to expand, and there was some "colour" coming into the city [by the 1970s]. I had some Chinese friends, but that was about it. [It was] pretty lily white."[42] There was a mix of perception and reality for these young suburbanites. Ruth Frankenberg's research on whiteness is crucial to understanding that whiteness and its corresponding privilege is fundamental in structuring race relations. In her landmark study, which features thirty oral history interviewees, many white adults admitted to never thinking about race as children and could not place themselves within the broader context of ongoing race relations.[43] In postwar Calgary and its suburbs, whiteness was naturalized, quite simply, as "the way it was."

Class and Suburban Childhoods

Defining class in childhood is complex. Inevitably, the social class of children is, and has been, defined by their parents' or a guardian's class. But as feminists have argued, a large part of the story is untold when a woman's class is defined based only on her male partner's identity. While this is problematic on a few levels, there really is no other way to determine childhood class other than within the familial context. Yet it is important to do so, as there is no more significant determinant of well-being in childhood than social class, despite race, gender, and ethnicity being powerful factors.[44]

Class can be determined on the basis of a person's relationship to work and on a parent's education level and household income. Children and adolescents were identified in terms of class by what their parents (in most cases what their fathers, as primary breadwinners) did. Yet postwar children and adolescents experienced several intersectionalities in terms of class, gender, age, and race relating to work, most significantly, children were limited in the amount of power they wielded in their relationships with their employers. Beyond paid work, most childhood and adolescent work was, and remained through this period, menial and unpaid. This work was typically under the direction and orders of parents and older siblings.

Some interviewees, for at least a portion of their childhood and adolescence, had mothers who worked outside the home. Recent research on women's postwar work indicates this to be unexceptional in many ways. While some women entered the workforce in unionized positions, other women, particularly new immigrants and Indigenous women, entered into more precarious work. Mothers entered the workforce in numbers not seen previously.[45] Despite the prevailing discourse that families were best served by Canadian women acting as housewives, which was associated with the male breadwinner model, this was not reflected in the realities of suburban lives in Banff Trail. These mothers worked long, unpaid hours in their homes, and many did paid work outside the home.[46] They often engaged in the double day, which saw them perform many of the household duties once they had done paid work outside the home. Working outside the home increased over these years for both single and married women.

In interviews, people discussed the work that their mothers did both inside and outside the home. Many mothers did not work outside the home until the children were older and their critical role of providing child care in the home was no longer needed. This speaks to the lack of availability of affordable child care in Alberta—which some interviewees mentioned—and the fact that, in many families, women's roles were based on working inside the home with a focus on taking care of their families.[47] When women had opportunities to work outside the home, these jobs were often depicted as part-time or occasional. William Wright said, "My mom was mainly a homemaker. She had a side career as a dietitian. She had a degree in home economics."[48] Allan Matthews recalled that his "father was in the oil business. He was a payroll supervisor. He worked at the job for his entire life. My mother used to work at a health food store. She worked part-time, which was pretty radical back then, it seems to me."[49] These memories are important, as many of these children were from working-class or lower-middle-class backgrounds. Their mothers' wages were likely important to total household incomes. Avoiding poverty, if at all possible, was part of a larger societal discussion often led by academic experts and other professionals such as social workers who explored the damaging effects of poverty on the poor, working or not.[50] Some experts believed that the "ills" of the family, particularly the families most in need, could be addressed directly through a greater participation in Canada's democratic way of life and that the time was near to challenge the voluntary structure—led by middle-class activists—with its potential as a critical training ground for good citizenship in a democracy.[51]

Doug Cass's characterization of what his parents did was typical of many: "My mother didn't [work outside the home]; she stayed at home. My father was in the construction business and started out as a welder."[52] Another participant also recalled that his father worked outside the home while his mother did not until he was much older: "My father was a lawyer and then became a judge. My mother was mostly at home, and she was also an English teacher. She wasn't teaching at all until I got quite a bit older."[53] With several siblings in the house, this pattern of women working primarily in the home before returning to professions or part-time work was not uncommon.

Jim Farquharson recalled his father's work and what all the male heads of household did on his block in Banff Trail in the late 1950s and 1960s. His father's job and the hours spent outside of the family home were similar to what a lot of suburban fathers did in this postwar period. His dad sold life insurance for thirty-five years and often worked from 8:00 a.m. until 10:30 p.m. On his block, he recalled that there were "a couple of welders, three firemen, Sears repairman, newspaper printer, truck driver, a couple in the oil patch, school teacher, janitor, shoe salesman, telephone lineman, garage owner, carpenter, farmer, pharmacist, accountant, optometrist, but mostly people did blue-collar work."[54]

Most of these fathers, whether blue- or white-collar, did not control the means of production in their places of work and, ultimately, had little control over their workplaces, which were often located outside the Banff

Trail suburb. This links them to untold numbers of commuting male suburbanites in this era, most of them fathers who did paid work far from
the suburban spaces in which they lived.[55] The trend of the home being
increasingly separate from the public sphere both physically (particularly
in the case of suburbia) and ideologically (across class lines) began in the
interwar decades and intensified in the postwar years.[56]

The following account by George and Elaine Skoreyko detailing their
family's move into the suburbs is typical of many experiences in Banff
Trail and in hundreds of Canadian suburbs in the period. It highlights the
challenges that many experienced as they moved to these nascent, expanding suburbs and built new homes:

> Lots were selling for $500.00 each and that was a lot of money those days.
> We managed to get the money together and were the proud owners of a
> "piece of land" ... [In] 1953, we started to build. Roy was a carpenter by
> trade, and we could save money by doing it ourselves. We moved in the
> first of June although it was far from being completed ... There was no
> heat, only the sub floor, wide boards with cracks, doors were still to be
> hung, and walls taped, but it was a home of our own.[57]

This family memory links their experience to that of earlier families in
other Canadian suburban spaces. Toronto's working people in the early
twentieth century were involved directly with building and renovating
their homes, with the entire family often involved, which was also the case
in Vancouver suburbs.[58]

Material considerations were most often the decisive factor, as the
suburbs were more affordable, and families could more easily purchase an
existing home or build a modest new home than in more desirable parts of
the city.[59] For some Banff Trail families, who struggled financially despite
the booming economy in the early 1950s, the process of purchasing a
family home was not smooth. Community lending institutions rather than
the "Big Banks" were sought to help with financing. In addition, community organizations provided furnishings for families who did not have the
means to purchase them. This anecdote, once again from the Skoreykos,
highlights the challenging material realities for a young couple seeking a
house in Banff Trail. Their description of their limited and second-hand
furnishings indicates the lack of material wealth, especially at this stage
in the family's life, were still felt in the suburbs, just as they would be in
an inner city or small town:

> The bank would not lend the money to us so we went to Tuxedo Credit
> Union ... We explained that we wanted to borrow money for a down payment

on a house ... After some friendly conversation, we told her a little bit about our background. Then she pulled the cheque book from her desk and wrote us a cheque for $1,500.00. We immediately deposited it in the bank just in case she changed her mind ... We could not afford a refrigerator so we bought an icebox which we used for two years ... We had plastic curtains ... We did not have any furniture so we used orange boxes for our storage cupboards. We also went to the Salvation Army to get ... a really nice rocking chair for one dollar and a standing bronze lamp for the same price.[60]

For other early Banff Trail residents, the lack of a sizable down payment and the limits this placed on their home choices, led them to Banff Trail. Their experiences were similar to what sociologist S.D. Clark observed in several Toronto-area suburbs in the late 1950s and early 1960s.[61] The heavy financial burden was long-lasting for many families, and the initial landscape was not impressive, as noted by Banff Trail residents who moved into the community, not yet two years old, in August 1955. Many looked at multiple houses and simply did not have a suitable down payment. Eileen Stearns recalled that they "took our future in our hands and signed an agreement to purchase a home. We were given a little green book ... by the insurance company that held the mortgage. It showed ... our monthly payments for the next 300 months ... We had a 'dirt' yard, no fence or trees, no sidewalk and a rutted mud road."[62]

Many Banff Trail families, like so many other postwar suburban families, were not wealthy. Some struggled to furnish their homes. They had saved and borrowed for down payments on houses that many readily admitted may have been beyond their financial means. There was a wide range of list prices in contemporary newspapers in the early 1950s. Houses in communities near Banff Trail listed in the $6,700 to $13,000 range, with most of them requiring a down payment of at least $5,000.[63] In context, across Canada, the average hourly wage earned from 1957 to 1970 was between $1.87 and $3.70 across all industries.[64] Alternative forms of housing were limited in Calgary, much like everywhere across Canada—public housing was not a top priority for any government, in any jurisdiction.[65] It was within this broader context that children and adolescents worked throughout this period in roles that linked them to other young people across time and place.

Children, Adolescents, and Unpaid Work

Household work, as noted by historians of childhood, is where working-class and middle-class children and adolescents made their most significant work contributions, not only in this period, but for the first sixty years of the twentieth century.[66] This work was highly gendered, something that applied throughout the twentieth century and earlier. The suburban home was first and foremost a workplace for women, but this was not the case for men in the postwar years.[67]

Interviewees often commented on the gendered nature of suburban household work, for both young people and adults. There was modelling done for children of all ages in many families. Doug Cass remembered that it seemed like the "natural order" to work, and he didn't mind it, as it meant he had less to do: "I was expected to cut the grass and shovel the walks. The girls were supposed to help Mom and help with the dishes. My mother did all the cooking until my sisters got to be quite old. All the cleaning, all the laundry for six people, she did all of those things exclusively ... I had to keep [my own room] tidy."[68]

A busy young girl helping out with a sizeable stack of dishes at her kitchen sink in Banff Trail in 1965. (Reproduced with permission of the family.)

Other interviewees also noted the gendered aspects of household work. William Wright mentioned that he and his brother did not have to do much of anything around his childhood home outside of some basic tasks and some outdoor yard work. He recalled that his "mom did most of it [the housework]. My brother and I were pretty spoiled. I remember a lot of yard work ... and I hated it. I don't remember any housework [except for] maybe making the bed. We had everything handed to us. I don't remember ever doing the dishes."[69]

Others echoed that the household work was not only gendered but also heavily weighted in that women and girls did much more of it. They noted that there was not a lot of structure and scheduling to work done either by young children or adolescents. Brent Harris said his mom did everything of consequence and that there were very few chores for him and his brother. He recalled putting laundry away and said, "I was certainly introduced to grounds maintenance ... walking the dog, picking up after the dog, shovelling the walk, cutting the grass, and pruning. We all pitched in, but we were certainly told what to do. There wasn't really a schedule. [Housework] was part of being a family member."[70]

There were real differences between the sexes where household labour was concerned: most boys did limited or no work in the female "domestic" sphere.[71] This sphere was almost exclusively indoors. Although in some circumstances women did the majority of gardening, men and boys did the bulk of yard work. Some of these families had as many as five or six children. Unsurprisingly, some mothers needed older daughters to help with familial child care and to perform other critical household work duties.[72]

In families with boys only, there were notable differences in the gendered allotment of chores, according to interviewees. With the same amount of work as in other homes, boys, out of necessity, did more work inside the home in comparison to families with both boys and girls. Additionally, fathers also seemed to be more involved than in other households, although this was not the case in all families. Allan Matthews, who did not have any sisters, recalled that his mother took care of laundry and ironing but that his "father was probably more helpful than the stereotype. He would do some of the cooking ... We had a vegetable garden, and that was his realm. We all learned to cook. My father would do most of the cooking when we were on vacation ... We all took turns doing the dishes or fighting to not do the dishes."[73]

Jim Farquharson's experience also demonstrate that a further split, beyond gender divisions, existed, and it depended on age. Older children, particularly adolescents, often did much more work than younger siblings and were models of working behaviour in the home. In his large family, which included five siblings, Farquharson said that housework was shared and chores were for all. He said he was "mowing the lawn and shovelling the walks. We all took turns washing, drying, and clearing [the] table of dishes. Every week we had to clean our rooms and make our beds daily. There were six kids ... It fell to the older ones to entertain the younger ones. The girls helped my mother quite a bit."[74] He made it clear that his parents, and in particular his father, believed that household work was important for learning the values associated with hard work and manual labour. It was conceived as character-building, and this conception was not exclusive to working-class families, as many middle-class parents required children and adolescents to help with household chores. His household also had student boarders who were attending university, so there were extra tasks that other families may not have had.

In many homes, there were gendered aspects to certain tasks, but not to all. Personal interests and initiative also mattered. In particular, by the late 1960s some girls seemed to have become more involved with tasks that had previously been done mainly by boys. The work done by adults was clearly delineated by gender. Michelle Macdonald said that everyone (except her brother) contributed to tasks, despite her mother working in the home:

> My mother always did all the cooking, baking, and cleaning ... My specific chores were always washing the dishes. I did that from standing on a stool so I could reach the sink, and that was from the time I was five ... My sisters dried, and my brother bugged us. He never did anything; he always got away with that because he was the oldest [laughs]. My father was a great builder, and he built our basement. I helped him ... measuring things, holding boards when he cut, but I didn't do the cutting. I enjoyed helping him out.[75]

In a 1959 Gallup Poll, housewives were asked if family members were doing as much as they should to help or if they could help out more. Eighty percent of Canadian housewives said that family members were doing all they should.[76] Clearly, of the women polled, the large majority felt supported in housework; however, the benchmark may have been quite low.

While the family home was the primary worksite for almost all suburban children and adolescents, one project drew together hundreds of Banff Trail children, parents, and teachers. The workspace was unique in Calgary and, quite possibly, the country. A Banff Trail resident remembered the building of the "the Worm" at Branton Junior High School. Work on it began because of a planning error: a portion of the school was dug ten feet deep rather than to the depth of a crawl space. It ended up being a 14,000 square-foot area filled with broken concrete, which was ultimately turned into a training facility, including a running track with banked turns. A resident, Amanda Queen, recalled that over five hundred young people and twenty-two teachers contributed to the building. Some work was done in physical education classes, with the rest of it completed after school and on Saturdays. She recalled, "Rakes, shovels, pickaxes, crowbars, and wheelbarrows [were] brought from homes ... The boys did most of the work, clearing the broken concrete left behind by construction workers. The girls helped by raking the area flat ... Because the school board did not support upkeep, the students watered and raked the pits every day."[77] The space was used for more than four decades but was eventually filled in due to environmental concerns.

Children, Adolescents, and Paid Work

While unpaid work was a critical component of suburban childhoods and adolescence in this period, paid work was very important to many. While some interviewees were indifferent about the paid and unpaid work they did as children and adolescents in their households, and outside of them, many discussed how their work contributed to their changing sense of identity. In both working-class and middle-class homes, suburban children and adolescents usually performed some work for wages during this period. With growing familial affluence, youngsters' incomes were more their own rather than a necessary addition to the family economy. This held true in Banff Trail. Children's wages were not necessary for the family economy, yet some suburban children worked a lot. There were many reasons offered for why young people worked, along with divergent stories on whether the impetus to work came from themselves or their parents.

The following poem, written by a William Aberhart High School student in 1961, broaches many of the values related to work and the work ethic promoted in both working-class and middle-class homes in these years, including perseverance, the "pioneering spirit," and humility.

> The prairie winds are calling
> Soft and sweet and low,
> They tell about the pioneers
> Who came so long ago.
> They tell about the struggle,
> The sweat, and work and toil,
> As day by day they tried to make

Their living from the soil.
They sing of perseverance—
The women and the men
Who came—and failed—undaunted still—
They tried and tried again.
They tell of humble homesteads
Surrounded by the snow,
While wrathful gods from up above
Made blighting blizzards blow.
They carol of the Springtime wind
That pushes back the cold,
They tell about awakening land
In hues of green and gold.
They whisper of the rising hopes
Of all the pioneers
To make this land the best of homes
Within the future years.[78]

Sprinkled throughout accounts there is language about the growth of
Calgary suburbs that harkens back to an earlier period in prairie history. This was an imagined and ultimately racist and ethnocentric history
that saw empty lands developed by hard-working white settlers who faced
nearly insurmountable obstacles in building the Canadian West.

Similar to the findings of historians, interviews and other evidence
demonstrate that some children in this period worked as hard as children
in earlier periods and at similar tasks.[79] Certainly, this held true in Banff
Trail, as both inside and outside the home paid and unpaid work were
important elements in the lives of children and adolescents. There is evidence of work remaining an important part of their youth for many of
Calgary's young people into at least the early 1970s. What changed was
that full-time schooling replaced child labour as the economy provided
ever fewer jobs for the very young.[80]

While there were standard jobs for most young people—babysitting,
delivering newspapers, and cleaning positions being the most common—
the reasons for working were wide-ranging. The following excerpt, titled
"Day Duty at a Service Station," captures some of the mundane day-to-day
activities in Calgary service-station jobs, held by countless adolescents:

Some people think a Service Station is a place where you go to work hard
all day long. But you can have fun if you set your mind at it. A customer
comes in and wants his oil changed. You start to drain it when all of a

sudden you accidentally step in the way of the flow of the oil. It flows all over your head ... It saves you from putting hair oil on your hair when you get home. Then you get sloppy and spill some grease on the floor ... Comes twelve o'clock and you sit down to lunch when in comes a car for gas. The old boy stands and talks to you so long your sandwiches have icicles on them when you get back ... Even if you do make ... LITTLE mistakes ... the public always gets served.[81]

Peter Baptie, the author, was no more than twelve or thirteen years old when he wrote this. As with many student articles and essays, there is a lot of humour here. While the work was likely quite repetitive, there were challenging moments, particularly for an adolescent just beginning his or her paid work life.

One striking theme found in the archival record, and noted by some interviewees, was that job opportunities were not limitless. In the 1950s, there seemed to be more work available; however, by the late 1960s this had changed. The enduring myth about this time—that there were more jobs than people—did not apply to young people. In other words, young workers were not spared from the cyclical lows inherent in capitalism. There were downturns through most of these twenty years, as described here in the *Calgary Herald*: "Large groups of men and women graduates from all faculties of ... universities still are unemployed according to the monthly report of the prairie region of the Unemployment Insurance Commission ... Alberta coal operators also were concerned over a lack of demand for coal and although Calgary's wholesale and retail business was good, no help was required."[82] This era is characterized by some as a time of uninterrupted economic boom and relative material comfort, yet this was not universal based on class, gender, race, or age differences.

Based on another article from *The Albertan,* "Students Exceed Number of Jobs," which appeared in May 1950, there were clearly employment issues for young people in their late teens and early twenties, even in the oil industry. Graduates who were specialists could find work, "but oil companies were showing a preference for men who had worked in the field and then returned to university for postgraduate studies ... The supply had become greater than the demand here, as Calgary had become a centre for hundreds of university graduates from various parts of Canada, U.S. and Britain."[83]

Much of this was echoed in the 1960s. Student employment for university and college students, dozens of whom lived in Banff Trail, was a key topic in the University of Calgary's student newspaper, *The Gauntlet*. This was not the entire student workforce, but low levels of employment were likely indicative of the broader picture in the city. Writing in 1963, student Beth Waters posed the question "Summer employment for university students?" As she commented, this was a "big problem ... about 1200 students applied to the employment service for jobs ... Sluggish construction in the city increased the difficulty for employment officials. About 50 per cent of students wanting employment were placed as compared to 68 per cent last year."[84] A lot of the work became more precarious in nature in that it was low-paying, often did not include benefits, and temporary.[85] The Canadian Association of Social Workers noted the challenges that youth faced in the mid-1960s in securing employment and emphasized that a large portion of young people were unprepared to assume productive roles as they reached adulthood.[86]

Five years later, young people across the country continued to be challenged in their job hunting. Agencies working on their behalf struggled to secure summer employment for students, especially in Calgary. In Montreal, only 25 percent of students who sought employment through Canada Manpower found work, and only 37 percent in Toronto were employed. The situation in Vancouver and Victoria was described as even gloomier. In Calgary, where an average of fifty-seven phone calls was required to place one applicant, Manpower employed only 11 percent of its applicants.[87]

A 1970 report prepared by Ken Brown for the Association of Universities and Colleges of Canada observed that students across the country faced many of the same issues with finding employment. Rather than seeing a great deal of difference between the early 1950s and late 1960s, there was some continuity in the general experiences of older teenagers. The transition to adulthood and work was not expected to be easy, nor were the final years of teenagehood, as Brown states in his preamble to the full report:

> Rather than put down in writing the comments used to describe the Canadian student's summer employment prospects—suffice to say that it is of national, as well as student, concern. Pressure must be placed on the federal government to find a solution ... Even here, the job prospects, especially for those with liberal arts degrees, are poor. The question that must be resolved is: Is university training for an education or for a job?[88]

Despite these challenges, there were young suburbanites who did find work in a wide variety of jobs, both part-time and full-time.[89] Motivation to work was varied. Very few interviewees said they worked to help support the family—in most instances, money earned was their own. Most of them did not recall knowing their family's financial circumstances.

Postwar research focusing on young people in a Toronto suburb also found the same. The authors wrote that "it is interesting at this point to note that the children (like many of the women) may have only a hazy picture of the family's financial standing, and that, because of this, they cannot approach the job situation realistically."[90]

Many young suburbanites worked. Wendy Glidden did significant paid work in her early teenage years. By the early 1970s, she had a job as a playground supervisor that required both dedication and time. The level of responsibility and accountability was also high, and she remembered it being hard work from a teenager's perspective. She was required to do a lot on a daily basis as a babysitter. The supervisor's position was even more challenging, as the kids came daily, and recreation activities and crafts had to be planned. She remembered "coming up with weekly plans ... We were in another community that was over about a half hour bike ride. We worked really hard for what little money we made. We had a lot of responsibility. I eventually became a supervisor [involving evenings, in later years, as an adult]."[91]

There is a long history of babysitting as work for the young in North America, and babysitters have been culturally typecast in many ways. In the early postwar era, they were viewed as irreverent "bobby-soxers" and by the 1960s as energetic and even sexually arousing.[92] Interviewees seemed to feel quite respected and valued in their roles. Ones who had babysat said that they babysat only for people that they knew in their community, which may have raised the respect level they received from their employers.

Babysitting was not immune to attempts to standardize and certify activities during this time. A 1950 article in The Albertan, "Urges Training for 'Sitters,'" called for formal training for teenaged babysitters and for babysitters to be a minimum of fourteen-years-old.[93] There were also several recommendations and guidelines from the Canadian Home Economics Association based on questionnaires sent to parents and students in nine provinces. Evidently, the association

> told parents to seek older women sitters through community organiza-
> tions, leave written instructions with sitters and don't let girl sitters go
> home alone after dark ... Some of the facts the association gleaned were: 1.
> The age range of sitters is 11–19 years. 2. Students spend one to 40 hours
> weekly sitting. 3. From 22 to 50 percent of girl sitters are allowed to go
> home after dark. 4. Only one-third of parents leave instructions with the
> sitter. 5. An average of 40 percent leave only a telephone number. 6. Some
> parents turn off the heat and the house gets cold. 7. Some parents do not
> lock the doors when they leave.[94]

Rising prosperity in Canada after 1945 allowed more working- and middle-class families to hire babysitters as a choice rather than as a necessity.[95] This invariably increased efforts by some, such as national associations, to have the "right" babysitter available for child care. Perhaps unsurprisingly, there was some resistance from teenagers about the work required when babysitting. Published in the *Aberhart Advocate* in 1964, a humorous piece titled "Babysitting" reflects some common sentiments about the challenges of babysitting. It also confirms that babysitting was not a positive experience for all:

> According to Mr. and Mrs. Turnip, babysitting is a plush job; possibly, the easiest in the world ... What they don't realize is that the minute they step out the door, Bobby Turnip dissolves into a blubbering pool of tears and Billy starts to break the flowerpots and trample the dirt into the rug, tear down the curtains and generally wreak havoc. In short the "angelic pair" have become a couple of little demons. It is eight o'clock; the sitter has been specifically ordered not to put the two to bed until eight thirty. What can she do? Let us follow the poor deluded teen-ager who has been shanghaied into sitting with Bobby and Billy as she pursues (and I do mean pursues) the course of an evening with them ...
>
> *[Following a series of incidents]*
>
> 8:59—Billy wants a glass of water, too. Our heroine takes an axe, murders them both, and goes back into the living room to settle down and watch "Outer Limits."[96]

While some look back with nostalgia to the postwar period as a time when babysitters were abundant and affordable, this so-called golden age of babysitters never existed, not even in the mind's eye of many 1950s and 1960s parent-employers.[97] For Mary Baker, babysitting, when she was in her early teenage years, was one of her few options for paid work. Female participants seemed resigned to their limited options but wished they had had more of them. The work was also important in helping to shape Baker's identity, both in terms of the tasks themselves and what the work allowed her to explore. She touched on her hopes. The timeless motivator for work for many in childhood and adolescence, having enough money to run away from home (mostly tongue in cheek), was mentioned. She recalled what she did for paid work as she moved into teenagehood. Her first job was babysitting, and she later took a job at the Bay in the grocery department. She saved most of her earnings but said she had "very different tastes from my family. I was a nut for Broadway musicals. I'd go to the library and read them. So, music. I spent money on fabric, made my own clothes, and went to movies, and after the age of fifteen bought cigarettes."[98]

Lisa Blair recalled starting her "own babysitting business when I was thirteen. I would buy material to make clothes with the wages, and I saved some."[99] This seemed to be a common age to begin paid work, especially for teenaged girls. Tammy Simpson also recalled when she began working: "I babysat when I was in junior high. I was around [twelve or thirteen]. I had been doing that at home for my mom, unpaid at home. For one summer, I babysat my grandmother. It was mostly to earn money."[100] Even for those from working-class families, the money earned as adolescents was retained for personal spending. Some mentioned giving part of their earnings to their parents, who felt they could contribute toward certain things, such as sporting-goods items.

While most babysitters were girls, some male interviewees mentioned babysitting in Banff Trail. Babysitting by teenage boys was not uncommon in North America, and as experts note, in fact, from the Great Depression to the new millennium male sitters were consistently portrayed as models of masculine identity for impressionable little boys threatened by feminized suburbs and female-headed households.[101] As Doug Cass remembered it, "I did a little bit of babysitting when I was in my mid-teens; that was very rare, if my sisters or one of the other girls in the neighbourhood wasn't available."[102]

In other words, he was not a first choice for parents, and people preferred adolescent girls owing to common gender stereotyping. He did not find the work unpleasant, but it was not something that he sought actively. This was similar to Jim Farquharson's experiences. He was solicited to babysit within his Banff Trail suburb when his sisters could not deal with young boys, and he accepted the role gladly. In some ways, this mirrored the contemporary education system, where men were principals and vice-principals and women were teachers. One role required more nurturing and caring while the other was focused on order and discipline. In talking about the work he did in his teens, Farquharson said, "I used to babysit. It was $0.15 an hour and, at Christmas, $0.25 an hour. My sisters babysat. Whenever they had trouble with the kids they babysat, I would be the next one to go around."[103]

Ultimately, teenaged boys were much less likely to babysit than were adolescent girls. Many boys delivered newspapers, as they did across Canada. Newspaper routes ranged in size from a minimum of forty or fifty papers to just over one hundred.[104] Frank Edward was one of several interviewees who delivered newspapers from a young age. He said, "My earliest paid job was a paper route ... It would have been an early morning job because *The Albertan* was a morning paper. From grade six through grade nine I was encouraged to save but not forced to put 10 to 15 percent into a savings account. I was able to blow the rest."[105] Allan Matthews also recalled that he "had a paper route. It was a *Star Weekly* route. I delivered the papers at Monday at noon."[106] Bruce Wilson remembered that he had worked as a paper boy: "By grade nine I had a paper route, flyer route that I was involved with and I earned some extra money. By grade ten, a high school teacher ... got us involved in Camp Horizon, the handicapped children's camp for one summer."[107] Interviewees mentioned what they did with their earnings. Frank Edward said he saved them and bought personal items from time to time. He had some guidance from his parents but, ultimately, the choice was his.[108] Growing prosperity within many working-class and middle-class families meant that some adolescents purchased clothes and other necessities with their earnings, but their earnings were not turned over to their parents to support the family as they had been in previous times.

Some interviewees recalled other types of paid work they did as teenagers. William Wright said he started a lucrative small business (with some initial earnings) with a friend. For him, as in the case of so many other young people, it was an important way to assert some independence as he transitioned from childhood to adolescence to adulthood. He remembered that he "used to mow lawns in the neighbourhood with a friend, and we had a little enterprise going, lawn mowing and edging in the neighbourhood." Both securing these jobs and then executing them were hard work, but "the job was fun; it was part of the independence thing."[109]

Sharon Johnstone discussed the importance of her musical work in that it was something that she excelled at from a young age; in fact, she was able to turn it into reasonably well-paid work. She enjoyed it, and it allowed her to be with groups of older people, who she identified with much more readily than her peer group in her adolescent years. The money she earned was hers to keep. In a more consumer-oriented teenagehood, few adolescents were saving their earnings—but she did. She remembered doing "a lot of singing gigs ... My sister and I got quite good at doing duets and playing instruments together. We would sing for certain banquets and weddings for pay, and that was quite exciting. The wages went into our account at the bank."[110]

Suburban spaces were not only connected to nearby cities; in some instances, they could be tied closely to rural areas in the province. While traditional forms of child labour were foreign to most young suburbanites, one exception emerged. A 1970 article in *The Albertan,* "Child Labor in South Beet Field Charge," reported on the work done by Indigenous families, and their children, near the southern Alberta town of Taber:

Conditions of work in southern Alberta sugar beet fields are forcing six-year-old children to labor beside their fathers and mothers ... Present conditions result in family breakdown and Indian cultural degradation for the approximately 2,000 workers in the sugar beet fields ... During that time, he learned that beet pickers are under contract to hoe fields, and net $17 per acre for first hoeing—with an acre determined as 23,760 lineal feet of sugar beet rows ... When the largely illiterate families arrive, they find it necessary to enter the contract with farmers ... To fulfill terms of the contract, children are forced into the fields to work alongside the father and mother, partially because there is no one to watch them if they stay at the housing accommodations."[111]

Many agricultural workers were Indigenous people who had limited choices in finding employment in Alberta. One interviewee, Jim Farquharson, said that a few years before this story was written, and prior to his tenth birthday, he had worked in these same fields. He recalled his experiences (his first paid employment) as a nine-year-old moving irrigation pipe in Taber. He said he headed south "for a summer holiday, and I hoed sugar beets. Hoed the fields every day from early in the morning. Get up early in the morning, move pipe, come in for breakfast, move pipe, come in for lunch, move pipe, come in for supper, and then move pipe before I went to bed."[112] He was being facetious in describing it as a "summer holiday."

Making the transition to paid work in adulthood was a prominent theme, even in junior high yearbooks in the 1950s and early 1960s. In nearly every yearbook at both the junior and senior level, national and local companies bought advertising space seeking potential employees from the student body. Secondary and postsecondary education, while increasingly important in this period, was not the ultimate goal for a significant minority of students. A Hudson's Bay Company advertisement excerpt, "For Graduates... Seeking a Future," from a Branton Junior High yearbook, is a good example: "There are over 50 varieties of jobs at the Hudson's Bay Company. Wherever your particular talents lie, buying, selling, personnel, accounting, publicity, or management ... at 'The Bay' you'll find a wonderfully diversified field of opportunity. Jobs-with-a-future, limited only by your own capabilities and initiative. Our Personnel Office will be happy to tell you more about the possibilities for a professional career."[113] Given the broader discursive focus on individual initiative and personal responsibility, there is an appeal here to the future and an emphasis on students being limited only by their own abilities. A strong work ethic, and its ultimate payoff, was emphasized in myriad ways.

In 1954, a Bank of Montreal advertisement at Crescent Heights, a school that many Banff Trail children attended prior to the opening of William Aberhart school, promised a bright future, good pay, and seemingly boundless opportunities for the young people who chose to seize them. Much like the Hudson's Bay advertisement, and countless other ones produced for young people in the 1950s and 1960s, everything in the advertisement focused on the future. Points of emphasis were the future, a pension plan, and steady increases—a "combination of opportunity and security."[114]

Young women were often targeted. Interviewees, however, discussed how, in some families, girls were often not expected to continue their studies following their high school years. Their options were limited into early adulthood. A Henderson Secretarial School advertisement was directed exclusively at young women, who were its entire clientele:

> Opportunities are better than ever. Prepare for a good position ... Everyone has heard of the "Way to Success"... It means a sound business training acquired from a modern up-to-date business school. Success results from planning ... so plan now to attend Henderson Secretarial School, and you will be following in the footsteps of hundreds of young Henderson graduates who have learned the secret of the "Way to Success." Enquire about our special summer courses.[115]

Work, both paid and unpaid, usually gender- and age-defined, was an important element in the lives of many suburban children and adolescents. Even in the absence of pressing family need, work was believed to be critical in shaping healthy young identities and, consequently, healthy future citizens. This dovetailed with some educational goals. Paid employment also allowed many young people to assert some independence as they transitioned to adulthood.

Conclusion

The postwar suburbs are often represented as being exclusively white, and Banff Trail, like many Canadian suburbs in this period, was no exception. Neither children nor adolescents seemed aware of the privilege associated with this whiteness, at least not from their perspective as adults. Race was a rare topic of conversation, although by the late 1960s it was discussed mainly in the context of the African American civil rights movement rather than in local or national terms. In the 1960s, nearly 70 percent of Calgarians identified their ethnic origins as either British or German.[116]

Banff Trail reflected this in that hierarchies of whiteness didn't emerge in the minds of young suburbanites. By the decade's end, immigration patterns into Calgary were changing, and the landscape in the 1970s was quite different, not only in Banff Trail but across the city.[117]

Banff Trail could not be categorized as either middle-class or working-class in these years. Most participants recalled no sustained experience of class differences, and such differences did not form part of their consciousness as children or adolescents. Despite their lack of awareness, class was the key determiner in their education, personal well-being, health, and so forth. Their relatively comfortable and homogenous suburban experiences tended to shield them from this knowledge. Across class lines, young people spent many hours doing both unpaid and paid work inside and outside their homes. Work was gendered, mirroring the adult world of work, but was nonetheless important to many in that it helped them make the transition to independent adulthood.

Chapter 4

The Serious Business of Play

Play and leisure time are fundamental to the way that children and adolescents define their childhood cultures, often without revealing much about their recreation activities to the most important adults in their lives. One participant remembered that his eighteen-year-old brother, on his motorcycle, chased him and his friends, in a form of tag, around the neighbourhood; they were terrified but nonetheless exhilarated: "That's a game I remember playing. [We were] just playing around the neighbourhood; the good old days when the evening seemed to go on forever."[1] This memory reflects a common notion that time had a different quality in childhood. Particularly for younger children, not yet on regular schedules, clocks and watches had not yet come to order their lives. School entry necessarily brought more time regulation, and adolescents, for whom work and extracurricular activities required scheduling, had to learn to organize their own time.

Postwar suburban children engaged in sports, recreation, leisure activities, and play. Popular culture and leisure activities were geared increasingly to children and adolescents following the Second World War as a result of modern ideas about organizing, formalizing, and institutionalizing youngsters' activities. While these ideas were in evidence during the interwar years, as more experts focused on play and recreation for their character-building propensities, the postwar period's focus on teaching Canadian citizenship values made them even more so. Nearly all children in North America were now spending more time at school and at play than at work. Nevertheless, play was not experienced in a universal, undifferentiated way. Class, gender and race shaped leisure time and recreation.

Among established organizations, the Girl Guides and Boy Scouts, dating from the Great War, were particularly strong in Banff Trail. Scouts and Guides were not church-based but did offer the promise of instilling the values of diligence, hard work, and discipline. Similar programs such as Hi-C and the Canadian Girls in Training were associated, to varying degrees with religion, helping to explain their popularity, at least among parents who encouraged their children to join.[2] These organizations were also critical in shaping distinctive gender roles by emphasizing traditional ideas of femininity and masculinity.[3] Unlike most young children, who had limited say in what activities they undertook, adolescents were permitted more freedom in choosing their own activities.

The postwar years served as a transitional period, across conventional racial, class, and gender lines, in that most young people had more time to themselves than did previous generations. Many older adolescents' increasingly busy schedules were filled with more leisure time and play activities; at the same time, there was a loosening of the hold of work and familial duties.[4] As discussed, suburban spaces, both in and outside of homes, were increasingly designated for children's and adolescents' use. The most profound change in the lives of Canadian children and adolescents, regardless of where they lived, was the movement toward a childhood defined by education, sports, recreation, and leisure. It was hardly "carefree," however, as young people had to negotiate difficult peer and sibling influences and challenges from several institutions, including their families and schools.

Childhood Recreation, Leisure, and Play in Historical Context

Age, gender, race, and class are historically important factors in the preferences and styles of childhood play.[5] These variable and others affected young people's access to recreational and leisure activities prior to the Second World War. In Calgary, in the late nineteenth century, early non-Indigenous residents were drawn for leisure and refreshment to the Bow River, where they enjoyed community picnics and shared family time.[6] The first organized hockey game was played in 1888, while even earlier, in 1884, soccer, badminton, tennis, rugby, and lacrosse were played on Sixth Avenue.[7] While younger children were not necessarily involved directly in these team sports, adolescents and young adults were often represented. In several pictures from the era, children are prominent and enthusiastic spectators at most major sport and leisure event, even if they were not participating directly.

For most Canadian children and adolescents, their first organized sports included discontinued games along with volleyball, football, informal hockey, and cricket, indicating the variety of team games played in early North American schoolyards.[8] Along with the natural environment, streets (for urban young people), homes, and schoolyards were, and continue to be, central to childhood and adolescent cultures. Contemporary experts asserted that young people acquired important social, physical, emotional, and cognitive skills through play and that play eased children's adjustment to their environment. Most importantly, they argued that it made life meaningful.[9] Outdoor recreation came to be one of many antimodernist responses to the ills of modernity. Antimodernists criticized the pace and direction of cultural change, the unchanging rhythms of modern living, and their impacts on young people, which they termed *overcivilization*.[10] Canada was at the forefront of educational pedagogy in incorporating Frobel's theories, with their emphasis on play as the central occupation of children, into the public education system.[11] Organized sports, in particular, were seen to build character, hone boys' masculinity and girls' reproductive capacity, address health problems, and maintain population growth among European settlers.[12] Modern trends such as urbanization and industrialization supplanted an older agrarian ethos about "natural time"—day, night, and the seasons. Urban dwellers were increasingly ordered by the clock and controlled by the factory or the business of cities.[13] Not everyone saw this as "progress."

The scouting movement had an important impact on youngsters' activities across the globe, in Banff Trail specifically. Founded by Robert Baden-Powell in England in 1907, scouting glorified the British Empire and emphasized the importance of the outdoors and its positive effects on young boys and girls. Scouting aimed to "make men" out of boys. The Canadian frontier was a suitable backdrop, as it provided a model for the "real man," who should be toughened, resourceful, and virile.[14] Baden-Powell's worldwide scouting movement embodied antimodernism in emphasizing the need for children to engage with the natural environment in a more meaningful and disciplined way. These values corresponded to the traditional values emphasized in principals' messages and curriculums throughout this period. Doug Cass recalled the ambitious programming in the 1960s: "It got to a point that it was almost every single weekend. We went for a hike around Old Forestry Road, Cochrane, Bragg Creek, and into the mountains. [There were] camping trips six to eight times a year."[15] Beginning in the early twentieth century, these activities gained greater value as leisure time was increasingly scheduled and was intended to hold greater purpose than it might have in previous North American childhoods. Some historians argue that in the case of nationally organized sports, which were spreading across the United States in the interwar period, these heavily administered activities became one of the most pervasive forces in the lives of many young people.[16] These same processes were at work in Canada.

Organized activities increased during the interwar years. Schools and a handful of private groups such as the YMCA, the Boy Scouts, and Boys and Girls Clubs shared in providing activities to both children and adolescents.[17] The City of Calgary provided a few modest programs, but the Parks Department was not directly involved until the late 1940s. However, by the 1930s, the Scouts and their activities were significant in Calgary, as reported in this 1939 *Calgary Herald* article:

> Calgary Boy Scouts, 1,000 strong, got out their bicycles early this morning and began calling at homes to collect toys for the Scout-Guide-Sunshine toyshop. During the first two hours nearly 100 homes were visited by Cubs and Scouts, the boys reaping everything from armless dolls and wheel less doll buggies to a shiny last year's model toy automobile, large enough to seat a small boy. For the scouts it was hard work. Their errands took them to almost all parts of the city ... But as one 12-year-old ... put it: "It's a lot better than spending the morning in bed. I get a kick out of going into all these homes."[18]

This toy-shop initiative reinforced the need for charity and revealed underlying class distinctions: these were predominantly middle-class adolescents gathering items for poor families hard hit by the Great Depression. There was a blend of leisure and "work" for these youngsters, who were openly proud in performing these duties. They practised precisely what organizers hoped they would during these drives, namely, helping underprivileged children. Civic duty, hard work, and contributing time and dollars to charities are often cited when former Boy Scouts or Girl Guides discuss these activities from the perspective of adulthood.

Throughout the early twentieth century, the ideas of Garden City planners influenced the way cities were shaped. In the context of childhood, planners, with their well-placed mistrust of the automobile and their disdain for the street, believed the solution to keeping children off the streets and under well-meaning surveillance was to build green spaces for them in the centres of large city blocks.[19] Many parks were built in Calgary. Edworthy Park, along the Bow River, was one popular leisure destination for families. Child experts of all kinds also contended that young people needed directed and administered activities. Left by themselves, or left idle, immoral behaviour, or even more serious juvenile delinquency, would lead them on the path to adult crime.[20]

Not all early twentieth-century leisure activities were carefree. Competitive sports, especially when part of the school curriculum, were not only important for physical fitness but also for promoting general education, quality citizenship, democratic living, and better sportsmanship.[21] In the Cold War context, these activities were cited repeatedly as weapons against the threat of communism. Healthy-bodied and healthy-minded young people would be better equipped to resist the menace of communism, yet young people still made important decisions regarding their time away from school and work. Often, spare time was theirs to fill, despite the efforts of parents, teachers, volunteers, and public administrators to guide them into directed activities. The immediate postwar years in Calgary saw a new emphasis on young people's activities as facilities and opportunities exploded in number, coinciding with the baby boom across the rapidly expanding city.

Leisure Time

One resident, Art Irwin, recalled constant action in Banff Trail as activities changed by the season. In "spring we always played baseball in our back yard until a window got broken. Then we had to go to [one of] the community park[s] to play ... In the summer there were picnics, fishing trips, kick the can at night. The fall was back to school and football on the crescent boulevard."[22]

For many young people, particularly preteenagers, the Banff Trail suburb was the main site for most activities. By contrast, teenagers' activities were not necessarily centred in the community. The latter's interests were more varied than children's, and they enjoyed increased mobility, as they could travel to other places. Because there were so many children in the immediate neighbourhood, if children wanted something to do, it was as simple as walking out the front door to find willing playmates.

Frank Edward said he "enjoy[ed] physical activity more than anything. I'd be out playing hockey for hours and hours in the winter. In the summer, throwing footballs around, throwing Frisbees. [Sometimes I was] riding my bike with friends or more likely by myself."[23] While there were always other young people to play with, he enjoyed and appreciated significant time alone. Unlike adults—especially women who did not work outside the home, for whom the suburbs might well have been confining and restrictive—children found ample space, and time, to spend alone. Many were content with the relative freedom of unstructured play.[24]

Elizabeth Davidson thought she might have been given too much freedom when she reached adolescence. She said she is much stricter as a parent: "I didn't have any boundaries. I would go out on the weekends, and she would never know where I was. She never seemed to be very concerned ... and I know what kinds of things I was up to."[25] Not having interviewed her mother, who was a single parent for some of the interviewee's childhood and adolescence, it is difficult to know if she consciously allowed her daughter to assert some independence at a young age or was too busy to notice, not overly concerned, or motivated by another reason. Her recollections also suggest that adolescents from working-class families likely had less supervision, given that their parents were absent for work more so than in middle-class families, which were patterned on the male breadwinner ideal. An important trend is that single-parent families were in decline in this period. The proportion of single-parent families (predominantly mothers) was 12.1 percent in 1941, 9.9 percent in 1951, and 8.4 percent in 1961.[26]

Scholars in the field of contemporary urban studies, such as Jane Jacobs, increasingly lament the absence of opportunities for young people to have time of their own, emphasizing that, more than any other age group except the elderly, they are historically at the mercy of convenience. By the late twentieth century, after attending school and participating in

A group of Banff Trail kids taking a short break from playing in the neighbourhood in July of 1958. (Reproduced with permission of the family.)

an expanded roster of organized activities, children had to wedge in outdoor leisure and play, which occurred incidentally.[27]

Many interviewees did not believe that they were as busy as young people today, yet several discussed how many organized activities they were involved in. Donna McLaren said she did "whatever was available in Tri-Wood; the baseball, soccer, and hockey [programs]. Soccer took over mostly. I belonged to the Y ... and did the stuff they had there. I golfed [and played] tennis."[28] While most of these activities had small fees, they were nevertheless geared toward middle-class children and adolescents and toward working-class families experiencing a modest increase in household income and available leisure time. McLaren enjoyed a mixture of leisure and recreation programs, but the larger point is that, similar to what Jacobs noted, children and adolescents were already enjoying self-directed spare time, demonstrating that this phenomenon is not new but emerged in the postwar era. Wendy Glidden said she could not recall any organized sports involvement and that "everything was very informal. We'd maybe get together and have a baseball game. Just a bunch of kids would say, 'Do you want to go to the park?' In high school, we did some bowling and those kinds of things ... We played outside all the time and played informal games all the time."[29]

Although Glidden did not recall there being any organized sports available, there were some (confirmed in school materials and by other participants) in Banff Trail and in the nearby Triwood community by the late 1960s. Regardless of adolescents' agency and desires, if parents or guardians did not allow, encourage, or facilitate formal extracurricular activities, they likely did not happen for some.[30] Their options were also defined by material circumstances.

While the suburban and urban landscapes provided a multitude of options for spare and leisure, there were also popular indoor options. The television set became the focus of leisure time for families.[31] An ever-growing array of programming for youngsters and families occupied much leisure time. While their reach was not complete, by the early 1960s, television sets were in 82.5 percent of Canadian households.[32] Where children's popular culture is concerned, 1955 was a watershed year in that *The Mickey Mouse Club* went on the air and was easily viewed in many Canadian households. In July 1955, Disneyland, an amusement park designed primarily for children, opened in Anaheim, California.[33] It immediately drew families from across the continent.

By the early 1970s, television consumed as much of young people's time as did school, and it penetrated their everyday lives to an even greater degree than radio or the movies had done in previous decades.[34]

Doug Cass recalled its importance, which was seasonal: "In the winter time, television was a big part of all of our lives. We had our favourite shows and routine around that. I never did any homework, so that was a major part of the schedule in the winter time."[35] In his suburban family, watching television was a family event, and households in the late 1950s and early 1960s rarely featured more than one TV set. Wendy Glidden also remembered television viewing as a shared activity: "We did a fair bit of TV watching as a family. There were a number of shows that we would enjoy [together]."[36] Jim Chambers remembered the contradictions between his own family and parents on popular television shows: "Your parents were not your friends, they were your parents, and they took the

The boys' choir from Banff Trail Elementary School in its production of *Columbus' Travels* was featured in this 1965 photo from the *Calgary Herald*. (Reproduced with permission of the University of Calgary Archives and Special Collection, NA-2864-1755-3.)

responsibility seriously. They were not remotely like the idiotic, syrupy parents in TV shows like *Leave it to Beaver, Father Knows Best,* and *Ozzie and Harriet,* where the kids ran roughshod over the grown-ups."[37]

Bruce Wilson recalled that even in childhood the television had become a way to make connections to a broader world, a world that seemed to offer so much promise and hope from a child's perspective. He remembered watching Walter Cronkite and that it seemed like "there was always something going on ... Apollo 13 or Gemini. There was always something being launched into space, and it was a big part of growing up, and watching it on TV. The landing on the moon in 1969, everyone was involved in experiencing that. That was a big thing."[38] He emphasized the shared experience that television established. Television broadcasting produced a shared culture for the young of this era that was unprecedented in its breadth, stretching beyond class and regional divisions.[39]

Television was also vital to the growing commodification of childhood. The popularity of *The Mickey Mouse Club* and Barbie illustrated the two major themes in the adult domestication of children's play throughout the period: commercialization and the co-optation of time and activities.[40] Yet this was not a universal experience, even in suburban childhood cultures. Jim Farquharson recalled that his family "didn't have a TV until [he] was in grade twelve. We did have a console stereo. We spent a lot of time listening to the different radio plays that were on like *The Lone Ranger* and *Hopalong Cassidy.*"[41] As one of the older baby boomers, he, along with his family, was different than most in not having a television set until the late 1960s. He did recall watching TV at friends' and relatives' homes throughout his childhood. Sharon Johnstone fell in the middle of the spectrum: "I enjoyed [watching] TV. We didn't have much [to watch on television], and we didn't have cable. We really weren't terribly interested in getting cable until we were way past eighteen years old. Our first colour TV wasn't until grade ten. When we were young, there were only two channels."[42] Not all children and adolescents were consumed by television, and as has been demonstrated throughout this book, young people were not merely passive recipients of intended messaging.

Discussions about television, its content, and its effects marked this era as TV sets appeared increasingly in most youngsters' homes. High school editorials in both the 1950s and 1960s offered adolescent perspectives on television, and these discussions are another example of the young inserting their voices into the debate. A 1955 article from Calgary Central High School's newspaper, the *Central Weeper,* was titled "T.V.—Good or Bad?" As the young writer discussed the situation:

T.V. or not T.V.—that is the question ... And whether it is good or bad, many people will still watch it (sometimes to the exclusion of almost all else). There are things to be said, both for and against television and both sides have their strong points ... the fact remains that there are a great many interesting programs which are not educational ... It is up to the individual to decide which he (or she) will be, a televidiot or a normal viewer.[43]

A survey of Calgary young people indicated that watching television and movies and visiting were the most frequent year-round activities.[44] Canadian audience numbers are limited for this period, but historian Paul Rutherford concluded that, in 1959, children (including adolescents) were in the slight majority of viewers from 4:00 p.m. until 6:00 p.m. and that they remained in substantial numbers until about 9:00 p.m.[45] These viewing times match up with the end of the school day and with typical bedtimes. Programming, particularly Canadian children's programming, was sparse. Locally produced children's shows received little critical acclaim. *Chatelaine* noted that for the on-air kindergarten that was *Romper Room,* the "guests are panicky preschoolers in their Sunday best, kept in line by a gimlet-eyed, syrupy-voiced lady."[46] National polling from these years reflected the changing attitudes of Canadians. Respondents were asked, "Do you feel that TV is a good influence on family life?" In 1956, 78 percent said that it was a good influence. By 1966, only 58 percent answered yes.[47]

Much like adult viewers, young people demonstrated that they were not passive recipients when reading "texts" such as television shows and movies.[48] While it is impossible to universalize adolescents' experiences with media, articles such as this one from the *Aberhart Advocate* reveal older teenagers as viewers who negotiated with, and could offer reasoned critiques of, the media:

One of the most repetitive and often boring pastimes nowadays is T.V. Most of the time you do not realize you are seeing the same thing over—it is cleverly disguised changing the names, gestures, and make-up of the guilty ... Now all we have to do is suffer thru the deodorant commercial, the alternate sponsor, the week from next Thursday's semi-annual sponsor, three station breaks and seven local commercials before the fun starts all over again.[49]

While there is no question that students received editorial input from older peers and teachers, critical thinking skills and an ability to engage with, or in many instances disengage from, television content is clear. Suburban adolescents were not unthinking sponges, merely soaking up the exploding 1950s and 1960s North American mediascape. Many viewers were active and engaged, even voicing reservations that some held about the "idiot box" and its effects on youngsters.

Spare Time

Most postwar children and adolescents, much like young people today, relished their spare time. The opportunity to do what they liked, obviously within certain spatial, legal, temporal, and ethical bounds, was extremely important to suburban children and adolescents. It was a time for free expression. Adolescents especially sought time to themselves as they made the transition to adulthood.

The importance of spare time to children and adolescents is clear. Two of the defining themes of childhood and adolescence in this period, which continue to this day, were ubiquitous scheduling and ever-increasing adult control over young people's time.[50] Surveys in Calgary at this time showed that the majority of respondents of all ages believed that teenagers were most in need of directed leisure activities.[51] Rather than spare time, many adults held the belief that more recreation and leisure activities would best serve idle youngsters. This belief was common throughout these two decades. In its 1951 annual report, the well-respected Calgary Boys Club opined that monthly socials should be supported "to keep the boys from seeking other and perhaps undesirable outlets. Dances should only be allowed occasionally and then under strict supervision, and should be confined to membership and their friends, *and not open to the general public*. On no account should adults (except as supervisors) be admitted."[52]

This type of discussion reinforced the popular idea that spare or leisure time should not be teenagers' own: it needed to be regulated and organized by adults. The delineation between childhood and adulthood was also emphasized. It was "necessary" to protect young people from one another and from adults who might prove to be harmful to them. The Calgary Boys Club was, at most times, aiding teenagers, not typically from middle-class backgrounds, who had had some previous difficulties at home, school, or with the Calgary Police.[53]

Lesley Hayes recalled having significant time to do what she wanted, despite the pressures and constraints put on youth. Spare time was spent "going to movies. We'd organize that. Reading. I was a voracious reader. It was often unstructured. Go out and see who you can find; get on your bike and go down to the tennis court with your racquet and see who you can find to play with. My mom wouldn't know exactly where I was, for hours."[54]

Despite widespread warnings about "stranger danger" and emphatic public discourses about the value of organized activities, many who grew up in the postwar suburbs had the freedom and latitude to create and direct their own activities during their spare time. There were real tensions between these larger messages and what in fact was happening in their lives. There was heightened awareness of the harm that could come to children, yet the suburban experiences of most interviewees, and their own writings, reflected little of this. Hayes, as she thought of it in the context of the era, was surprised to recall that her mother did not know exactly where she was for hours on end, from time to time. The availability of spare time was essential to doing other activities, yet class and material circumstances were often vital factors in what many of these children could and would do. Contemporary studies in Calgary reflected this as well, as time was the major requirement for participation in desired activities for teenagers, followed by money, equipment, and facilities.[55]

Reading was mentioned by many young people in their memories of their day-to-day lives as children. Youngsters read influential books that became instant classics. *The Catcher in the Rye* and *Lord of the Flies,* for example, were published in the early 1950s. One baby boomer recalled in a memoir that "it was a great decade for fantasy, with J.R.R. Tolkien's epic *Lord of the Rings* trilogy in 1954–55 and *The Lion, the Witch and the Wardrobe* by C.S. Lewis. Science fiction peaked in the fifties with ... works by Ray Bradbury (*The Martian Chronicles, Fahrenheit 451*), Robert A. Heinlein (*Tunnel in the Sky*), and Isaac Asimov (*I, Robot*)."[56]

Doug Cass remarked on the importance of reading and how he "fell in love with *Mad* magazine and ... [I] read a huge amount of fiction by Jules Verne, books that were serious books about grown-up things but meant for children. I read all the *Dr. Dolittle* books. I would find an author at the library and go through everything they wrote."[57] Much of this had been his dad's influence and they read and shared books until his death. He mentioned getting a lot of books from the public library, something that distinguished working-class and middle-class homes. Extensive personal libraries were not often a part of working-class homes in this period.

From the late 1940s, the importance of books was encouraged and nurtured, mainly by middle-class parents but also in advice columns for teenagers. In 1950, the syndicated column "Teen Topics by Sally" featured some not-so-subtle advice on reading habits and materials:

> Do you go for comics exclusively? Do you skim through the picture magazines? Don't you EVER settle down with a good book? Good books aren't necessarily the classics ... A lot of popular current literature is fine

reading—well-written and interesting ... At least one of the reprint pub-
lishers has a line of junior books—new editions of teenage stuff that has
been best-selling material. These junior paper backs are tops in entertainment. Mystery stories, western, career books, joke collections. So shop
your corner drugstores and stationery shops, kids.[58]

This advice was representative of the hierarchizing of reading materials at the time, with comic books and pulp fiction almost always placed
much lower than "literature." It was in the early postwar period that comic
books, especially those associated with horror, terror, sex, or crime, were
demonized as direct contributors to the perceived rise in juvenile delinquency. One notorious case in New York led to the banning of some comic
books in the mid-1950s.[59] In terms of hierarchizing, cost was a factor since
middle-class adolescents were much more likely to have the money to purchase books, whereas buying lower-priced items and borrowing books were
likelier options for working-class teenagers.

William Wright did not recall the specific titles of books, but he did
remember reading much more in his childhood and adolescence than he
ever did as an adult: "[I] remember a lot of television. Way more reading
than I do now. Comic books. And I was into a lot of drawing and cartooning.
That would be a lot of my free time."[60] In both the literature produced by
high school students themselves, and in interviews, no female interviewees
recalled reading any comic books. Some romance books were mentioned,
with a mother's reading habits sometimes influencing these choices.

Mary Baker recalled that spare time was often spent with friends,
with a focus on quality and reflective time. She would meet up with her
best friend, and they "would walk every night. [There was] lots of walking, yakking, and hanging out. Not necessarily planned activities ... I was
involved in church stuff, every church activity, choir, Guides. I did not
enjoy teenage social activities. I wanted to be Greta Garbo."[61] She mentioned Garbo and the movie star's influence on her young life. For some,
these iconic representations offered hopeful examples of lives outside the
suburban existence. Quite simply, some mainstream teenage activities
were too boring for her. Other female interviewees mentioned seeking out
activities with younger adults rather than spending time with their peers.

Going to movies was a large part of adolescent life for many adolescents and children. Doug Call recalled that in the early 1960s downtown
theatres "had Saturday matinees for $0.25, and we [he, his sisters, and
friends] took the bus. It would stop right by the Bay, and we would walk
from there. We did that up until the time I began working."[62] Movies for
and about youth hit screens across North America. A memoirist recalled:

"Movies like *The Wild One, Rebel Without a Cause, Blackboard Jungle, High School Confidential!, Teen-Age Crime Wave, Reform School Girl ... Teenagers from Outer Space* made it seem that youth ... was everywhere on some kind of dark, disturbed rampage."[63] This was all part of the larger trend that made popular recreation increasingly a consumer product, dependent on a growing network of related forms of consumption for young people. From clothing to grooming to the new technologies, youngsters took part in and contributed to the creation of a mainstream modern youth culture by the mid-1950s.[64]

Going to theatres and movie watching were most often for entertainment purposes, but for some they were more than that. William Wright recalled seeing several blockbusters from the era and that he "used to live at the North Hill Cinerama. It used to be this great old theatre. That was kind of my haven when I was growing up. There was also a theatre at the Brentwood Mall."[65] Space was vital to adolescents as they created their own cultures centred on their preferred activities and their peers. The new shopping malls, which housed many of these theatres, became key places where adolescents could express their youth cultures, independent from home and school; unlike adults and young children, teenagers existed increasingly in separate spaces, separate worlds.[66] While movies targeting young people were very popular, music made for and by young people, also kept many children and adolescents occupied. Many participants mentioned the excitement Elvis and the Beatles generated with their television appearances and that this music was instantly popular with nearly all teenagers.

It is clear that music was important for adolescents, and this was reflected in their own writings. A 1964 article in the *Aberhart Advocate,* titled "Modern Music Dictionary," discussed the wildly popular Beatles and their influence on adolescent cultures at the time: "What's the hottest group in teenage music today? Silly question, isn't it? Several new words have imposed themselves upon the Queen's English and some of you out there in Beatleland might like to pass this around to your poor, innocent, uninformed, uncorrupted acquaintances ... Beatle ... Beatlemania ... Beatlemaniac ... Beatlenausea ... Beatlephobia ... Beatlephonia ... Beatlephonic."[67] The fusing of music and popular culture was just one process. Others remembered the importance of music and recalled the Festival Express tour that went across much of Canada and came to Calgary's McMahon Stadium in 1970.[68] McMahon Stadium stands a few minutes' walk from Banff Trail, and the concert featured some of the biggest acts of the late 1960s and early 1970s, including Ian and Sylvia Tyson, Janis Joplin, Jimi Hendrix, Bob Dylan, and the Grateful Dead. As Jim Farquharson remembered, "It was loud enough and close enough to our home that we just sat in the backyard and enjoyed the concert. An Eagles concert was so loud and created so many complaints by the neighbourhood that Calgary brought in its antinoise by-law that still exists."[69]

Teenagers were also involved in writing and performing their own music. Brent Harris said that in his "junior high and senior high years, [he] drove down to Mount Royal College for that practical and theoretical trumpet lesson."[70] It was not only adults who travelled to work from within their suburban communities; teenagers lived important parts of their lives outside their suburban communities. Sharon Johnstone noted that, "beyond singing and piano, I enjoyed drawing and painting."[71] Her singing took her across the city as she performed with family members at functions. It was what she enjoyed doing, and she had some say in what she would perform and where she would do it.

For some, spare time was some of the most memorable moments of their childhoods. Because the countryside was easily accessed by car, and most suburban families had one, the opportunity to take extended Sunday afternoon drives was a highlight. Allan Matthews said that was his biggest joy as a young child: "My parents, I remember when I got older, wished I quit coming. To me, it has always been amazing. That was probably the

Rock music fans at Festival Express concert, held at McMahon Stadium in Calgary in July, 1970. (Photographed by David Cunningham. Reproduced with permission of the University of Calgary Archives and Special Collection, NA-5689-5-15.)

real joy that I had. Sundays. My father would always find some new place to go, or even just going to get the eggs on Sunday, he would find a new route to go."[72] Simple pleasures, such as walking and talking with friends, were mentioned. Other children enjoyed highly organized activities with very clear goals. But there have always been young people, just as there are many adults, who prefer some solitary time. It was a recurring theme that children and adolescents appreciated the opportunity to spend some time alone or, at the very least, to be able to daydream without feeling, or being told, that spare time was wasted time.

Shopping

Shopping, in many forms, was an important part of young peoples' lives. Ever-increasing consumption and shopping are often associated with urban, and especially suburban, living in the immediate postwar period. While there was increasing prosperity, it was uneven in that it was not experienced universally by all families, more specifically, it was not experienced by all children and adolescents. One key indicator of this is the fact that membership in the Boys Club in Calgary reached six hundred boys by 1960. Membership in the Boys Club has always been overrepresented by children of the unemployed and working class. Granted, Calgary's population was increasing, but there were a number of young people in need. The Calgary club was the largest not only across the Prairies but also west of Toronto.[73] Even though the commodification of childhood in the broader context of consumerism is a popular topic among historians of childhood, a significant number of young suburbanites did not embrace shopping, particularly spending on consumer products. For some, there was not much choice in this, as they had no disposable income. A 1960 editorial in the *Aberhart Advocate* expressed resistance to and questioned the commercialization of Christmas from a suburban teenager's perspective:

RADIO, TELEVISION, NEWSPAPERS, CHRISTMAS LIGHTS, SLOGANS, POSTERS, TV, COMMERICIALS, ADS, MAIL, and anything else business can dream up as an advertising media, has been informing me of that singular fact for the past six weeks. Did you notice that some of the stores stuck fat, jolly, red, Santas on their windows and counters with the same tape that one-half minute before had held glaring black cats and grimacing pumpkins in place? I get so tired of our commercial Christmas. Gaudy lights blink obliquely at the masses of silent, expressionless people plodding through the streets for their personal Grail; the gadget they saw advertised on TV that would be just the thing.[74]

This article expressed well the dizzying array of media, older and newer, that young people engaged with, coupled with marketing and advertising on a new level. The process of commodification was not new, but the volume of advertising was unprecedented.[75] There was no break in the advertising onslaught: Halloween decorations were just put away and Christmas decorations replaced them immediately—a phenomenon that continues today.

Throughout the postwar era, there was a concerted message, delivered more widely than ever by the growing mainstream mediascape. What were once deemed lowbrow—radio, television, and the movies—became the new arbiters of style and taste.[76] The communication channels were often one-way, although they were mediated by young people as they were consumed. New technologies also became a productive tool for some creative youngsters. William Wright recalled getting a movie camera for his tenth birthday: "It changed my life. It was something I wanted, and I petitioned for years. I developed a really early fascination with the movies. That shaped my childhood in that I was given an incredibly creative outlet at a very early age ... I was just so obsessed with this hobby."[77]

Radio, feature-length movies, and popular literature in this era also inspired countless toys and games.[78] Newspapers also continued to be significant influences. The *Calgary Herald* made several recommendations for Christmas shopping in 1951—reinforcing traditional gender ideals in the types of gifts described:

> You can let the children play at either war or peace this Christmas ... Many boys ... will want guns or ships for routing the enemy and girls like C.W.A.C. or other uniforms. They also will enjoy playing cowboy and Indian, and the Indian seems to have scored a big advance over the cowboy this year ... You can help to develop aptitudes and prepare for peacetime careers with all types of building toys (road building equipment holds new interest) and mechanic's or carpenter's kits for boys. Girls may develop dishpan hands at an early age, for even two-year-olds will like a new toy kit which includes dish rack, garbage can, mop, brush, wash cloths.[79]

The themes of war and conflict are also prominent in this article, reaffirming that there was no time in the Cold War era when any childhood or adolescent experience was unequivocally carefree. The utilitarian nature of certain gifts emphasized that toys were important tools in creating good citizens.

Commodification, however, was not a simple process of transference that imposed consumerism on independent, individual children and adolescents, nor was it something that blackened "pure" childhoods; instead, it came to form one of the major building blocks of modern youth culture.[80] Bruce Wilson remembered childhood leisure time that involved nearby suburban shopping spaces such as the North Hill Shopping Centre as well as other large malls located in the south of Calgary:

> There was the Big Boy hamburger place and Sears [in the North Hill Shopping Centre] were the big ones. Market Mall, by the high school years [in the early 1970s], was the big thing ... I still remember that Chinook was the big draw ... I remember the Woodward's store had the big display [and at] Christmastime sitting and watching the angels display; downtown, not so much. Movie theatres were only available downtown, the Palace and some of those older theatres. We'd hang out and chase around there.[81]

Clothing and style were notable in nearly all yearbooks from the period. While many interviewees did not recall the importance of clothing style, some did recall that shopping for clothes was "fun" and a way to "express oneself" by early teenagehood. This fits with what Toronto's

Lady Baden-Powell visited and celebrated with Girl Guides in Calgary in 1955. (Photographed by Jack De Lorme. Reproduced with permission of the University of Calgary Archives and Special Collection, NA-5600-7075B.)

Crestwood Heights young suburbanites experienced. It was noted that clothing, for both teenaged boys and girls, had become an important symbol of changing status.[82] Several yearbook pages were dedicated to teen fashion. In the 1950s, cashmere sweaters, polo shirts, saddle shoes, and corduroy pants were the height of high school fashion. These styles were featured in print ads aimed at teenagers and in popular catalogues from this period—Eaton's and Sears being two widely distributed ones.

Local spots such as the Chang's grocery store, with its lunch counter, and the Wig Wam, with its milkshakes, were also spaces where adolescents would gather to eat and socialize. In these years, the types of local shops and stores that youth had access to varied greatly, depending on where they lived. One youngster recalled that "that was the glory of living in a world that was still largely free of global chains. Every community was special and nowhere was like everywhere else."[83] This changed in later decades when development was dominated by large companies and chain stores, which dominated suburban landscapes. Department-store shopping was prominent in both the school culture (in dozens of advertisements in school yearbooks) and in the memories of a large majority of participants. Sears was mentioned several times, as it was an anchor store in the new North Hill Shopping Centre, which was built in 1959. In the United States, Sears and Roebuck actually extended credit to older children and adolescents, who, with regular allowances, were able to apply for their own Sears credit card.[84] Wendy Glidden recalled that shopping was very much a social outing with her mother, whereas with her father it was more basic.[85] This was echoed by others who mentioned the gender dynamics of shopping within their own families.

At times, families enjoyed a meal as part of the shopping experience, whether it was at newly built malls or in the downtown core. Glidden discussed going to the North Hill Mall on the bus with her mother; they dressed up and treated it as a social outing, as the Sears department store was "quite fancy." She also recalled going grocery shopping to "Co-op every Friday night. So we would terrorize the downtown Co-op, and we would run up and down the stairs. They had a little counter, and we would get a dinner—a burger and fries ... We used to go to downtown a lot for shopping too."[86]

For young boomers born into postwar affluence, the Western world seemed to have a near endless ability to produce material goods and meet their wants.[87] Retailers were eager, in most instances, to service young consumers. Not all young people, however, felt welcomed in all stores.[88] Ageism can take several different forms. Glidden recalled that in Banff Trail "there was a drug store and the Chang's corner store right across from Aberhart [High School] ... and the [drug store proprietor] hated kids.

He'd always try and kick us out of there. The Chang's guy was pretty darn friendly."[89] There was obvious conflict at the everyday level of adolescents' lives, with noisiness, shoplifting, or loitering (actually carried out or just the possibility of it) a likely reason for the owner's disdain, despite the business that teenagers brought into the store. What is most notable is that youngsters' consumer cultures took shape in a morally contested space. The degree to which this occurred changed over time, but it is, nevertheless, a process that happens wherever and whenever the market intersects with children and adolescents.[90]

Conclusion

Childhood play, in myriad formats, remains a key way for children to express themselves individually and in their childhood cultures. The postwar years were transitional in that most young people had more spare time than did their cohorts in previous generations. Regardless of where they lived, their lives were increasingly defined less by work, paid and unpaid, and more by education, sports, recreation, and popular culture. Youngsters' activities were more organized and formalized, although many participants discussed how much they enjoyed the playtime they themselves organized as children. A majority of young suburbanites found both the space and the time to relax and roam on foot, bicycles, and, later, in their cars.[91]

Chapter 5

Healthy Minds in Healthy Bodies

Gender, sexualities, bodies, and overall health were areas of concern to young postwar suburbanites. The Second World War had drawn attention to the importance of health and fitness, and because of more affordable medical care and municipal public-health nurses who visited homes, more families could access care before it was too late. Also important were postwar attempts to return to traditional gender roles, especially for women, who were required to re-adopt a feminine style after wearing the overalls and uniforms of war service.[1] As Wendy Glidden expressed it: there were ongoing tensions concerning dress, appearance, and bodies that needed to be negotiated by young people as early as junior high. Branton Junior High, she commented, was very "straight-laced": they "still had to wear dresses. I can remember taking skating in grade seven, and the community hall was right across the street. The assistant principal was horrified that we had worn pants. He made us go change for the ten minutes of home room. Then we had to go change for skating across the street."[2]

Glidden was one of the younger baby boomers, so this was not a memory of events dating to the early postwar years. Some of these school policies and practices continued well into the 1960s and even the 1970s. This reveals that more progressive attitudes and their accompanying practices did not come easily to some educators and administrators, and as the most vulnerable age group in society, children and adolescents have often had to endure the prevailing, and restrictive, attitudes and practices of their time regarding gender, bodies, and sexuality.

Boyhood and girlhood experiences, and representations of them, were distinct throughout this era. These distinctions reflected influential and idealized postwar adult gender roles in many ways, although everyday practices did not always reflect these ideals. Among influential experts, including psychologists, medical doctors, and academics, the health and wellness of young people also came into sharper focus and took greater hold in schools and families by the early 1970s. By the late 1960s, public discourses on sexual education, both formal and informal; multiple definitions of sexuality and gender, and who defined them; how childhood sickness and injury were experienced and treated; and, finally, a growing emphasis on diet all became critical to understanding postwar childhood and adolescence.

Gender

Gender is a central topic in the historiography of North American suburbs and their residents. There are long-standing intersections between gender and suburbia in historical context. In John Stilgoe's influential study on the nascent American suburbs of the nineteenth and early twentieth centuries, he concludes that women not only contributed much of the philosophy underlying early borderland life but also actively shaped the landscape.[3] They were integral to the well-being and care of the inhabitants and to the environment itself, both built and natural.

Historian Suzanne Morton located ongoing class and gender conflict in working-class suburban households, but more importantly she ascertained that the idealized model of homes headed by a male breadwinner conflicted with the realities of female-headed households and broader employment opportunities for women.[4] Another key finding was Morton's conclusion that gender was experienced in different ways at different ages.[5] This is a salient point in the context of gender, childhood, and adolescence—something participants reflected on myriad times.

There have always been alternatives to gender-defined play, and the unstructured play of boys and girls, often segregated, has been a gender-integrated activity at many turns.[6] In the interwar years, younger girls faced educational restrictions, less rewarding job options, and limited political opportunities.[7] Conversely, adolescent girls were more likely to do well in school and to graduate from high school.[8]

As early as the mid-nineteenth century, the divide between "male" and "female" was considered so wide that influential child-advice books were aimed solely at one or the other. Emotions were the key difference, as little girls needed to quell emotions while boys had to master them without losing that vital competitive edge that they might bring to their adult lives.[9] This was a simple binary for advice givers, as there was no discussion of anything other than male or female genders, whether in adulthood, adolescence, or childhood.[10]

As institutions worked to impart certain values to young people in the first part of the twentieth century, gender differences were emphasized. Historian Sharon Wall notes that one of the key features of camp life leading up to the post-Second World War period was its sex-segregated nature.[11] In getting children and adolescents out of cities, there were attempts to cultivate the true "natures" of boys and girls; organizations targeting boys addressed waning urban masculinity while those targeting girls tried to keep them appropriately feminine despite socioeconomic opportunities opening up for women.[12] Robert Baden-Powell's scouting movement initially focused exclusively on boys. It had a profound effect on shaping boyhood in the twentieth century as it aimed to produce men, and the frontier provided the framework for the "real" man in waiting: virile, resourceful, and tough.[13] In contrast to postwar boy cultures, which stressed competition, construction, and physical play, girlhood cultures focused on love, playing with dolls, hairdressing, and grooming.[14]

As the postwar suburbs took shape across Canada, these large tracts of new housing embodied a separation of the sexes that had women mainly responsible for home and family and men responsible for economic support and leadership in the new communities.[15] This separation of the sexes was not uniform, however; in many new suburbs, local community associations had to be formed, and it was women who typically led the way,[16] if not always providing figurehead leadership. Brian Rutz remembered that women, especially his closest friends' mothers, shaped his early childhood through their prominent roles in the homes he visited and played in as a child. This was echoed by nearly all of the participants. Rutz recalled, "My sense is, when I think about going to my friends' places, there was always a mom there. It was just understood that a mom was doing all that stuff [necessary and vital caregiving work within the home]."[17] Historian Neil Sutherland determined that young girls being a "mother hen" to other young people was so important to many girls' childhood experiences that being female and child care were bound inextricably.[18]

For most mothers, work included primary child care, at all times of day. With limited formal daycare providers in Calgary at this time, children benefitted greatly from an informal network of mothers who provided varying levels of supervision.[19] This reality reflected broader constructs associated with gender and idealized roles. The need to live gender-specific lives was a key theme in many important and influential books circulating across Canada in the postwar era. The formal ideologies and theories behind this idea were legitimated by the functionalists who dominated the sociology discipline as it established itself in Canada.[20] These functionalists focused on consensus in Canadian society and how important institutions such as families, schools and the state produced order, stability, and productivity in a well-functioning, modern society.[21]

Bruce Wilson recalled that expectant mothers, who were also teachers in Banff Trail in the 1960s, never taught in the classroom for very long after becoming pregnant: "I'd say ... [gender roles] were very different than now. Women were not considered to be included in certain roles or job expectations. I can never remember a teacher even being pregnant. As soon as they were, I guess the teacher was gone. I knew there were some in the younger grades."[22] Suburban children noticed these things, even if some aspects were not discussed openly with their peers, their parents, or even with teachers themselves. This suggests that even the basic facts associated with gender and sexuality were not necessarily common knowledge.

Fatherhood, boyhood, and masculinity were also tightly interwoven.[23] While girls had serious challenges to overcome, based on gender, so too did boys, if not to the same degree.[24] Mary Baker said that, in the end, "it was much easier for girls to be bolder than it was for boys to be more timid ... For guys it would have been deadly for them to take on a more female-type role."[25] Fathers, while often well-meaning, had to meet the idealized role of fatherhood as well as contributing to the shaping of their sons with both everyday actions and words.[26] These fathers of postwar children and adolescents, suburban and otherwise, were part of a generation that married comparatively young, gained residential independence earlier than their own fathers, and fathered children during a baby boom. There were significant differences between their personal childhoods and their parenting years.[27]

Why adults chose the suburbs, and Banff Trail specifically, was a point of discussion. Other than the relative affordability,[28] William Wright recalled that his parents decided that the proximity to the new University of Calgary and good public schools was a key motivator.[29] Other fathers frequently spoke of the positive values of the suburban experience for their youngsters and emphasized, in particular, the opportunities for outdoor play and the natural environment not found elsewhere.[30]

Generally, work inside the home fell to mothers and girls. Most boys did very little or no work in what was traditionally the feminine sphere; when parents did ask sons to do some work inside the home, they normally did not expect the same levels of good performance.[31] This was not universal, but most female participants, and a handful of male participants, confirmed that this was the case in their own suburban homes and in the majority of the homes in which they spent time as young people. Fathers modeled this gendered behavior for their sons. Very few fathers contributed much inside the homes, outside of repairs, some basic renovations, and light maintenance and cleaning.

Experts on childhood and adolescence continued to gain influence over parents throughout this time, and never more so in the history of Western childhood and adolescence to that point in time. Most organizations adopted the basic tenets of emerging child-development theories in crafting their guiding philosophies for what boys and young men needed. A report titled "Free Time Needs of Boys," from the Boys Clubs of Canada and commissioned by the City of Calgary in the mid-1950s, illustrated this well:

> Every boy in any community should have the opportunity of free time activity; the companionship of boys in a good environment under good leadership ... Every boy should have the opportunity of receiving physical training ... Every boy should have the opportunity to learn and practice wholesome health habits. Every boy should have opportunity for education on a personal interest basis, to develop vocational skills, and to uncover [the] latest vocational aptitudes. Every boy should have the opportunity to develop his interest and skills in hobbies and cultural activities ... Every boy should have the opportunity to experience outdoor life.[32]

The overwhelming focus in this excerpt is physical activity, health and wellness, and learning "proper" values.[33] For young people, this idealized version of masculinity was learned by interpreting the actions of others, through implicit messaging, and from overt instruction, as outlined in the Boys Club advice. There was also an intrinsic pastoral element to this idealizing, in the common belief that the suburbs offered the promise of better health because of their open spaces and outdoor opportunities, in comparison to urban settings nearer downtown cores, which were marked by rapid expansion and crowding. Gender roles could be confusing and confounding.

Girls transitioning to adolescence recalled the difficulties, and at times, sadness, in doing so. Some reflected on the inherent societal power imbalance. Mary Baker echoed this in recalling gender in the late 1950s and early 1960s in the context of school: "Hitting grade seven [at Branton Junior High], it all changed. Girls' roles were gone. There was a huge shift, particularly for someone like me, who had gotten to do whatever I chose."[34] She saw the shift to adolescence, occurring in junior high school for almost all young people, as signalling a life stage defined largely by gender. Whereas many tend to associate greater autonomy with an increase in age—later bed times, the ability to do more things unsupervised, greater activity choices, and so forth—she believed firmly that her situation did not improve as she reached adolescence. The acquisition of power and autonomy by boys and girls as they came of age was not necessarily a steady progression toward independence. This point is key to understanding the complex and often uneven shift to adolescence from childhood for boys and girls.

Tammy Simpson remembered that play in elementary school seemed relatively undifferentiated: "We all played together because I enjoyed the outdoors so much. We were playing army, snowball fights. They might try to say, 'Oh, I'm a guy, you're a girl.' The backhanded compliment I would get would be that you can run as fast as a guy or you can throw a ball just as far as a boy." Simpson, along with many others, said that sexism in late childhood and adolescence was overt. In her peer group, it was just assumed that as a girl she was not welcome to participate in certain games and activities being played by boys. Much of this was modelled on adult gender roles, which stressed passive femininity for young women and active masculinity for young men. She also mentioned that when she got older she "never took up golfing, and I think the guys were happy about that so I wouldn't go along."[35] She likely challenged them not only because she was a girl but also because she was a very good athlete who might have beaten them on the golf course.

Bruce Wilson also noted the transition between the elementary years and junior high years: "By junior high, we started formulating our ideas about how girls couldn't do the same things as boys."[36] This distinction is important, and while there are likely several reasons for it, the effect of the peer group was as big a contributor as all the other information circulating in this period that emphasized fundamental gender differences. Tensions arising from adolescent sexuality were an important influence as well. The influence of the peer group did change over time, but in the junior high years it seemed to take on added importance and for some extended even into their high school years.

But young people had minds of their own and certainly questioned the values and norms presented to them. Bruce Wilson remembered seeing things that did not make sense, even from the perspective of a young adolescent. He recalled that the nearby "Highlander Motor Hotel was a place where my parents sometimes went to have a drink. There was a men's, ladies, and escorts entrances. That always got me."[37] Postwar baby boomers, writing fiction in adulthood, have also discussed gender constructs through their characters. Elaine in Margaret Atwood's novel *Cat's Eye* remembers that the stories from school textbooks represented an idealized gendered suburb that she never actually knew. She recalls that "the father goes to work, the mother wears a dress and an apron, and the children play ball on the lawn with their dog and cat."[38]

For several interviewees, gender inequality was simply not something that was discussed, particularly with young children. Wendy Glidden said,

"It was more informally with us. This is what boys do. This is what girls do. I don't remember my parents ever telling me I couldn't do anything because I was a girl."[39] This easing of prescribed gender roles represented

Students often emphasized their milestones and expected behaviours and practices in their student publications in sketches, poetry, and short stories, as shown in this 1956 drawing of an idealized prom scene. (Calgary Central High School newsletter, June 1956, and reproduced from the author's personal collection.)

an important shift for young girls and demonstrates that at least in some postwar suburban homes the highly gendered adult world wasn't necessarily replicated and encouraged in childhood and adolescent cultures.[40]

A 1957 editorial titled "Equality versus Supremacy," from a Calgary high school newspaper, illustrates some of the tensions surrounding gender:

> Men have been educated to the fact that everyone is created equal; yet they seem to think that they have certain privileges ... At almost every party, the men swarm into a corner to swap jokes ... Women are also considered to be naïve in regard to business. True, there are few great women scientists, business heads or politicians. This is because women have been tending the home, which is natural and right ... Women in previously all-male occupations are either looked upon as unfeminine or are told that they are wasting time and energy because they will only get married anyway.[41]

What this young writer demonstrates well is that adolescent girls, like herself, were thinking about some of the wider tensions that marked gender relations, regardless of existing age divisions. She also highlights some of the practical challenges that girls and women faced in social situations. The author laments the fact that men will often hive themselves off at parties to discuss "masculine" topics that they believe to be, patronizingly, unsuitable for mixed company.

Wendy Glidden acknowledged the pervasiveness of traditional gender ideals: "There was lots of informal ways of making sure that girls did things. I remember when we finally got to wear pants to school, and we got to be a little more normal. Finally, they are kind of waking up; wearing dresses and being super feminine [was unnecessary]. I remember that for junior high, when it actually shifted ... There was a little shift in thinking."[42] The shift was about more than just wearing pants. It was about choice and knowing that identities, sometimes based on gender, could be linked to these choices or to their absence. From the perspective of adolescence, these were not trivial matters. This happened at Branton Junior High in the late 1960s, a time that we often idealize (in the wake of the sexual revolution) as being progressive on the issues of gender and sex. For adolescent girls, freedom to choose their attire reflected their agency.

In 1969, an unsigned editorial in the *Aberhart Advocate*, clearly written by a young woman, captured the frustrations of adolescent girls who felt wearing skirts to write a ninety-minute exam was illogical. The writer asked, "Why does this administration spend so much time and energy on such trivia as dress rules when administration members and guidance counselors are so overworked that most students who need individual attention simply don't get it? ... Most of us learned how to dress our-selves before we entered grade one."[43] Students were annoyed about the bureaucracy, the ongoing regulation they faced, and their limited power to address other issues with adults. The writer, using sarcasm to good effect, underlines that teenagers are not small children and that they are capable of making their own wardrobe decisions.

Gender issues did not simply pit men against women and boys against girls. Male and female participants recalled that they were conscious and supportive of feminist causes in the late 1960s and early 1970s. Despite the popular view of suburbs as bastions of convention and conservatism, the interviewees revealed elements of progressive thinking in several households.[44] Asked about gender and what it meant in his childhood and adolescence, Frank Edward remembered that "my parents were very lib-eral and very convinced of the equality of the sexes ... We probably talked about it in the context of those idiots that didn't meet that line of think-ing ... We talked about it in what would probably be considered a very mod-ern way."[45] While some interviewees were clearly influenced by attitudes in the present, others corroborated that there was a growing consciousness about gender inequalities, which was captured in adolescents' own writ-ings at the time, as indicated in their school newspapers.

Adolescent Sexualities and Bodies

Closely related to gender were the issues of adolescent sexuality and bod-ies, subjects of much concern as postwar parents and teachers grappled with changing ideas and new theories. Baby boom children and adoles-cents, particularly in the 1950s and early 1960s, were generally met with silences, misinformation, denials, and deflection regarding their changing bodies and emerging sexuality. Mary Baker, a baby boomer born in the 1940s, described her sexual education as beginning, like that of children for centuries past, in a barn when she was four years old:

> You know, really, by the time we got anything in school it was useless ... I was not sexually active, but I had more knowledge and experience than I needed to have. Nobody gave you anything useful, like this is a condom and this is how you put it on ... Girls just disappeared. I can think of two good friends that gave up their babies ... It was criminal to do that. And to the boys that lost their children too ... I have nothing good to say about how sex was dealt with.[46]

She touched on many themes, mentioned by other interviewees, that have been broached by researchers working on this era. Noteworthy among them, and echoed by older boomers who were in elementary school in the early 1960s, was the lack of information and the lack of dialogue between generations, and even between teenagers themselves, especially in the 1950s. The forced "invisibility" of pregnant teenagers was a powerful and damaging statement to other adolescents.[47] Teenage pregnancy rates are difficult to quantify, as we know that pregnancies did not always end in births. The topic of unwed teenage pregnancy remained at the forefront of media coverage across the country in these years.[48] The rate of reported teenage pregnancies—referred to as "illegitimate" until the early 1970s—has dropped since the late 1960s and early 1970s, as reflected in official health statistics. In 1974 there were about 57,000 teen pregnancies, in 1992, 38,000.[49] Even so-called legitimate pregnancy was "hidden" from public view, as witnessed earlier in this chapter in Bruce Wilson's recollection of never having seen a pregnant teacher in the classroom.

When asked about formal sex education, the lack of meaningful information was echoed by another participant. According to Allan Matthews, "There were lots of things you never talked about. I didn't know anything about sex until I had a conversation while washing dishes with my mother one night ... I had female cousins that I'd meet under the stairs and a couple of girls in grade six that I met behind the school; that's how I got my sex education."[50] Donna McLaren, born in the 1950s, said sex education and personal relationships didn't get talked about at home. She recalled "asking my mom about fish fertilizing their eggs ... and I don't think the answer was clear ... I felt pretty much in the dark about it ... in junior high. I did fool around with one boy ... As a ten-year-old, I shared a bunk bed with my five-year-old cousin and was terrified that I would be pregnant."[51] One memoirist remembered that "nearly as bad as having sex was thinking about sex. When Lucille Ball on *I Love Lucy* was pregnant for nearly the whole of the 1952–53 season, the show was not allowed to use the word 'pregnant.'"[52]

When it came to formal sex education in this period, adolescents were often segregated by gender for the lessons, but there was little difference in what they were being taught (or not being taught). Parents did not seem to be more open- or tight-lipped with boys or girls. Earlier twentieth-century discourses on youth and sexuality were influenced greatly by members of the highly regarded medical and religious communities.[53] But those receiving this information do not necessarily accept it; they filtered and interpreted it. For targeted children and adolescents, there was usually little opportunity to discuss the received information in a give-and-take process with adults. Information was often simply withheld.

By the 1950s, both psychological and medical professionals were urging parents to confront the sexualized body and sexuality itself as part of the normal course of development and maturation.[54] Later, high-circulation periodicals, such as *Chatelaine* magazine, featured liberal feminist pieces and editorials and articles on general interest topics such as abortion, birth control, lesbianism, and women's sexuality, bringing into many middle-class Canadian households information that was mostly new.[55] But it appears that at least some suburban mothers and fathers, at least until the mid-1960s, still chose not to discuss the body or sexuality with their pre-adolescent or adolescent youngsters. Michelle Macdonald succinctly recalled that, for "sex education, we got shown the videos, and you could read the materials. No discussion. There was no discussion with parents, siblings, and friends. Nothing."[56] Others remembered it in a similar way, particularly the oldest boomers. Barry Matthews said that "there was no sex education; [it was all] street talk."[57]

These memories suggest a shift in pedagogy and curriculums by the early 1960s in Calgary. In 1962, an article in the *Calgary Herald* titled "Early Sex Schooling Urged" revealed some of the discussions from a three-day teachers' convention held in Calgary, where it was concluded that sex education should begin informally in grade one with teachers taking spontaneous questions. It was noted that "only one discussion group favored integration of sexes during instruction on sex education. Children should realize from the beginning, the group argued, that they are different, and these differences should be explained in each other's presence."[58] Notably, children and adolescents were not consulted in any of these discussions. In keeping with prevailing discursive constructs regarding masculinity and femininity, no decision was reached on integrating boys and girls.

Formal sex education in Calgary schools was implemented by the early 1970s. Bruce Wilson, who became a Calgary Board of Education teacher, recalled the first attempts to teach sex education at his school, Senator Patrick Burns, in 1967: "It was all of us in one grade in the gym. Three hundred kids at least. There was a question box and teachers. It was a whole new thing. Lots of conversation; all the kids were involved with it. I think it helped the parents open up the conversation."[59] As mentioned by other interviewees, the dialogue was constrained, but these attempts at discussion at least prompted some conversations between teachers and students, among students, and possibly at home between adolescents and parents. Sex education films made for the classroom and for different age groups were introduced in other jurisdictions around this time, linking these childhood experiences across the country.[60]

As most people divulged when prompted, there were alternatives to formal sex education that permitted young people to gain knowledge and experiences. Comics, "girlie" magazines, and pulp fiction suggested other ways to make sense of sexuality, ones that could potentially unsettle the dominance of a family-based, monogamous heterosexuality.[61] William Wright recalled that "sex education was learned in the schoolyard ... I don't think I ever had any sex education chats with my parents. It was avoided in the 1960s and 1970s ... it was never discussed in my house, mainly through friends; or, the truth is, it's your brother's *Penthouse* collection."[62] Again, his memory illustrates that, despite some larger changes to sex education curriculums and what seemed to be an opening in dialogue, adolescents found ways to get "educated."

Other interviewees recalled "necking," some "heavy petting," and awkward attempts to "go beyond second base" by their junior high years, and this fits with recollections from other suburban baby boomers. Some of this activity was while dating, but much of it was explored in unsupervised moments, which increased in adolescence. For the book *Crestwood Heights,* young interviewees from the Toronto suburb told researchers that mixed-gender parties and kissing games could begin at the age of eleven, if not earlier.[63]

Allan Matthews gained sexual "knowledge" from the period's burgeoning men's magazines, illicit (for teenagers) sources that objectified female bodies and that were never intended to educate adolescents, although they likely served similar purposes for many adolescent boys throughout the postwar period. As he remarked, "I remember one of the guys had a *Playboy* collection, and that's kind of where I learned the anatomy of a female. I could never talk to my father about that kind of stuff."[64]

What these other sources provided was something counterhegemonic. When children and adolescents were exposed to "normal" sexuality, as prescribed in postwar advice books, magazines, movies, and sex education curriculums, it was inevitably conceptualized as the preserve of married, adult, heterosexual couples, who produced children. This was a necessary lesson for teenagers as they prepared themselves to fit into that societal framework.[65] But there was resistance to these prescribed roles and behaviours. Allan Matthews discussed sexuality and some of the alternatives to the dominant heteronormativity of the time. He had a brief, homosexual experience with a friend—just experimental—that never led to more. He added that "there was also a kid in junior high school at Branton that I look back on as flaming. He must have led a very lonely life, though, unlike today, no one seemed to even be aware. I know I was not, though [I] later found out that his interest in Petula Clark was a giveaway, but who knew?"[66] It was a thoughtful admission. Given that the legal system criminalized homosexuality until the late 1960s, combined with strict religious teachings and societal taboos regarding homosexuality, the topic was probably not broached by many adolescents. Yet children and adolescents are naturally curious; it is probable that this person's experiences were not isolated.

The social norms promoted in schools, particularly those regarding obedience and appropriate attitudes about gender, class, and race, depended on disciplined and normalized bodies.[67] This early socialization in "correct" gender and sex roles and body discipline meant that children implicitly understood that behaviours, bodies, and minds all needed to be normal to be healthy and socially acceptable. Based on polling in the late 1960s, Canadian society was split on the acceptance of homosexual behaviour. A 1968 national poll asked participants whether "homosexual behavior, if it is conducted in private between men aged 21 and over, should, or should not be a criminal act?" The results were almost evenly split: 49.7 percent of interviewees said yes, while 50.3 percent said no.[68]

Brian Rutz echoed this lack of public awareness or acceptance of other sexual identities. He recalled that during these years it was "unthinkable" to be gay. Yet he and his friends liked both the rock band Queen and Elton John: "With Queen, as completely obvious as it is, I don't remember any connection to them representing gay. One guy who wasn't part of my inner circle, I remember him as 'stereotypically' gay, but I talked to friends later that it didn't even cross our minds."[69]

There seemed to be little acknowledgement of lesbian or gay adolescents even though, obviously, there were some gay teenagers in Calgary's suburbs, but they were almost certainly closeted, given the times and the repercussions.[70] Rutz indicated that it was not part of his individual consciousness, or of his larger dominant peer groups, to identify whether someone was homosexual. There was a disconnect between some of the earliest pop music icons who directly associated with homosexuality and how people perceived them. He used the words *suppressed* and *unthinkable,* indicating that the Calgary suburbs, on this matter, were representative of the dominant mainstream, heterosexual culture.

There were, nonetheless, some rare instances of resistance to that "norm." According to Mary Baker, adolescents were aware of alternatives to the idealized heteronormative family, which was presented to them uncritically in most instances. She remembered details about a designated day, "Fruits Day," every Thursday, created by adolescents to express their nonheterosexuality. In wearing green, you were a "fruit." She said that "speculations [abounded] about various teachers, most of which were probably spot on ... I remember one guy positive he was not attracted to women—the car, the girlfriends, the whole thing. He could have had a better life if he had been able to explore what he might have wanted."[71] This is yet another example of some young suburbanites subverting dominant messaging and, in doing so, shaping their collective experience.

This adolescent cultural practice and other related ones were absent in school yearbooks and newspapers in the 1950s and 1960s, reflecting the editorial controls placed on student editors by older students and teachers but also the types of students who may or may not have been involved with school publications. It also demonstrates that universalizing the adolescent experience is highly problematic because of what may be missed in the "official" records and when exploring everyday practices. In many ways, however, adolescent patterns, whether sexual repression or expression, can reflect the adult world, regardless of intent. The increasing influence of psychoanalytic theories in the early postwar period also meant that heterosexuality was an expression of "maturity" that determined the individual's claim to normality, that integral element of postwar social classifications.[72] Teenagers were theorized to be malleable and easily influenced—characteristics that could make them either model sexually responsible adults or deviants and delinquents.[73] Yet they questioned what was presented to them by adults charged with guiding young lives. As historian Mona Gleason discusses, this process of mediation, in the instance of embodiment, was influenced as much by individual experiences, desires, and needs as by imposed ideologies and official pronouncements.[74]

The process of mediation was demonstrated in the reactions of teenagers to a 1969 visit from a high-ranking Calgary Police Force officer, who spoke to a sociology class. As reported in an *Aberhart Advocate* article titled "Andy Little," the officer spoke on a range of topics, from homosexuality to drugs. He had a "very harsh attitude towards homosexuals" and did not support the pending legalization of homosexuality in Canada. The article noted that the officer "stated that sex offenders are incurable and should be locked away where they cannot do society any harm ... Although some students found the inspector's attitudes objectionable and his arguments feeble, his visit was a great success."[75]

The officer represented dominant adult attitudes as expressed by individuals in authority. The criminalization of certain behaviours by marginalized individuals based on their sexual orientation meant that self-identified homosexuals, along with other sexual outsiders such as transvestites, were defined medically and culturally as mentally ill and as a real threat to the safety of adolescents and children.[76] In this instance, the medium—a Calgary police officer—was also the message.[77]

As noted, while most of the oldest boomers did not receive much, if anything, in the way of formal sexual education, this was changing in Calgary's suburban junior high and high schools by the late 1960s. With the ever-increasing professionalization of its administrators and staff, schools gained power and influence late in this period. While this process did not occur overnight, these changes are reflected in the following excerpt from a Calgary Elementary Education Committee report that focuses on what individuals require to live in modern society: "Society is turning to the institution it created specifically to take charge of the formal education of the young with the request, sometimes the demand, that the school become consciously involved in the education of children in personal and interpersonal relationships, specifically those concerned with family life, including sex education."[78]

By the end of the 1960s, the topic of sexual education for teenagers had entered the mainstream flow of information, and the tone of the official message was decidedly different in its new frankness and openness. A shift in pedagogy was taking place. A doctor—part of the committee to present the brief on sex education to the Calgary school board in the late 1960s—spoke with students at William Aberhart High School. Dr. Hatfield's visit was noted in the school paper:

> [He] pooh-poohed the idea that sex education would rob the home of its natural roles, stating that too many kids were simply not getting it at home and the course could act as a supplement, not a replacement, for what the parents had already taught ... He claimed that sex education would be only a small part of a much broader "family living" course, that would include financial management, driver training, drugs, alcohol and especially personal relationships ... The doctor maintained that any opposition to sex education was an emotional response.[79]

By the end of the 1960s, the topics of sexuality and personal relationships had finally become part of the everyday conversation in schools; in reality, it caught up to the activities that many teenagers had been engaging in long before. It also reflected societal views: a February 1964 national poll had 76 percent of respondents approving a course in sex education for students in high school.[80]

Dating and Relationships

By the early 1950s, dating and "going steady" were mainstream teenage practices and no longer emergent modern trends.[81] One journalist called Calgary a "hotbed for teenage dating" and argued that it existed to a greater degree in Calgary than in other centres in Alberta, a claim that seems anecdotal and not backed by research. The article detailed findings from a 1950 youth conference that involved delegates from twenty Albertan urban centres:

> There was a lively discussion on the question of intimacy between boys and girls. It was generally agreed that a boy should not kiss a girl on the first time out together. However, after that, kissing was definitely considered a part of dating. The girl should set the limit in embracing ... In summing up it was felt that in all phases of a boy and girl relationship, the girl should set the standard and the boy live up to it.[82]

On the surface, it might seem empowering that adolescent girls were deemed responsible for setting limits on physical contact, but this advice reflected the simplistic, misogynistic, and enduring belief that "boys will be boys."

Some refuted the sexualizing of all male-female adolescent relationships. Donna McLaren said that she "wanted a boyfriend just so I could throw a football with him."[83] She couldn't find other girls who were interested in sports to the same extent that she was, so having a boyfriend allowed her to indulge her passion for sports, especially during a time when organized sports for young women were limited. She did get some unwanted adult male attention; she recalled that in her junior high years "there was a janitor that took a little too much interest in me at times. So there was a little bit of that going on."[84] Unsurprisingly, this was not isolated. According to Mary Baker, "There was all this snickering, teasing passes made to me regularly by guys driving me home from babysitting. Were they legit or not?"[85] Even at school—or while engaged in the most common part-time job for teenage girls, babysitting—sexual harassment compromised their sense of security.

Many postwar teenagers were dating but also debating whether going steady was the best choice. A 1957 article in the *Central Collegiate Institute Weeper*, titled "This Steady Business," presented one girl's arguments against the practice:

> Why go steady when you are young? When teen-agers go steady they miss all the fun of meeting different types of boys and girls. Far too much time is spent in each other's company and hence the school work suffers. Going steady means that you have to adjust to the other person's life ... Besides, if your mother is anything like mine, she wholly disapproves of it ... "Variety is the spice of life." This quotation explains why young people should, as we say, "play the field."[86]

The author reiterates much of the advice that adult advisers, in numerous roles, offered to students: focus on school marks, maintain individuality, and avoid the pitfalls of paying too much attention to a single member of the opposite sex. Canadians, generally, agreed with this. A 1963 Gallup Poll found that 91 percent of respondents believed that high school boys and girls should date "different boys and girls" rather than being allowed to go steady.[87] The majority of interviewees reinforced that this was the more common practice. Most of them did not have steady boyfriends or girlfriends in their junior and senior high school years. While some mentioned having friends that did so, the general trend seemed to be not going steady in Banff Trail.

While information about personal relationships flowed down to young people, there was also information gained and exchanged between teenagers about personal relationships. A short piece, "How to Find a Mate," that appeared in the *Aberhart Advocate* in 1963 reflected what teenage boys and girls were looking for in a potential partner:

> We found that 80% of those asked put personality in top place, and that intelligence and looks shared the other 20% equally. Second position revealed 80% intelligence, with 15% personality, and 5% looks. Third place had 50% looks, 35% popularity, 10% intelligence, and 5% personality. Popularity rates 65% in fourth position, with looks taking the other 35%. Therefore, the most popular order is personality, intelligence, looks, and popularity.[88]

The survey reflected much of what participants recalled when they discussed gender, sexuality, and personal relationships. Adults may tend to marginalize the emotions and personal relationships that developed in teenage years—think of the dismissive term *puppy love*. This school-based survey suggests that teenagers were seeking something more. While questions remain about how adolescents measured intelligence and personality, the responses demonstrate something beyond a focus on looks and the ever-present high school social hierarchy.

Donna McLaren recalled that she had several friends who experimented sexually with boys in their teenage years in the late 1960s and early 1970s but did not necessarily date the boys on a steady basis: "I would always go along [for parts of the evening]; I don't think I felt jealous. I wasn't the one doing it. I wasn't one of the girls meeting up, and it was okay with me, to a point."[89] While she didn't remember engaging herself, she did express some regret that she didn't take the opportunity to do so, or that she was never asked to do so by her male peers. This type of dating activity actually reflects the broader Calgary data from the period, collected in a 1966 City of Calgary survey. High school respondents said that they tended to date more than four times per month and did not show a strong inclination to date one person in a steady relationship.[90] Local dances and larger concerts were always popular choices for teenagers. When successful bands such as Bill Haley and His Comets came to Calgary, hundreds turned out—whether on a date or simply out for an evening to enjoy some rock and roll.

Some young people did continue to date on a steady basis,[91] but dating patterns did change over time. The pill was also available by the 1960s and had a profound effect on the sexual practices of people of all ages, if they chose to use this new form of contraception. Interviewees indicated that access was not necessarily easy, at least for teenagers in the late 1960s. But a national Gallup Poll found that 64 percent of Canadians favoured it in 1960.[92]

Lesley Hayes discussed her personal relationships with both her parents and her peers in the context of recounting what happened to a

Bill Haley and His Comets performing at the Stampede Corral in June 1956 for hundreds of fans from across the city. (Photographed by Jack De Lorme. Reproduced with permission of the University of Calgary Archives and Special Collection, NA-5600-8113A.)

classmate who got pregnant in grade twelve, which was not a topic of discussion with her close friends: "I always stayed friends with my parents ... If I had a boyfriend, I could always tell them. I was also seventeen [when she first had sex] and not twelve ... I felt I was old enough to make a reasonable decision ... I didn't feel like I was going against social norms or that it was particularly risky."[93] Like some of the other participants, she had a reasonably healthy relationship with her parents. There was good two-way communication in many regards, but when it came to certain topics, quite simply, they were never discussed. Parents didn't ask, some youths did not feel the need to share certain personal experiences with adults, and many mothers and fathers in this period made it clear that they were not particularly interested in full disclosure from their changing and maturing adolescent children, regardless of gender.

Sports and Outdoor Recreation

While there were an increasing number of indoor activities geared to young people in this period, and activities centred on the exploding car culture of the 1950s and 1960s, sports and outdoor recreation were important parts of young suburban lives. And given the baby boom and that many working adults had more free time to be involved in their children's activities, adults began to lead and direct them more than ever. These activities were designed to be safer, with the overriding goal of shaping children and adolescents into disciplined beings who would become orderly, responsible adults. Leaders transformed some play into managed activities in groups such as Little League Baseball, the Scouts, and Boys and Girls Clubs.[94] Sports, particularly competitive sports, had come to be viewed as having the power to promote physical health, democratic living, good citizenship, general education, and appropriate sportsmanship.[95] Certainly, much of this was a middle-class phenomenon, but working-class families could access some of these activities, especially those that were community-based or church-based and therefore less costly.

The disciplining nature of many of these activities was reflected in adults' stated goals as they designed programs for young people. In several instances, older teenagers designed and delivered programming for pre-teenagers and young adolescents. Women and girls appeared to maintain some influence related to recreation and leisure in Banff Trail and nearby communities, where they worked occasionally. They held leadership roles and appeared to make several key programming decisions. Many of them had heightened sensitivity to younger children, but there were clear directives being set out here.[96] A 1950 *Calgary Herald* article laid out what was happening in the city's supervised summer programming, taking place within expanding local parks and playground systems:

> Playgrounds, 22 of them giving blanket coverage to the city, opened their two-month season as hundreds of fun-loving youngsters poured into summer having a good time. Kids, ranging from bewildered six-year-olds to belligerent teenagers set on being "first for scrub" gathered ... to take advantage of the city's organized sport and recreation program. The city's summer program ... has a three-pronged objective: 1. To introduce and develop within individuals a varied range of life interests. 2. To provide a program of purposeful activity. 3. To carry over into the spare time of the children those activities which had had their start in the curricular program of the schools ... The real purpose of the program is to have fun.[97]

Although they appreciated the organized programs available to them, many recalled that it was the ability to choose their own activities, along with the opportunities to organize themselves, that they preferred. Barry Matthew's fondest recollections were "when we played football in the park or walked to the skating rink. I did play a little bit of organized hockey ... We were given freedom. We spent lots of time out and about. The bikes would go as far as they would go. Later, as teens, we rode our bikes to Banff. [It] took two and a half days to get out there."[98] In this respect, Matthews expresses the importance of independent thought and creativity in choosing outdoor activities, despite, or perhaps in response to, the growing trend to organize and discipline young people. Surveys of Calgary teenagers reinforced this in the mid-1960s; over half of the respondents indicated a preference for more informal recreation while one-third preferred organized recreation programs.[99]

Nonetheless, there were tens of thousands of young people using these summer programs in Calgary on an annual basis by the early 1950s. Although the future Banff Trail community was just beginning to take shape, there were a growing number of houses in the area and recreational programs available in and around the burgeoning community. An article in *The Albertan* detailed the profound impact that these programs had on children, particularly those from families who did not have the means to afford more costly programs, which were available in increasing numbers not only in Calgary but also across the country. As Valerie Korinek has noted, while an increase in postwar affluence is undeniable, it should be seen more as a 1960s phenomenon.[100] Certainly, it was not universal, as many working-class people continued to struggle financially throughout the period. Public parks were important:

More than 95,613 children took part in the sports at the 21 playgrounds this summer Alex Munro, Parks Superintendent, told the January meeting of The Alberta Council on Child and Family Welfare Friday in the Hudson's Bay Company store auditorium ... Wherever a new subdivision was opening up the Parks Department was asking for a block or more be reserved for playgrounds. The city develops these playgrounds and then the community takes over he explained. There are now 58 skating rinks, 47 hockey rinks, 16 major playgrounds and five smaller ones, he said.[101]

This article reveals how these new playground facilities were administered following their construction. After a short period, the new community associations, directed and led by local parent groups, were responsible for the upkeep of expanding play areas. A broader network of community associations developed over time and worked together; however, this was a localized phenomenon. Given the number of young people growing up in these communities, these spaces teemed with teens and adolescents, irrespective of the season.

All of this participation, in many ways, contradicts historian Doug Owram's argument, made in his history of the baby boomers, that the rapid decline of religion and the weakening of activities like Scouts and Guides revealed that youthful "barbarians" were not fully under the control of adults.[102] An excerpt from a Calgary Boys Club annual report in 1961 captures much of the purpose of outdoor activities, particularly for boys: "Camping is one of the most rewarding experiences in the life of a Canadian boy. Learning the art of simple living in the out of doors, and the practice of learning to live together with boys of their own age is the central purpose of Camp Adventure. The activities were planned around the natural interests of the boys."[103]

Scouting and guiding played a large role in many young lives in Calgary. An excerpt from a 1952 *Calgary Herald* article reveals the movement's relevance and popularity across Canada: "Appreciation of Canada's contribution to the world Guide movement was expressed Thursday by world Chief Guide Lady Baden-Powell at the annual meeting of the Canadian Council, Girl Guides Association. The meeting was told that Canada's Guide population, third largest in the world association, numbering 87,762 has seen an increase of 9,034 girls."[104] Organizations such as the Canadian Girls in Training and the Girl Guides were designed to exploit the "character-building" possibilities as well as providing opportunities to shape adolescent girls into feminine, domesticated, responsible, and faithful citizens.[105] However, young people also used these organizations and associated activities for their own purposes.[106]

Allan Matthews recalled that he excelled in the scouting program not just to earn the intrinsic rewards but also to explore the wider world outside of Banff Trail, the city of Calgary, and, at times, Canada. He said that by fourteen he had earned "the highest badge you can get, a Queen Scout. I was about two years younger than anyone else. I went to a world jamboree. I went to a national jamboree in the US. Later, I did an exchange visit with a kid out of Montreal, and seven days on a train at fifteen or sixteen by myself was kind of cool."[107]

By the early 1970s, newspaper articles were contributing to new representations of guiding by arguing that Girl Guides were doing much more than the prevailing stereotype of selling cookies door to door as their primary mandate. In a *Calgary Herald* article from 1970 their broadened role was presented officially: "Selling cookies is just part of the game, say the 300,000 Canadian Girl Guides who celebrate their diamond jubilee this year ... Today, mini-skirted Calgary Guides assist at blood donor clinics, collect books for libraries on Indian reserves, work on local Safety Council campaigns and donate carefully made layettes to the Providence Creche ... Recreation and outdoor activities are an equally important part of the contemporary program."[108] Many of the activities had been part of the guiding program for decades, but in ongoing efforts to recruit new members, articles such as this one, of which there were many in the daily press, emphasized community activities over recreation and outdoor pursuits, which had always been prime features and draws in Scouts and Guides programming.

Health and Wellness

By the 1950s, young people's health had improved steadily since the late nineteenth century. Canadian governments and practitioners focused on the national importance of saving babies and young children, the field of pediatrics expanded, efforts increased to erase high infant mortality rates, and disease control gave way to concerted efforts to prevent illness with science and technology.[109] In the immediate postwar years, psychologists also explored the dangers of unchecked mental health issues and what they might mean to Canadian society.[110]

Postwar young people were subjects of concern, and in Calgary headlines blared warnings about such issues. An article titled "Cancer Takes Toll among Children and Teen-Agers" appeared in the *Calgary Herald* in 1950, despite the fact that childhood cancer was relatively rare. Parents were encouraged to look for early symptoms; the writer emphasized that cancer was second only to pneumonia as a cause of death from disease among young people.[111] As with most of the period's expert advice, the onus was placed on parents to be vigilant in monitoring their children for potential cancer symptoms.

For young people growing up in Calgary's suburbs, the environment was touted as one of the best possible places for them to thrive and prosper in their formative years. Yet, in 1950, Calgary's spending on children's health, and health care more generally, was not as much as other municipalities. A 1950 newspaper report revealed that "while Calgary spent $1.05 per citizen on medical health services, Toronto spent $2.40, Vancouver $2, Hamilton spent $1.78 and Winnipeg $1.60."[112] This reflected the provincial funding associated with these cities, which affected all young people, including young suburbanites.

Suburban life has often been and continues to be held up by developers and city planners as a healthy lifestyle alternative to more crowded and possibly unhealthy urban sites. This motivated many postwar families to move to the suburbs.[113] The suburban ideal includes an inherent view about the healthy influences of a rural lifestyle.[114] This ideal built on a concept of pastoralism that grew as an antimodernist response to the urban and industrialized spaces of modernity. Yet for the first part of the twentieth century, Canadian cities were not healthy places.[115] In Calgary specifically, large

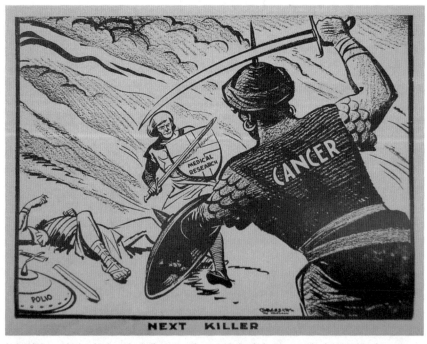

A sketch from a high school yearbook illustrating the ongoing battle between medical research and cancer. (Crescent Heights High School yearbook, 1957–58; and reproduced from the author's personal collection.)

areas were marked by squalor and poverty, forcing many poor families to live in dismal and unsanitary surroundings, in contrast to the better neighbourhoods with their relative prosperity and individual affluence.[116] This was not unique to Calgary, in terms of the unevenness of suburban development; as late as the 1920s only about half of all suburban homes on the Prairies had sewers.[117] The suburbs, regardless of what city they were associated with, have not always been the promised islands of health and wellness. By the early 1950s, however, new suburbs such as Banff Trail benefitted from the ongoing development of infrastructure and services, which contributed to a healthier environment. While the Banff Trail development was a relatively modest one, its residents were part of a broader network of family-oriented and affluent migrants whose suburban lifestyle fostered concern and interest about the local community and its environment.[118]

In the immediate postwar years, polio was easily the biggest health scare, regardless of where people lived.[119] Newspapers from the early 1950s featured countless articles on polio and its far-reaching effects on the everyday lives of young people. A 1952 article, "Students' Long Holiday

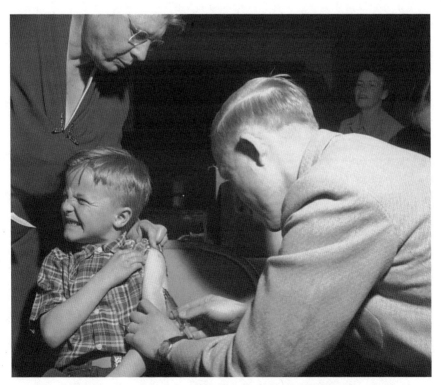

A young boy receiving the polio vaccine in June 1954. (Photographed by Jack De Lorme. Reproduced with permission of the University of Calgary Archives and Special Collection, NA-5600-7434A.)

Ends," detailed what the outbreak in the late summer had meant to thousands of youngsters who returned to classrooms, ending "three extra weeks of summer vacation, ordered because of the 1952 poliomyelitis outbreak. Three new cases were reported in the city during the weekend—only one of them a school age child... Although the opening has been sanctioned by the city board of health, some parents are still worried about polio and are keeping their children away."[120] While many baby boomers were not yet of school age, this did affect the oldest ones and continued to impact lives even after the Salk vaccine was introduced in 1954.

Advice on dealing with illness and treating others with health issues was a popular topic in newspapers, magazine articles, and popular literature.[121] Advice like this from the Teen Topics series, which ran nationally and in the *Calgary Herald,* is illustrative:

> How do you treat the sick, the injured, the crippled? ... The basic rule is to act toward the ill and injured as you would wish them to act toward you. First, don't pay them so much attention that you embarrass or tire them. Then, fit your services to the patients' needs ... Don't try to wait on him hand as well as foot ... Unnecessary aid will depress and annoy him. Never give a sick person medical advice kids. And don't tell him the story of YOUR accident or ask details of his.[122]

This type of advice was widespread in these years as basic medical advice and popular psychology permeated public discourses. Psychology's technologies of normalcy—represented by the modernizing school system, the child guidance clinic, Canada's public health care system, and television, radio, and magazine coverage—conflated the normal with social norms and values.[123]

Suburban adolescents also engaged with health issues on an intellectual level. Teens discussed most contemporary health-related topics. The issue of euthanasia received some thoughtful treatment in a 1962 *Aberhart Advocate* school newspaper article that also explored some of the religious aspects:

> Can it be considered a crime to release a person from misery through an act of mercy, to allow that life a painless escape from what can no longer be thought of as life? ... If a person has strong beliefs in a Supreme Being ... and uses the Bible as the basis of these beliefs, it is doubtful that that person could ever reach an opinion on killing in the act of mercy for it states in the Bible ... "Thou Shalt not kill" ... I for one fail to see how a human being, compassionate towards his fellow man ... could refuse a

man or woman eternal peace through a simple act of mercy which would be unconcernedly administered to any dying animal.[124]

This analysis reflects careful consideration of the religious and moral implications associated with euthanasia. The writer appeals to the spirituality of religious persons in that they take the act of euthanizing to be something God-like in its merciful nature.

Teenagers also raised the topic of smoking—increasingly contentious by the 1960s. One 1962 letter to the editor of the *Aberhart Advocate* focused on a survey, conducted by the City of Calgary, of high school students:

> It was found that about 46% of the boys and 32% of the girls smoke. This has aroused a grand campaign to take the cigarettes out of the mouths of babes. Before you print anything in your puritan paper, I would like to condemn this campaign. In the first place it has not been conclusively proved that they do any harm ... Besides, when one can smoke in a crowd it gives you a feeling of belonging and quiets your nerves. They also taste good. My parents both smoke as do my brothers and they live normal healthy lives as I'm sure I will. COUGH, COUGH.[125]

Smoking was socially acceptable in this period.[126] But many interviewees mentioned that they recalled discussions, particularly by the mid-1960s, that began to focus on the health-related issues associated with long-term smoking.[127] The teenager who wrote this article focused on the social benefits of smoking along with the lack of data supporting smoking as being harmful to health. Many messages were positive. One memoirist recalled that, according to some advertisements, cigarettes actually made you healthier by soothing jangly nerves and sharpening jaded minds. "Just what the doctor ordered!" reads an ad for L&M cigarettes.[128] While there were some tensions, even within the health industry regarding smoking, by the end of this period the antismoking message had gained some momentum.

Advertising continued to target teenagers throughout this period, though, as it would be another two decades before changes were made to 1908 legislation regarding the sale of tobacco to adolescents.[129] Doug Cass recalled there being a growing consciousness of the links between ubiquitous smoking and its adverse health effects. His father was a heavy smoker. He recalled most men smoking and that secondary smoke was something that everyone had to deal with. He said smoking caused his "father's health problems ... I don't think people thought of it as a big health issue ... I don't remember any other fathers having quite as severe a health scare with smoking ... I think a lot of people started to cut back, maybe into the 1970s."[130] He recalled that second-hand smoke and its potentially harmful effects did not seem to be part of people's consciousness. Unquestionably, smoking was common. In a 1963 national poll, 17 percent of respondents smoked over a pack of cigarettes per day; another 32 percent smoked but less than one pack per day.[131]

But, as early as the late 1950s, some adolescents were aware of the latest research and of advances that linked some kinds of cancers with smoking. A 1959 *Aberhart Advocate* article asked readers whether they smoked or if they were thinking about starting. It discussed the link between smoking and cancer based on laboratory testing and argued that smoking was gambling with health.[132]

Adolescents grappled with health issues from many different angles. For some, the discussion merged with their personal experiences with the smoking habit. Nor was smoking only an issue for adolescent boys, as adolescent girls also struggled with smoking and its effects on their everyday lives. An article that appeared in 1965 effectively described what many teens experienced by linking smoking to body image:

> After we moved to the big city, I stopped [smoking] mainly because there was no-one here who smoked and no place to smoke in secrecy. Well, I woke up the other day and decided it was time to start again ... I admit that I cut down on my food, I quit biting my fingernails, and I quit fidgeting quite so much—but I must also admit that the smelly fingers, the lousy taste in my mouth, the crummy taste it gave to the food I did eat, the sting in my eyes, the coughing, the stench in my room, and the general unsuaveness of it all was driving me out of my skull. Finally, I decided. What would you rather be—a skinny, calm corpse, or a fat fidgety quick?[133]

The perception was that urban young people were not smoking as much as rural kids and that there was nowhere to smoke without detection in the city. There are no strict numbers from the era in terms of a rural-urban split; however, anecdotally, it does seem that the practice may have been less scrutinized and somewhat more acceptable outside of cities.

Some interviewees recalled having various ailments, childhood diseases, and injuries as both children and adolescents. Doug Cass recalled that his family was pretty healthy and that he didn't "know that anybody had any chronic illness. [There were] typical childhood diseases: measles, mumps, chicken pox. I broke my arm once when I was sixteen, out tramping around in the mountains and fell down a cliff. Other than that, nothing of any note. None of us had any operations."[134] This was a very typical response from a small majority of interviewees who remembered being healthy children and adolescents, along with most friends, classmates, and family members, although this should be seen as a generalization rather than a universalization. Bruce Wilson said, "I never missed a day of school for ten years. Grade one, had the measles, and grade two, the chicken pox, and I never missed another day ... Other than colds, I never really was sick."[135] Much of this correlates with advances in medicine and treating childhood diseases and ailments, more accessible and affordable medical care, and the rising standard of living. The first childproof medication cap was invented; Rh immune globin was developed, thus eliminating Rhesus disease; vitamin D was introduced into milk; and important vaccines for mumps, measles, rubella (German measles), and polio were available by the early 1970s.[136]

Tammy Simpson, born in the early 1960s, remembered it being the same for her: "My health was pretty good. I was quite active. I did have hay fever and allergies, so I had to be careful with the dust."[137] Brian Rutz recalled: "I was pretty healthy. I was very into bombing around on my bike. I had a few bad wipeouts ... there were two concussions out of those. Overall, not very sick; no allergies or anything like that. I didn't spend any time in the hospital."[138] Outside of some relatively minor conditions and accidents, the majority of interviewee responses indicated that children and adolescents were relatively healthy in this period.[139] If needed, some of them mentioned going to the nearby Foothills Hospital regularly, or to one of Calgary's other hospitals on a consistent basis, to get treatment for ailments or injuries or to visit patients. Outbreaks did happen from time to time, including a German measles outbreak in the mid-1960s across North America that led to wider discussions of childhood disease and vaccinations in widely read publications.[140]

Most families, as noted, had better access to health services, especially after 1964, with the establishment of a national Medicare system and the expansion of the welfare state.[141] The number of physicians in Canada increased, and, more importantly, the ratio of Canadians to physicians also improved significantly. There were 17,221 physicians in Canada in 1955; 25,481 in 1965; and, with Medicare well established, 31,166 physicians in 1970. There were 934 Canadians for every physician in 1955, 779 in 1965, and 689 in 1970.[142] Many childhood diseases such as mumps, measles, and chickenpox had also been effectively eliminated by 1960, while diphtheria rates dropped dramatically from high rates in the interwar and war years.[143]

While many of these youngsters' parents had lived through some harrowing economic times, this was not the case for most of these baby boomers, even in working-class families. There had been provision for poorer families in Calgary's history, as the Junior Red Cross had opened its doors in 1922 and was designed to provide care to the young people of families

Table 5.1. Number of Physicians in Canada, 1955–70	
Year	**Physicians**
1955	17,221
1965	25,481
1970	31,166

From: Statistics Canada https://www150.statcan.gc.ca/n1/pub/11-516-x/sectionb/
B82_92-eng.csv.

who could not afford to pay for medical care.[144] Its small hospital was housed in a three-storey house, until 1950, when it moved to the Richmond Road location; it was operated by the Red Cross until 1958 and then by the Alberta government until the 1970s.[145]

While many participants did not recall being ill as children, or others being ill, there was some notable differentiation regarding health. Some of these discrepancies speak to the tensions that can exist between memory and lived childhood experiences. Mary Baker said that she "used to see sick people, and people used to die. I had a good friend die when I was in high school of cancer. My mother had polio. My aunt ended up in a wheelchair and never got out... My mother was very overweight, so she was always very conscious. She said she married a tall, thin man so she would have tall, thin children."[146] Some of this speaks to the way some families dealt with illness and death. In this era, most hospitals had policies in place that would not allow children and adolescents to visit ill family and friends, and many children did not attend funerals, particularly before their teenage years.

Brian Rutz described what health and illness meant to him as a child, at nine or ten years of age:

My mom got really sick. She had a bad problem with her uterus, and she was in the hospital for a while. I remember there was a feeling she might not make it. I remember going there every day, and my dad would buy us a glass bottle of Coke. We'd wait in the waiting room. We never saw her in the hospital, and my dad would sit us down in the waiting room, and he would visit her. It was for at least a couple of weeks ... I didn't know how sick she was ... I didn't hear until later ... I don't remember thinking this could be bad ... I was probably just shut down."[147]

Other participants shared similar sentiments. They recalled that they often felt very isolated, even alienated from friends and other ill family members, when they were in hospitals. This was most trying for children, and, to a lesser degree, adolescents, who were often unable to spend time with family and friends when they were hospitalized. For Michelle Macdonald, the hospital was an intimidating place, one that she feared a great deal: "I remember my father was very ill, and I remember spending a lot of time going to the hospital... It was a scary place."[148] This particular illness and hospitalization were experienced in the early 1970s, so practices and regulations were beginning to change, as many hospitals were altering their architectural design and everyday regulations and practices concerning visiting hours and protocols.[149]

Tammy Simpson recalled some of her angst associated with an ill brother. She knew that something was wrong and that her anxiety was quite high, as she could intuit her parents' worries: "He was really ill when he was about four. He was hospitalized, and I remember being left with a babysitter because my parents would go to visit him at the hospital. I was worried because my parents seemed to be very worried and ... I think probably at that time, there was a policy that I couldn't go."[150] She did not specify which hospital her brother was admitted to. Many hospitals were working actively to change their policies. Family practices and informal rules, however, did not always change with official rules and regulations. Some families simply did not feel that it was appropriate for young children to spend time in hospitals unless it was believed to be absolutely necessary.

While not mentioned as often, some young people truly enjoyed being ill or injured because it could have unintended consequences, many of which were positive. Lesley Hayes said, "To be sick was great. You got to watch TV. Once my Mom was working, you got the house to yourself, and you got the TV."[151] The increasing draw of the television is clear—it had become an important point for parental control as adolescents sought to exercise some agency in their television-viewing choices. Being home from school, particularly for adolescents who were unsupervised, and having the "run of the house" allowed for this, as there was suddenly no competition from siblings, friends, and parents when it came to what could be watched.[152]

Mary Baker recalled "thinking this could be a pretty sweet deal. I got a lot attention. My father liked me sick; he would pay attention to me in ways he wouldn't otherwise ... Mother was a frustrated nurse with no one to practice on ... I was aware that this was a favoured role and that this could be something I could play."[153] For some young people, in other words, it was much less about the illness or injury and much more about how you were treated and perceived when somewhat needy. This person knew that her condition would give her attention she would not otherwise receive from her father and that the way she felt as a result was actually "dangerous" to her. She knew that she could manipulate these situations and the actions of others. This is a key gender experience, as this type of attention seemed to be sought only by adolescent girls, perhaps because strength, power, and action were masculine attributes, while the sickly, weak woman in need of care was also a long-time construct.

Diets were also discussed by interviewees, as this era saw items such as processed foods, in various forms, marketed to families more aggressively and on a widespread scale. Cheez Whiz, Tang, and other processed foods were popular products by the 1950s. While food processing had been around for decades, there was a confluence of growing wealth for many families, an exploding commercial food industry with aggressive TV advertising, and a growing appetite for fast food.[154] Bruce Wilson recalled that his family went on different fad diets, as the entire family had weight issues: "Fresca was one of the first diet drinks, and I hated it ... [We] consumed a lot of chocolate bars and things that were frowned upon ... A lot of kids spent their extra money at Chang's, and no one was really supervised ... There was a lot of extra calorie consumption going on there."[155]

There were competing discourses, with parents, advisers, and educators; the growing fast food industry; and children and teenagers often pitted against one another. Vitamins were marketed to all family members. Advertising copy stressed that people were eating too many empty calories; even if meals were well-prepared and healthy, it warned, they often went uneaten because children and adolescents had made poor food choices.[156] Like adults, young people chose to use their disposable income for things they wanted; some youngsters spent it on candy and fast food. Tammy Simpson recalled that this was an "era where we lived on Kraft Dinner and fried bologna. My sister, seven years older, was a bit of a hippie, made homemade pizza and threw home-cooked ground beef on it ... She was my first exposure to looking after yourself."[157] Sharon Johnstone recalled the defining features of diets from the era from the perspective of childhood: "One of the things that was dreadful was the amount of canned vegetables and that fresh vegetables really weren't bought ... The processed foods were terrible, and people didn't realize it."[158] Tammy Simpson echoed this: "Like many families, we ate white bread, processed cheese, and nobody thought anything of it. We had fresh vegetables, but it wasn't a focus."[159]

Family schedules, the seasonal availability of foods, and changing family incomes and tastes were some of the factors affecting household diets. With many mothers working outside the home by the 1960s and early 1970s, older children and adolescents often prepared more meals for themselves. The TV dinner can be traced back to the Second World War and the US Army, but it was in the late 1950s that it entered into many homes.[160] Some families, especially those that identified as middle-class, seem to have had stable eating patterns, and it was almost always mothers who led the way in at least trying to provide healthy meals and fewer processed foods for their families, especially by the late 1960s, when articles began focusing on children's diets and their importance to good health and wellness.[161] Most interviewees recalled dinners that involved the entire family sitting down to share a meal, unless extracurricular activities collided with meal time.

William Wright commented: "My mom was a dietitian and focused on nutrition and on diet. I remember her saying when I was seven or eight, 'No more white bread. No more sugared cereal.' I don't remember a lot of discussion. We definitely were really well-fed as kids."[162] Wendy Glidden recalled that, "when we were kids, we weren't super overweight. I don't remember that being an issue. Certainly, my parents wouldn't have brought it up. We had a big garden. A lot of what we ate was healthy and out of the garden ... We weren't devoid of salads and vegetables."[163] Several interviewees made direct links between their relatively healthy diets and the lack of childhood and adolescent obesity in the Calgary suburbs, although the topic was discussed in the mainstream media by the mid-1960s, again pointing to tensions between oral histories and what was found in newspapers from the period.[164] Most participants mentioned the relative rarity of overweight young people in the early postwar years, and there were few references to weight issues in any of the school literature that young people wrote.

A national poll on the most urgent problem facing families in 1960 found that fewer than 10 percent of respondents thought it was their own health or the health of others.[165] There were no contemporary studies on diet and weight in children and adolescents, likely because weight was not at the fore of medical inquiry. This is in stark contrast to present-day discussions on teenagers' body image, diet, and exercise. This does not mean that issues did not exist, but yearbook pictures show most, if not all students, in the "picture of health."[166] Sharon Johnstone said that "her mother was very conscious of eating good food. I don't think health as a general topic was talked about ... None of us were overweight. My mom said, 'Eat well and get outside and get some exercise.' It was a stock phrase."[167] Barry Matthews, one of the older baby boomers, recalled that fast food was not as prevalent in the early to mid-1960s in Calgary: "I don't remember any soda pop, I don't remember much of that kind of thing. The local fast food wasn't prevalent then."[168] Restaurant meals were not a regular family event for most interviewees. Other children who grew up in the 1950s echoed this, recalling that there were not that many choices dining out. Jim Chambers recalled, "Think of almost any well-known restaurant chain. Very few of them existed in the fifties. Most restaurants were one-of-a-kind or part of small local chains."[169]

Outside of home economics and the introduction of programs such as Participaction in the 1970s, students did not receive a lot of guidance at school about health, diet, and so forth. Although the Canada Food Guide was established in 1942, and while it was in wide circulation due to various educational campaigns, interviews and brief references in the archives indicate that it was largely ignored.[170]

Conclusion

Experiences and representations based on gender remained distinct in many ways throughout this era. Adult gender roles modelled, both knowingly and unknowingly, by young people certainly influenced childhood and adolescent cultures. The health and wellness of young people also came into sharper focus and took greater hold in institutions such as schools and families by the early 1970s. There was a distinct change in formal sex education over this period, although knowledge about sex was learned in different ways by young adolescents. Informal sexual education remained the primary way that both males and females explored their emerging sexualities.

Class mattered in the health of young people. Health improved drastically in this period owing to numerous scientific advances, and the working- and middle-class children and adolescents in Banff Trail were obvious beneficiaries of these advancements. While not spared from illness, injury, and death, they nevertheless enjoyed comparatively healthy, young lives. Despite such improvements, adolescents in this period, especially young women, struggled with certain aspects of being young. For young women, this was not a struggle that started or ended in this period—representations of young women throughout the twentieth century and early twenty-first century continue to be problematic.[171] There were inadequacies in many ways, and the last word must go to Mary Baker, who graduated from William Aberhart High School in the late 1960s. She remembered sitting for her grade twelve exams and thinking that if she left, she'd escape it all: "I was not one of those people that fit into suburban gender roles. I had friends. I was in lots of clubs." But none of it gave her "the capacity to do what I wanted to do."[172]

Chapter 6

Things That Go Bump in the Night

Darkness and shadows marked the lives of many postwar suburban youngsters. They were ever present for some young people, by choice and otherwise. Margaret Atwood, in describing some men in postwar suburbia in *Cat's Eye,* wrote, "These are not ordinary men but the other kind, the shadowy, nameless kind who do things to you."[1] One student's poem also captured some of this angst:

> I am a child of darkness
> Of darkness and the sea
> I am a child of darkness
> No one cares for me
> In my mind I am alone
> With no one to love and trust
> And the key to my heart
> Long ago turned to rust[2]

While children and adolescents have clearly been influenced by adult practices and discursive constructs throughout time, they often demonstrated remarkable resilience and agency in negotiating these powerful influences. The balance of power did not fall in their favour always, but young people did not simply accept what was presented to them by the adult world.

The night has often held negative connotations for young people, particularly from an adult perspective. Darkness signals a time when youngsters, particularly pre-adolescents, are supposed to be silent and unseen. Yet nuance needs to be added to this perception, as the "everynight" period for some adolescents is an important time, a time of day when some of them believe they can escape piercing adult gazes, usually well-meaning but at times disapproving, restrictive, and constraining. It marks another division between childhood and adolescence, as it is adolescents who are especially active under the cover of darkness, experiencing the added freedoms that crossing the threshold from childhood typically bring.

At times, suburban adolescence was marked by crime, delinquency (although some of it was relatively harmless), and violence. There was a gendered aspect to the violence, and suburban boys perpetrated much of it, and more than occasionally, although not exclusively, it was girls who were victimized by these male perpetrators. Conversely, there were times when young women were involved in delinquent behaviour. Adolescents resisted and rebelled in countless ways in postwar suburbs, as in North America at large, as they helped to define a modern youth culture that allowed them more freedom from adult regulation than youths had enjoyed in earlier periods.[3] Adolescent experimentation with alcohol, illicit recreational drugs, and sexual activity was not uncommon. Much of this is reflected in the literature that teenagers produced. Many young people were not reluctant to explore new-found freedoms in different ways, and for various reasons. Parents and other authority figures were left to deal with this, not just in suburban Calgary but across the country.[4] Nighttime, under the cloak of darkness, was when much of this took place.

The Night

Nighttime has always been associated with unknowns for people, positive and otherwise, as well as with potential dangers, regardless of age or personal circumstances. Yet darkness, for many, has offered sanctuary from the everyday, the opportunity for people to reveal inner impulses, and, in some instances, the opportunity to realize certain desires, both in their waking hours and in their dreams or nightmares, however innocent or evil in nature.[5] As dusk turned to evening in postwar suburbia, some preteenagers used the encroaching cover of darkness to spend additional time with friends. Quite simply, it was an opportunity to express themselves through playing with friends, away from the watchful eyes of adults. Michelle Macdonald recalled that at night she would climb out her window and "collect [my closest friends]. We'd play in one of their yards. My sister was my accomplice; she'd help me back in the window. I was usually sneaking out at 8:30 p.m. as it was getting dark. It was always me going to fetch the two of them."[6]

The act of sneaking out the house reflects the benign nature of some childhood resistances associated directly with fading light and the shift to nighttime. But it is significant as it represents initiative and action, in direct opposition to adult expectations. Bedtimes were often not negotiable, particularly for preteenagers, and with the increasing regulation and compartmentalization of children's daytime activities in the twentieth century, the cover of night was an opportunity to play as they alone chose.[7] Sneaking out to play after dark may not seem noteworthy, but in the minds of preteens, escaping their parent-dominated homes to spend time with friends, without adult rules and in secrecy, was significant, demonstrating a clear instance of their otherwise limited agency.

Curfews and other restrictions on youngsters' movements, well beyond individual family rules, are not a modern phenomenon. By the late nineteenth century, with a new focus on children's and adolescents' welfare and physical and moral well-being, anxious stories of children roaming the streets after nightfall abounded.[8] Canada holds the distinction of being the first country to legislate a juvenile curfew; the first was established in Waterloo, Ontario, in the 1880s. By the 1950s, although the suburban landscape may have been deemed "safe" for youngsters by parents, experts upheld a long and good night's rest as essential for a healthy mind and body, and middle-class families increasingly became acquainted with and adopted their views. For some young people, although the night was marked by potential dangers, they were balanced by its potential freedoms.[9] Suburban spaces by the late 1950s and early 1960s were well lit; there was enough artificial light from homes and street lights that children could easily find space in which to play and return home safely even as darkness fell.

Older teenagers were also freer to express themselves at nighttime. Suburban high school students were inspired to create artistic expressions associated with darkness, dreams, nightmares, and the night. One poem explored themes of redemption and love associated with the magical qualities of the night from the perspective of adolescence:

> The night
> descends from the twilight sky
> in coils of endless
> black thread
> weaving dreams
> and sewing together
> the day's torn hearts.[10]

There is an abundance of literature exploring the nighttime through the viewpoints of childhood and adolescence.[11] What this poem suggests is that youngsters' distinct experiences were often not shared with adults for various reasons. Whereas adults may have seen the nighttime as dangerous for children and teens left unsupervised, it often inspired and positively influenced youthful creativity, reflected in poems and sketches, for instance. Freed from daytime conventions, nighttime's shadows could, in fact, shield the oppressed from the intense glare of power; it provided a space for the individual's realization through acts of resistance.[12]

The importance of nighttime to claiming both time and space is noteworthy, especially within the context of the postwar suburbs. Some participants noted that while nighttime was important for its liberating possibilities overall, they could claim suburban spaces for their own use at night by the late 1960s. Much of the activity was escapist; for instance, William Wright recalled going to the University of Calgary at night, when it served as a teenage playground; he spent a lot of time just "hanging out" with his peers.[13] Brent Harris echoed this, recalling that on weekend evenings he would go to the movies over at the social sciences theatre at the University of Calgary with friends from Banff Trail.[14] For these young teenagers, this time and this space allowed a chance to spend time with older teenagers, free from parental supervision, before North American campuses developed sophisticated camera surveillance to monitor space and activities. This claiming of space by adolescents can be seen in the context of a transfer of power after nightfall: power can shift from the mighty to the meek.[15] Some adolescents were prompted to create alternative experiences based on shadows, darkness, and the night; nighttime space and time were thus significant in helping some of them navigate the struggles of teenagehood.

Not only did the cover of night spark imaginations, stimulate creative writing and art, and serve as pure escapism, it also provided a lifeline out of problematic suburban experiences. For some, connections with others did not come easily, and some of the alienation experienced by adults in the postwar suburbs was a reality for adolescents—possibly even more so because they were at a developmental stage often marked by social awkwardness.[16] Mary Baker recalled that she had only a few close connections with classmates and friends within her suburban community, and she expressed a general resentment of her suburban childhood. For her, it was stifling, marginalizing, and limiting. It constantly reinforced her feelings of difference. Suicide was attempted more than once, and she was diagnosed as clinically depressed in her teenage years. She also expressed that she was "simply hanging on" as she approached adulthood, in the hopes that her life would improve once she left her teenage years. She talked about the importance of the night and how the nighttime—specifically "the midnight movie"—helped her cope with complex everyday realities:

The TV was outside my basement room, and I could sneak out every night. I discovered Judy Garland, Marlene Dietrich, Greta Garbo, all these strong women ... I used to say I was raised by the movies ... I was an insomniac, so I watched pretty well every night. If my parents did know I was doing this, they never said anything ... When my friends were going on about Sandra Dee, I would say why would you want to be Sandra Dee when you could be Greta Garbo? They'd say, 'Who was Greta Garbo?' ... It was a lifeline to me. It gave me a sense that there was a bigger life [than] I could have here.[17]

Although she wasn't leaving her suburban home physically, the cover of night allowed her to move beyond both time and space, which were normally constrained. The basement, as it was for so many teenagers, could be a refuge. For her, this space, and the nighttime freedoms enjoyed in it, may have even been a lifeline of sorts. Movies are often seen as an escape from the everyday, but in this instance movies reflected a kind of life that she sought so desperately. She brought her own meanings to these movies, and they had a profound effect on her young life. Unable to find strong female role models in her daily life, in what was a very bleak time for her, she found hope in some of these iconic actresses from early Hollywood movies.

Sharon Johnstone mentioned that time spent alone wasn't isolating but was necessary for improving her mental health: "I actually enjoyed being quiet and at home. I wasn't really into going out ... It wasn't until I was twenty or twenty-one that I was involved in going out."[18] This memory reflects some of the differences between teenagers that simplistic constructs and generalizations can never capture about any age group, but especially a group that did not have the same access to power nor the same agency as did adults in their lives. While several participants mentioned curfews, in-home groundings, early bedtimes, and similar constraints, sprinkled throughout the archival record is evidence that some young people circumvented these regulations with varying motives.

Brian Rutz recalled the importance of shared nighttime experiences as he entered his teenage years. While some relished time dedicated to themselves, others, like Rutz, viewed nighttime as an opportunity to spend time with their peer groups in a private setting. He recalled, with some fondness and nostalgia, that there was a co-ed social group of five girls and five boys that formed: "There was a steady stream of birthday parties ... Invariably, there would be a rec room in the basement of these houses, except for mine ... Luckily, my parents would leave [if he hosted]. We'd go down in the basement to socialize."[19]

Time and space, uninterrupted by adults, was important. For some, it was an opportunity for boys and girls to socialize outside of the classroom, in an informal, private space that many suburban homes could provide. Recreation rooms were increasingly common in suburban homes in this period, and they were often co-opted by young people for their own use, regardless of the time of day. As Rutz recalled, his parents would leave the young teens at home to socialize without supervision. His parents likely knew most of them personally, and contrary to some of the prevailing myths and discursive constructs of the period, these young people simply enjoyed one another's company without adults hovering nearby. Most participants revealed that some activities were not readily shared with parents and guardians.

Not all parents and guardians placed their trust in children and adolescents. Historically, across North America, coercive strategies such as criminalizing young people's presence in public spaces after sundown were reinforced by perceptions of the night's dangers and youngsters' vulnerability.[20] While the sensationalism and drama of nighttime crime, delinquency, and vandalism has held the attention of many adults over the past two centuries, there are no hard statistics to support the belief that more delinquent or criminal activity occurs after dark. Typically, most young people are not out after dark, which severely curtails their ability to organize and commit criminal acts. In recent years, as more study has been undertaken about "juvenile" crimes and misdemeanours,[21] findings demonstrate that most crimes committed by teens happen during the daylight hours.[22]

Until teenagers had access to cars, their after-dark activities, both indoors and outdoors, were limited, a fact discussed in contemporary student publications.[23] An *Aberhart Advocate* editorial from 1962 noted that there were unsolvable challenges in appeasing parents and local law agencies when it came to trying to find nighttime activities for teenagers across the city. Places that students wanted to go to were often licensed and therefore unavailable to high school students, who were not yet twenty-one years old. The editorial mentions that Red Deer would be hosting a new teen night club: "If such a club can be established offering food, fun and friends under one roof, we say let's support it."[24] Transportation, travel, and safety were concerns, however, since Red Deer was 86 miles north of Calgary.

The automobile, whether it was borrowed or owned, changed the suburban experience for those that had access to it. Barry Matthews, one of the older baby boomers, was straightforward: "We got cars, and life changed. We'd go to parties. I didn't hang at the mall or anything like that. We were also big sports fans and went to sporting events."[25] Others said that the ability to drive gave them even more freedom to go where they pleased with no supervision.

While parents could and did shuttle young people, it was not to the same extent as in many North American households today. Young people often walked or biked to activities and informal social events after dark, even well into their high school years. Allan Matthews recalled that in his preteen years there were "games in the park like kick the can and raiding the occasional garden."[26] Public green space was a key marker for sub-urban and small-town young people, as access to parks and open spaces was limited in some cities—they simply did not exist in some places. Garden spaces, outside of very small plots, were rare in most inner-city Canadian neighbourhoods.

As youngsters aged and matured, enjoying house parties was com-mon, but going out with friends was the most important nighttime activity for most. School newspaper articles reflected the adolescent night life in suburbs, as evidenced in this excerpt from a 1957 poem titled "I Won't Be Back":

> When night is almost done,
> I hurry home to bed.
> That party sure was fun,
> But I am almost dead.
> The house is locked up tight,
> There's no way to get in.
> I'll be out here all night,
> Oh! Where's the aspirin? ...
> I think that I'll skip town ...
> This life has got me down,
> I won't be back no more![27]

Recurring themes of escape, nighttime parties, and possible alienation from family and home, along with the ever-intriguing pull of simply escap-ing ordinary life for adventure, were all emphasized.

Jim Farquharson recalled that neither he nor most of his close friends had curfews. When he was very young, he played hide-and-go-seek in the dark in parks, back alleys, and swamps until called in by parents. As he got older, it was "just walking different places. I used to go to older parties with an older crowd. I suppose in grade ten I was going to grade twelve par-ties ... It was just social parties."[28] Interviewees were split on curfews—a small majority had them while many did not.

Nighttime activities often involved just wandering around and exploring spaces that appeared different than they did during the day. One poem, titled simply "The Night," which appeared in a 1966 Aberhart yearbook, explored some of the activities associated with walking in the park, some of the dullness of teenage life, alienation among others (presumably adults), and the trials and tribulations of being a young person:

> The night is very dull and dark
> And as I walk through the park
> The people stop and stare
> They wonder why and where
> I do come from ...
> Only others of my kind and race
> Know all the hardships that I face
> Love and opportunity ...
> That's all I want.[29]

The author suggests that she saw age and her generational cohort—her life stage of adolescence—as significant identity markers. Here, the night serves as a metaphor for adolescent alienation.

By the early 1960s, newly built shopping malls alongside the smaller strip malls also offered teenagers more opportunities to see the popular movies of the day at theatres. While movie going was an established interwar pastime for children and youth, the postwar years, as discussed, featured an even greater focus on adolescents, with movies being designed for their consumption.[30] Escapism and science fiction were common themes in many films. In his popular memoir, one man recalled the nature of movies in the 1950s: "We might equally be attacked by flying saucers or stiff-limbed aliens with metallic voices and deathly ray guns, and [movies] introduced us to the stimulating possibilities for mayhem inherent in giant mutated insects, blundering mega-crabs, bestirred dinosaurs, monsters from the deep, and one seriously pissed-off fifty-foot woman."[31]

William Wright recalled how important the North Hill Shopping Centre and its Cinerama were: "I used to live at the North Hill Cinerama. That was kind of my haven."[32] Wendy Glidden had similar memories of the late 1960s and early 1970s when "we would go to a lot of movies."[33] Brent Harris recalled: "We had a movie theatre in the Brentwood Village Mall, and that was the first kiss with a girl. Saturdays or Sunday evenings we would go to the bowling alley in the North Hill Mall."[34] For some, after they could drive and had access to a car, drive-in theatres were another popular option. Otherwise, drive-ins were popular as a family activity, up until a certain age.

The night was not only about leisure activities. We know that teenagers continued to do paid work outside the home in the 1950s and 1960s.[35] Some of this was evening and nighttime work. In earlier times, children's use of the streets at night blinded some middle-class observers to the fact that they worked at night or very early in the morning out of sheer necessity.[36] Nor had this practice ceased entirely by this period; one interviewee immediately associated work with the nighttime, particularly as he reached his late teens.[37] Throughout these years, there were references to teenagers and nighttime work in the local newspapers. A 1950 *Calgary Herald* article discussed the perils of young people working at night on city streets. The reporter noted that "Calgary's night-riding telegraph boys are being illuminated so that motorists driving along dark streets can spot the dark-uniformed cyclists about half a block away ... All of the telegraph boys ... must have generated-operated headlamps and tail-lights, in addition to the reflector-type tail-lights."[38] Others recalled brothers, sisters, and friends who worked in fast food restaurants, which was much more common by the mid-1970s, as the service economy employed young Calgarians in low-paying jobs.[39] Teenagers delivered countless newspapers in the early morning hours. While it was not nighttime work, it was certainly work performed under the cover of darkness, especially in the late fall and winter months.

Some teenagers experimented with alcohol and drugs (the latter seemed more common in the 1960s than in the 1950s) at nighttime. Parks and other quiet, out-of-the-way suburban spaces were popular sites for this. Once again, the adult gaze could or would not often reach teens using spaces that were otherwise dedicated to recreational activities such as walking, hiking, skiing, tobogganing, and cycling during the day. As Tammy Simpson noted:

> Some parents were stricter than others, so it was simply easier for all to be out of their parents' place and spend time in Confederation Park ... There was a place called the Pit ... that was built in 1967 ... It had a built-in fire pit ... We'd smoke cigarettes and maybe dope, hang out, flirt, and stuff grass down the chimney. The whole valley would fill with smoke, and the fire department would show up. We'd also do something that wasn't healthy; we'd hyperventilate, take a couple of deep breaths, someone would come up behind you and squeeze you, and then you'd pass out.[40]

Despite ongoing adult suspicions across time, teenagers did not spend most of this idle, after-dark time engaging in illicit activities. Curiosity and experimentation were key motivators. For many teenagers, the night was an opportunity to socialize with peers, oftentimes solely within this group. At most other times, adults, particularly in middle-class families where both parents were not working full-time hours outside the home, were present or nearby. For still others, the night was an opportunity to have time completely to themselves.

Delinquency and Crime

Without question, juvenile delinquency marked suburban adolescence, as it did in both urban and rural areas in a broader Canadian context. Jim Farquharson said he never ended up in a juvenile home—implying that his actions didn't cross certain lines. He recalled that some kids started out with small motorbikes at Branton Junior High and that the cops would be there once or twice a week to deal with various incidents: "Those same kids in high school formed motorcycle gangs ... Some friends were docile. Others were on the borderline of getting in serious trouble. I was comfortable with both groups, much to the chagrin of my mother."[41] He describes a side of the post-war suburban experience that saw young people operating right on the line of lawfulness or just crossing over it.[42] While they were not characterized by serious crime, vice, and peril, Calgary's suburban spaces were sites for delinquency and more major crime than was typical of life in the suburbs.

Adult attempts at social control are as old as humankind itself.[43] What is often lost in broad discussions of delinquency in historical context is that youngsters account for a fair percentage of property crimes, such as shoplifting and various nuisance actions in public spaces, although their nature and extent are often exaggerated.[44] Violent crime is committed, overwhelmingly, by adults, not by young people.

Public preoccupation with the transgressions of juveniles, which some-what accelerated in this period and continues to the present day, makes it difficult to picture a time when young people were not collectively perceived as deviant; however, before the mid-nineteenth century they were rarely a target of public concern.[45] By the early twentieth century, federal and provincial regulations and rules regarding the policing and incarceration of juveniles were codified.[46] This basic framework would remain in place until the early 1980s, when the federal Young Offenders Act replaced the earlier federal Juvenile Delinquents Act (JDA), originally passed in 1908.

The JDA asserted that young people could be liable to arrest and punishment and subjected to forced treatment of the condition that was believed to cause their transgressions.[47] Under the JDA, delinquents were not only defined as youngsters who broke a law; they could also be children presumed to be abused or neglected and, therefore, deemed likely to break existing laws or become corrupted by their immoral families. Additionally, they could be acting in a manner deemed inappropriately adult, given their age; delinquency was, and remains, a flexible concept, measured in ideological terminologies.[48] It must be emphasized that the definition of *juvenile delinquency* changed over time and that these definitions were interwoven with class, gender, and, as time passed, race.[49] In the case of the JDA, the foremost qualifying category was age. Changes to definitions were done in the context of modernist impulses; the female delinquent came about as the product of new and expanding knowledge from the fields of medicine, sociology, and psychology.[50] In many ways, the juvenile justice system in this period dealt with young women as malleable and identified teenagers who were deemed capable of being reformed.[51]

The Second World War saw the production of a continuing discourse on delinquency as a harmful social ailment caused by wartime pressures on families and schools.[52] In large cities such as Montreal, schools mobilized young people, fostering an increased effort to create productive youngsters and patriotic citizens.[53] The larger point is that delinquency was not dealt with solely by punitive measures. There were also attempts made to prevent delinquency and to address root causes in an effort to redirect delinquents.

The understanding that delinquency is socially constructed—rather than an unchanging, scientific, or morally absolute measure of right or wrong, moral or immoral—is not new.[54] The fact that delinquency is socially constructed means that its definition has changed over time. The "delinquent," as a criminal category, was established within a network of power relations that reflected prevailing definitions of civilized, acceptable, and moral standards of behaviour.[55] Importantly, in the postwar period, categories changed in just a few brief years. In the 1952 Calgary Police Force's juvenile report, smoking was listed as an offence alongside theft and damage to property.[56] By 1955, smoking was nowhere to be found as an offence, and new categories such as possession of an offensive weapon, cruelty to animals, and shoplifting had emerged.[57] By 1968, the juvenile delinquency detail report had categories such as narcotics, glue sniffing or nail polish sniffing, and annoying phone calls.[58]

As the 1950s began, Alberta changed how juvenile delinquents would be treated. Social workers attempted to address delinquency as a social disease that could be cured by professional social-work techniques.[59] The province reduced the juvenile age for boys from eighteen to sixteen, resulting in less protection for older adolescents. The *Calgary Herald* supported this measure:

> For too long police court magistrates have been frustrated by Alberta law which, contrary to other provinces, sheltered sixteen and

seventeen-year-old hoodlums from the weight of justice. Now these mis-
fits can be properly sentenced and placed in the Bowden institution ...
where they can be disciplined and re-educated apart from hardened criminals ... The government has taken a progressive first step. We trust there
will be more in the future.[60]

While this 1951 editorial does not advocate young people being put in with
the general prison population, there is tacit approval of a more disciplinary
shift in the treatment of juvenile delinquents, the term *progressive* being
an ironic descriptor. These changes were in line with other constructs of
juvenile crime, which was presented as a relatively new and disturbing
issue. Canadian teenagers, it was claimed, were being corrupted by postwar prosperity, a shift in morality, loosening family ties, and so forth.[61]
Some editorials emphasized that it was a national issue in Canada by way
of discourses on wayward youth being pampered in Alberta while boys of
sixteen years or older in Saskatchewan or Ontario were being sent to the
criminal courts and treated as adults.[62] Other articles, in magazines read
widely across Canada and the United States, discussed what measures
needed to be taken to address the problem.[63] Not all wanted delinquency
dealt with harshly. Some argued for a return to positive community and
familial influences to help in the prevention of delinquency.[64] Others
focused on the need for patience and understanding some of the underlying issues often associated with delinquency.[65]

In 1952, the City of Calgary determined that levels of juvenile delinquency required a dedicated unit of officers to deal with juveniles who
ran afoul of the law. The Calgary Police Juvenile Investigative Force was
initially composed of four men. These first staff members were chosen for
their ability to relate to young people, along with their previous job experience in the force. By the early 1970s, this detachment had increased to
fourteen dedicated officers.[66]

From inception, the force received significant coverage in the local
press. This favourable publicity focused on the new relationships being
formed between youths and officers as a result of this necessary initiative. One article stated that the unit was created "jointly by civil and
provincial authorities in the hope that it could ... stem the rising tide of
juvenile delinquency and replace it with young people who had a healthy
regard for the law and a ... desire to become good citizens."[67] Media support, however, was not consistent over time. By the end of the 1960s, the
Calgary police's youth department was described as a farce, as ultimately
ineffectual in fighting delinquency, and the blame now placed on a lack
of parental control and broken homes.[68] In 1961, *The Albertan* claimed

that "the best shoplifters are in the eight, nine and 10-year-old range; housebreakers run between six and eight-years-old and the ones who wreck buildings under construction usually go to about age 15."[69] These criticisms did not take into account the near tripling of Calgary's population from the late 1940s through the early 1970s. It grew from just over 129,000 people to over 400,000 by 1971.[70] In addition, the large majority of offences, although potentially troublesome, were relatively benign in their nature and scope.

There was a persistent and familiar discourse that harkened back to a time, roughly twenty years earlier, when youth delinquency had not been a serious problem.[71] In a 1955 Calgary Boys Club report, the circumstances surrounding the origins of the city's chapter, seventeen years earlier, were held to be a response to delinquency, which had reached such alarming proportions steps had to be taken to do something for the boys with delinquency records as well as those whose social circumstances meant that they needed help outside of their families.[72] Other Children's Aid Department reports characterized juvenile delinquency as a social disease that was running rampant and nearly unchecked in the communities of many of Canada's major urban centres.[73] Social workers, both in Alberta and across the country, called for increased funding and the ongoing professionalization of social work, upholding education as a bulwark against juvenile delinquency and other social diseases.[74]

Some newspaper articles provided graphic details that spoke to the violence that defined teenage gangs in the early 1950s, many of which continued into the 1960s in a variety of forms. Gangs, as some suburban baby boomers discussed, did reach across urban spaces, and the gangs' exploits were featured in dozens of local newspaper stories. It was common for gang members to be described as "brutal" or "cowards." One perpetrator was said to have "had his hand encased in roughened strips of leather which tore the skin each time he hit ... They use large rings, knuckledusters, key chains wrapped around their hands and carry 'shivs' ... to intimidate youths and girls who arouse the ire of gang members."[75] *The Albertan* quoted a teen gang leader of the 10th Street Boys, who were alleged to be attempting a "terrorist" campaign among high school students and perpetrating assaults on young people: "We don't see how the cops can break us up."[76] These stories illustrate that some adults could be led to believe that these described behaviours were the norm rather than the exception among teenagers. It seems, though, that many parents were able to strike the right chord regarding discipline. A 1960 national poll asked nearly seven hundred Canadians about their parents' strictness; 80 percent indicated that it had been "about right" while only 11.7 percent believed it was "too strict."[77]

One content analysis of postwar samples of national and local newspapers in Canada demonstrated that most stories about adolescents had a negative orientation in focusing disproportionately on deviancy.[78] Popular movies such as *Blackboard Jungle, West Side Story,* and *Rebel Without a Cause* only reinforced this negative orientation with their iconic images of adolescent gangs, violence, and disregard for authority.

The meagre statistics available are also inconclusive, as reporting changed during this period. As discussed, the age of juvenile males, for the purposes of being classified as juveniles in the justice system, dropped by two years, and the city's population, both in the urban and suburban areas, exploded. In one case of housebreaking in 1950, seven juveniles were held responsible and dealt with by Children's Aid. In 1949, one year before, the number of housebreakings had been ten. In the case of shop breaking, the Children's Aid dealt with seventy-five juveniles in 1949; in 1950, this number was a comparatively low at twenty-four.[79] The Calgary Police Court, which handled juvenile delinquents, saw fifty males and seven females dealt with under the Juvenile Delinquents Act in the same year.[80] These numbers reflect a very small proportion of Calgary children and adolescents, even with some crimes going unreported. Some of the reporting lumped overlapping age groups together; one report indicated that 185 young people between the ages of fifteen and twenty had been arrested for more serious crimes such as assault and arson.[81] It was in this context that many Calgarians believed that their city was witnessing an explosion of the juvenile delinquency that was also plaguing other North American centres.[82]

Despite a disproportionate amount of negative publicity, there were counternarratives contending that delinquency was not the problem that some journalists, social workers, psychologists, sociologists, and the police and public said it was.[83] There were a few newspaper stories in the early 1950s that explained that the numbers didn't support these discourses of fear. One *Calgary Herald* article in 1951 explained that the city's "delinquency in 1950 was the lowest it has been for 20 years."[84] Later in the decade, even as tales of affluent suburban young people engaging in sex and drug use emerged, most did not assume that the adolescents of exclusive enclaves such as Toronto's Rosedale were dangerous potential criminals.[85] National polling in 1961 reflected some of this ambivalence. When asked what the most serious problem facing the country today, apart from unemployment, only 5 percent of respondents mentioned juvenile delinquency.[86] This did not mean that young suburbanites were not victims of crime.

Despite the quietude that is associated with suburban life, suburbia could be the site of violence, and it was often gendered. As teenaged Elaine, the main character in Margaret Atwood's *Cat's Eye,* explains about walking home: "We've been told not to do this alone, and not to go down into the ravine by ourselves. There might be men down there."[87] While men were often thought to be the ones most to fear, certain older male suburban teenagers were believed to be potentially dangerous. Mary Baker remembered that when she was eleven years old a violent incident happened in a relatively secluded space between the nascent suburbs and the nearby countryside:

> I was grabbed by an older boy. I knew his sister. He was seventeen. I was dragged off to a little wooden structure, and there was another boy as a lookout. It was not a good situation. My next younger brother ran home, hysterical. The most instructive thing was my reaction to not scream ... I also had a sense you wouldn't necessarily be helped. I remember thinking to keep my wits about me, and making some smart-assed comments. He said he was going to have some fun. I don't recall how long it was. My older brother and his friend came tearing down and caught this kid at the end of the field. I got home, and my mother was on the phone ... She didn't get off the phone. All she said was, "Did he put his thing in you?" ... My father went to talk to his father. My father said he didn't want to see the boy's life ruined. My thought was, Whom did he go after next? He was a rough customer; it was a rough family. He got information that this was okay from [a person of some authority]. My quintessential moment of my childhood—it's not safe to depend on men. They'll circle the wagons and protect the guy ... I sure knew that all of this crap, that women don't have to do anything because men will take care of them [wasn't true] ... That's the underbelly of the niceness of the fifties and "we will look after the girls." Bullshit.[88]

It was a heartbreaking revelation, one that exposed what could, and did, happen to some young women and almost certainly went unreported in many cases. It would be naïve to believe that this might have been an isolated incident—other participants mentioned similar incidents with other older boys and men. It also brings up questions about why it went unreported and the perception that involving the police might bring shame on the family. Baker gave no indication that she ever spoke about this to friends, extended family, or anyone else in the community afterwards.

There was limited recounting of sexual abuse by interviewees. Other data nevertheless suggests that sexual abuse was more widespread in these years than many then thought. Significant evidence of abuse can be found in case reports prepared by social agencies, in reports of court cases, and in survey data.[89] Despite the fact that there was underreporting, there was increasing concern about sexual assaults against young people. This led people to look for new ways to deal with the issue, reflecting a dominant view that sex criminals suffered from a mental condition rather than criminal indifference to fellow citizens.[90]

While the topic of delinquency and crime in the postwar suburbs remains relatively unexplored, we know that suburban girls in Toronto were, at times, eager to escape rough home conditions or felt the draw of youth cultures beyond their own communities.[91] There were echoes of the latter from some participants. Some made their way to downtown Calgary to engage in activities that their parents certainly never knew about. Wendy Glidden discussed her activities, which included minor legal infractions, although she never had any contact with Calgary's juvenile authorities. She recalled getting together with a friend in downtown Calgary: "A few times we hitchhiked, shoplifted, once or twice, little things like that. Not in any big ways [were we delinquent or rule breakers]; we had a lot of freedom. I went to clubs with my brother ... He would have been in university, so I was thirteen or fourteen ... to listen to groups and bands."[92] As the official juvenile delinquency statistics from the period indicate, most often, young people were caught for committing minor indiscretions—in line with definitions of delinquency rather than criminal activity.

This era came to be defined by the belief that delinquency could and should be addressed by new rehabilitative methods.[93] Although they had a presiding judge, juvenile courts and families depended on psychological experts and social caseworkers who observed court proceedings, assessed youngsters' emotional well-being, identified causes of conflict, and, ultimately, recommended the most appropriate individual treatment. Despite this professionalism, the delinquent's class, gender, and race were huge influences on how justice was meted out. Additionally, in instances of identifying and dealing with "problem girls," though supposedly based on unbiased casework procedures, the professionalism of social caseworkers was interwoven with their moralism. Often, final assessments were based on hearsay as much as on "scientific" determinations.[94] Parents were also targeted, as their neglect of parenting duties was cited as a fundamental cause of delinquency.[95] While parents may have been targeted and scapegoated by some Canadians, in a national poll in 1965, nearly 77 percent of respondents disapproved of parents either paying the fine or serving the child's jail sentence for unlawful behaviour.[96] While young people did not face an adult system geared exclusively toward incarceration and punishment, the Calgary Boys Club executive director's report for 1957 suggested the prevailing viewpoint: "When a boy is referred to us, individual attention is given to his need, and soon we are able to help mould his character into a channel leading to good citizenship. Boys' Club is known for its patience and tenacity in dealing with so called problem boys."[97]

The term *good citizenship* is loaded with problematic connotations, yet the focus was not so much on ensuring that young people would "pay the price" for their transgressions as it was about preserving a certain vision of Canadian society. This was a system that was not responsive enough to social issues such as health, poverty, and housing.[98] Social workers' reports openly discussed the fact that the public, at least from their perspective, did not support social assistance; many regarded welfare recipients as lazy, shiftless, and unworthy of social support.[99] Social workers, generally, had a firm belief in their work, and their reports are heavily infused with clear statements that such programs were vital for strengthening family life by means of counselling services and so forth.[100] The preventive role of child protection services was characterized as being of vital importance to family cohesion.[101]

Growing belief in the social sciences as the way to progress was especially notable from the late 1940s through to the early 1960s.[102] In literature from 1947, Children's Aid social workers were part of a larger cohort who believed that most youngsters in need, "given the proper type of training, could be saved and moulded into very useful citizens."[103] The goal was not unsettling the system but reinforcing it and producing young adults who would contribute to it as proper "citizens." Advice was never far away, at times coming in magazine articles for harried parents. Parenting had taken a real beating in the previous twenty-five years, they advised, and while parenting should not be based on terrifying children, as it had been for these parents as children, parents should not be terrified of their children either.[104]

Suburban spaces and teenagers were also touched by broader gang activities in this period, a topic that was popular with the movie-going public and touched on in feature films. One person recalled that adults were not privy to these happenings in any meaningful way. Violence among teens after school was not uncommon, and it is well established that much of the history of childhood and adolescence is a hidden history. The level of surveillance that has emerged in recent decades was absent. Jim Farquharson remembered that when a cop car was spotted outside the junior high school, people knew who they were coming to see—kids who were known delinquents, for things like theft: "We used to have belt fights in grade seven where you'd take off your belts and whip each other. First one to draw blood won ... In those days, after school, there was always scrapping ... For me, it was entertainment. They were your friends and you weren't going to let anyone beat them up."[105] Several of these boys who met regularly were never charged with delinquency. While this kind of activity may not have constituted delinquency per se, the year it happened and, quite frankly, who was involved influenced whether events became a statistic in a juvenile delinquency detail report. Schoolyard fighting seems to be as old as schools themselves, but its organization, the use of weapons, the age of the participants, and so forth also factored into its naming. The fact that some of these activities took place on school grounds in these new suburbs has not been widely reported through the lens of childhood and adolescence.

While some gang activities (which seemed to be only casually associated with Banff Trail) were based around the wider Calgary area and prompted much discussion about male delinquents,[106] postwar suburban spaces were also sites for delinquent and violent behaviours. These activities were not new. Early twentieth-century memoirists often recalled that streets, playgrounds, and unoccupied lots were frequently sites for conflicts and at times fisticuffs; they were a kind of youngsters' battleground—especially for boys.[107] William Wright, growing up in the late 1960s and early 1970s, recalled that he "had one bad experience where one guy who terrorized us went on to be in a penitentiary for killing his wife—the school bully who became the murderer."[108] Bullying was recalled offhandedly by a few interviewees, and it was mentioned only briefly in some student publications. Several participants recalled that teachers seemed to turn a blind eye to it. It may have been normalized and tolerated in the period, but the sheer numbers of young people comprising the baby boom cohorts might have made it nearly impossible to address the problem regularly.[109]

As the 1960s closed, the Banff Trail community was rocked by a murder committed by a local teenager on a summer morning at William Aberhart High School. A seventeen-year-old Banff Trail teenager was charged with noncapital murder in the slaying of a fifty-year-old caretaker at the school. The teenager was a former student of the school and had graduated the previous spring. The caretaker was shot in the abdomen with a .303 calibre rifle shortly after arriving for work. Police found him on the first-floor landing close to the main entrance of the school. Detectives noted evidence of a break-in: the main floor window on the west side of the high school had been smashed. The caretaker had been employed at the school for seven years and was described by school principal Larry Parker as a "really nice man."[110] The motive for the killing, if any, was not released publicly in any Calgary newspapers or included in the police records from 1968. The incident reveals the deep complexities of suburbia, adolescence, and childhood in this period. When interviewees did mention the murder, it was almost surreal for them. There was a strong sense that it was an unfortunate yet isolated incident that certainly did not define the community.

Juvenile delinquency and larger crime statistics were not broken down into districts in this period, but we know that the most highly reported offences occurred in more densely populated urban areas, especially because they were mixed-use spaces that had more stores (for shoplifting and store break-ins).[111] The downtown business core was the site for much of this activity, as this is where the larger department stores and businesses were located until strip malls and larger shopping malls were built in the suburbs later in the postwar period.

The bulk of delinquency, committed by suburban young people or otherwise, was not serious in nature throughout this period. One former resident, Faye Esler Hall, recalled that in 1956, the year that Branton Junior High School was built, young vandals smashed the courtyard windows and that this was the talk at school for months.[112] This suggests that these types of delinquent acts were not common in Banff Trail. Brent Harris discussed what was involved in his delinquent activities: "Store security saw me changing a price tag on a tape, and they caught me. My parents got called in, and it went to juvenile court ... where the judge just slapped me on the wrist ... That scared me straight.[113] Much like Wendy Glidden, who said she committed some petty crime, the offences committed by suburban youths such as Harris were inconsequential for the most part; these kids were not hardened criminals in the making. Boredom and cheap thrills, more than anything else, seemed to be the significant contributing factor.

There are dozens of contemporary student articles from the period responding to how teenagers were portrayed in public discourse. In one, resistance from young people to these representations is clear. Delegates to a Y-Teen conference, a group that Banff Trail teens were part of during this period, believed that the public did not distinguish between law-abiding teens and juvenile delinquents. One city teenager is quoted as saying, "The press and radio [should be] criticized for giving adverse publicity to the teen-agers by allegedly playing up the actions of delinquents and giving little publicity to the good side of the picture."[114]

By the mid- to late 1960s, a shift had occurred across Canada, as voices of displeasure with the operation of the Juvenile Delinquents Act were loud and clear. They were made by legal reformers, social activists, politicians (often at the bidding of families who had had negative contact with the juvenile justice system), and important reform organizations such as the Elizabeth Fry Society, a charitable organization first established in Ontario in the 1950s to support some of society's most vulnerable populations, including women, girls, and children, dealing with the justice system.[115] Canadians were divided in their views. In a 1963 national poll, 49.5

percent said there was less "juvenile delinquency in this community today, than there was, say ten years ago," while 50.5 percent held the opposite view.[116] Influential organizations weighed in.

The Vanier Institute of the Family was founded in 1966 and began to hold annual meetings. It funded various groups around the country, including Calgary, to spur a renewed commitment to the family and human values.[117] In the 1960s, official government inquiries may not have remade the system, but they did produce moments of re-evaluation that spurred political events that would mean significant change in the next fifteen years.[118] By the 1970s, criticism had become the basis for a widespread attack on the juvenile justice system's overreliance on subjective evidence, heavy use of nonlegal personnel, lack of public accountability, and absence of due process.[119] The 1984 Young Offenders Act would mean a different era in Canada, one where delinquent young people were offered more protection than older criminals and rule breakers, although there were more similarities to the broader justice system than there had been under the Juvenile Delinquents Act's regime.[120] Delinquency, and at times crime, did exist in the postwar suburbs. While many of the activities were benign, young people were both victims and perpetrators. Certain events changed young people's lives and remained with them into adulthood. Children and adolescents, however, also engaged in other forms of resistance.

Resistance

> I questioned a lot of things as a kid. In elementary, I was leaning toward being an agnostic ... My mother, being an academic, allowed me to ask those questions. I asked for permission to leave the gymnasium during school assemblies when they recited the Lord's Prayer. I was dutifully asked to leave the gymnasium in front of the whole school ... My parents certainly stood up for me against the school administration ... and this was grade five. It was an interesting challenge for a young fella in the late sixties.[121]

This recollection, by Brent Harris, reveals a comparatively mature form of resistance to the prayer recitation that was very much a part of daily school routines not only in Calgary suburbs but across the country during these years. He spoke admiringly of the support of his parents, and especially his mother, in this matter with the school administration and teachers. In the popular media, parents were also seen to be catalysts for young people's general rebellion.[122] While parents are often the focus of resistance by adolescents, this anecdote reminds us that they could be allies under certain circumstances.[123] The idea that young people are somehow naturally inclined toward resistance and nonconformity is a relatively recent one in the long history of childhood. The beginnings of this idea can be traced back to the world spawned by the Industrial Revolution.[124] Empirical evidence makes it clear that over the past century only a minority of adolescents experienced their teenage years as a time of rebellion, or as a significant break with the past.[125]

It's also noteworthy that the "creeping conformity," thought to aptly describe the postwar years, was not a constant in the long history of Canadian suburbs. Not only were left-wing politics fostered in some suburbs in the early twentieth century but some radical movements in modern Canadian history began in working-class suburban communities.[126] As we have seen, even if political radicalism did not define Banff Trail or most other postwar suburbs, postwar suburbs did include many working-class homeowners who were, in many cases, from working-class backgrounds.

One act of resistance that cut across age lines and realized a goal that came to define the area for some residents in this period was attempts to foil a plan to have one of the city's main landfills placed a few minutes' drive north of Banff Trail. Several people remembered their parents lobbying to have the site located elsewhere in the city, and some participants, children at the time, attended meetings to protest the plan. It was their first taste of local politics. One resident, Roy Farquharson, recalled that when the City of Calgary announced the plan, the "neighbours were naturally up in arms. A committee was formed and I was one of those representatives who fought this horrendous plan. We were finally successful in its defeat."[127] Ultimately, the Spy Hill site was chosen, and the proposed site became important to both suburban young people and adults by the late 1960s, as it had been for the earliest Banff Trail residents. With the exception of a public park, the large area was left in a relatively natural state and became a park. In 1967 the green space was formally recognized and became Confederation Park.[128] As we have seen, Banff Trail was not an exclusive suburban enclave defined by professionals and wealth. Many residents were working-class people with blue-collar jobs mixed with some lower-middle-class families; they didn't enjoy the privileges that often accompany wealthy and more influential residents when they get involved in "Not in My Backyard" campaigns.

In understanding the most important institutions in children's and adolescents' lives, there can be no denying that the balance of power lay with adults during this period, as it did historically. Older teenagers began to enjoy increased levels of power and autonomy as they aged: being able to drive, working for pay outside the home, not always reporting their whereabouts to parents, and making choices within their social circle. Power, nevertheless, was not fully in their grasp. Well-functioning relationships are defined as much by instances of resistance—such as a youngster who questions his religious faith as an elementary student— conflict, and negotiation as they are by co-operation.[129] Debate, disagreement, and true dialogue cannot be characterized as rejection, as it sometimes is by adults.[130] On an individual level, this means that some children and adolescents constantly try to resist, challenge, and remake adult influences according to their individual goals and personal traits.[131] Along with the family home, the school was the most likely site for young people to exercise their agency. At times, this was evident even among the youngest schoolchildren.

With the Cold War being waged, and despite constant claims about the need to reinforce freedom and democracy, students were not seen as partners in their own education. Historians of education in Canada have shown that progressive tenets did not necessarily flow down to everyday classroom experiences.[132] Even the initial walk to school for five- and six-year-olds could become an opportunity to test childhood bounds. Michelle Macdonald recalled that she was shown her walking route to and from her classroom and was then expected to follow the route every day: "The first day, I went the wrong way [of her own accord]. I confessed to my mom that I had gone the wrong way. It was the first time I had broken the rules."[133] Often these acts of resistance were small acts far from an adult view, but from the perspective of childhood, and well over forty years later, a single event could still stand out as an effort to make an independent decision.

Allan Matthews recalled that in elementary school he got into trouble purposefully because there "was a teacher ... who I was in love with; she had great boobs, and I liked her perfume. Like any grade four boy, I was naughty so I could get detention and spend extra time with her."[134] Some boys started to model some adult behaviours (boorish and otherwise) at a very early age. But this was not exclusive to boys. Some adolescent girls also sought attention from older male teachers. Donna McLaren recalled: "I would do things to get detention ... With one teacher, I had to sit beside his desk for months, and I wanted to do that ... The teachers ... were all young, had long hair; they were stylish for the times. I was really interested in their attention, but they thought they were giving me detention."[135]

Older teenagers also expressed resistance through their writing. Speaking to former editors, teenagers clearly did not hold final editorial control on school newspaper columns, yet they often voiced concerns. In 1969, an *Aberhart Advocate* editorial on discipline focused on three main points:

1. Many schools have complex and intricate systems of disciplining students.

2. Most forms of punishment are silly and ineffectual. They serve only as negative reinforcement of unacceptable behavior patterns. By enforcing detentions, and suspension, the administration success-fully wastes their time, the student's time, and the teacher's time. Meanwhile, they have done nothing to solve the original problem.

3. There is a great deal of discrepancy between the way students are treated in one school and the way they are treated in another.[136]

The writer goes on to argue that the consequences were uneven among high schools; Banff Trail's Aberhart High School appeared to be rather lax in its discipline. For being late, students had to report to the office; after three occurrences, they were spoken to about the issue. For skipping classes, they were punished by the vice-principal. For participating in unauthorized activities, they could be suspended. Finally, although having long hair could result in expulsion from Western High School in this period, at William Aberhart it only garnered snide remarks from teachers. In effect, provincial guidelines, student handbooks, and other official documents could be interpreted and enforced in different ways at the everyday level. These discrepancies came out through a student-conducted survey that sought information from eighteen students at other Calgary high schools. Dress codes, restrictions on hair length for males, and so forth were prevalent across North America, and some of these regulations were in response to the 1960s counterculture, which permeated society and influenced multiple age cohorts.[137]

Teenage students were also critical of the education system at an intellectual level. Suburban and urban teens were interviewed for a 1966 *Calgary Herald* article and expressed frustration with both content and pedagogy in their curriculums. While not a large sample size, the paper surveyed forty-eight students in nine high schools. The graduating students questioned both the value of their education and its administration. The report also found that the "majority of students questioned whether the system was accomplishing its main purpose ... to induce learning. Several ... said their education ... particularly during high school years, seemed to be little more than cramming and memory work ... The most serious problem ... was the lack of necessary guidance.[138] These particular students, likely heading to postsecondary institutions, believed that they needed additional guidance from adult experts. This was not a radicalized group of adolescents.

Other students did focus on questioning and resisting teachers and administrators. Some of the school newspaper's leaders decided to sponsor a grievance bureau for those students who felt they were treated unfairly in certain circumstances. The bureau sought students who were willing to speak objectively and honestly about what they had experienced. Ultimately, they posited that the purpose of the "bureau [was] to find out whether there is injustice within the school system, and if you can help us with this research the results may also be beneficial to you."[139] The 1969 article in which this development was reported revealed a shift in tone and focus from school newspapers of the 1950s. Unquestionably, we see young people influenced by, and beginning to influence, social movements across North America. Students were coming home after school to horrific images from the Vietnam War and violent student clashes on television. As the 1960s progressed, adults were more and more scandalized by the anti-Vietnam war protests and civil rights activism of young people, with their long hair and their countercultural attacks on what they termed "the establishment."[140]

A cascade of these images flowed across television screens and newspapers on a regular basis. While it may not have been on a twenty-four-hour basis, and as ubiquitous as they would be in later decades, suburban adolescents were exposed to national and international movements around the world. The New Left, composed of a broad range of left-wing activist movements and intellectual currents, had gained prominence in western Europe and North America by these years. The 1968 uprisings, led by students, were prominent in print, on the radio, and on television screens.[141] Many of these activists chose to represent themselves as youthful as a conscious political choice—as part of broader politics in the 1960s and early 1970s.[142]

Young people fuelled much of this social consciousness, and student writings reflected an escalation of adolescent engagement with social issues in these years, given the larger unrest and the break with the past. Responding to some of the student protests in Quebec, some suburban students argued in the *Aberhart Advocate* that the "epidemic of student rebellion is only an indication of the infection that has for many years been part of the educational system ... Unless students, educators, and administrators can collectively come up with some solutions, 1968–69 may be the year of a national student rebellion. Vive l'ecole libre."[143] As with so many other issues, teens were divided on what kinds of actions could, or should, be taken.[144] This divide was reflected nationally: 43 percent of respondents in a 1968 survey thought students should "have a greater say in the running of university affairs" while 57 percent felt they should not.[145]

Many *Aberhart Advocate* articles were cryptic when it came to why student groups were seeking change. Intrepid reporters, students themselves, remained unconvinced that such groups needed to exist in suburban

Calgary and questioned their relationship to student "revolutionaries" in other countries. A 1964 article focused on the secrecy of the Student's Revolutionary Council and what it might mean to the school and the broader community. The newspaper's stance was clearly one of appeasement; it did not want there to be anything as "dreadful" as a strike, as there had been recently at another Calgary high school to protest construction noise. The writer hoped the group would "respect law and order, and not act in an unseemly fashion. Student riots have occurred in the USA; students helped to overthrow the Bolivian president; the radicals always include groups of students. It would be a pity if anything like the strike at Henry Wise Wood [High School] ever occurred again in Calgary."[146] Whether that Wise Wood group ever stuck against something more controversial than distracting construction noise was not mentioned.

Nevertheless, broader events influenced student behaviour. Regardless of residency, there were varying degrees of engagement with these issues. Unsurprisingly, the level of sophistication was uneven. Similar to many adults, some students seemed to grapple and identify with certain issues and causes. For others, this engagement was facile and superficial at most. As others have emphasized, in many ways the significance of the emerging youthful counterculture was the increased politicization of the nonpolitical.[147] Much of the idealism of the era, focused on young people, meant that important (from primarily an adult perspective) causes or social concerns—Vietnam, international coups, Indigenous issues, educational reform, women's liberation—could gain the support of young people who did not identify as political activists.[148] In Banff Trail's classrooms, the Vietnam War, educational reform, and the women's movement were discussed in several instances. Discussion of the Vietnam War held additional meaning to many, as there were some American schoolchildren who lived in the Banff Trail area and across the city in the postwar era.

At times, emotions did become heated, to the point where some teenage students needed to remove themselves from activities that were of vital importance to them. In 1969, some of the students running the school newspaper believed they could no longer continue in their duties, and the *Aberhart Advocate* was transformed into the *Lead Balloon* because of several student and administrative concerns. Students expressed grievances about several issues they faced as school newspaper contributors. Ultimately, students believed they could no longer produce a newspaper that accurately reflected their viewpoints because of the unreasonably heavy hand of the school administration. They also argued that their right to elect their own editor had been compromised, as the administration was imposing a hand-selected choice onto the newspaper staff. Finally, they argued that they had been "threatened with dissolution if we took our 'bitches' to the principal ... Viewing this and the treatment we have received ... we can no longer bring ourselves to contribute our efforts to the school paper. Therefore, we dissolve rather than sacrifice our values and self-respect to this ... institution."[149] All of this took place in the final months of 1969, and the student newspaper was relaunched in 1970. The tone of yearbooks and school newspapers did seem to reflect the broader countercultural ruptures of the late 1960s in that they questioned institutions that seemed to many in society to be increasingly unresponsive.

Some of this resistance also took the form of teenagers and older preteens experimenting with recreational drugs. It was not a universal experience, though, as several adolescents had no interest in experimenting with drugs in any form. Bruce Wilson noted a shift among his peers by the late 1960s and remarked that "things changed with the drug culture coming in. I wasn't involved in that at all. But some of your friends kind of separated apart. There was a real division by that time [at William Aberhart High School]."[150] Discussions were held across Canada and the United States on drug culture, and the legalization of marijuana was discussed by doctors in *Life* magazine. As usual, adolescents' lack of life experience as well as their developing life habits were cited as potential issues when it came to legalized drug use. Because teens were able to get cigarettes easily, the argument followed that they would have easy access to legal marijuana.[151] The same argument was made in Canada: the RCMP viewed marijuana use, within the larger drug culture, as a grave danger; increasingly visible marijuana use, they argued, would be an inevitable gateway to the use of harder drugs. They worked to develop support in the medical community for not legalizing marijuana.[152]

Increasingly, the daily newspapers also began to shift their focus from gangs and gang violence to the drug problem that parents with teenagers now faced.[153] Conferences, symposia, and discussion groups were held to address the issues, although there were no formal Canadian numbers on drug use among adolescents in this period. It is difficult to quantify use accurately, particularly illegal substance use, but as with many other adolescent issues, it seems plausible that information from US Gallup Polls also pertained to Canada. In a poll from 1969, the first year that Gallup asked Americans about drug use, only 4 percent of American adults said they had tried marijuana. Thirty-four percent said they did not know the effects of marijuana, but 43 percent thought it was used by many or some high school students.[154] As usual, in Calgary, parents were targeted as one of the major causes for a lack of education regarding drugs, despite having limited knowledge of drugs and their associated problems from an adult perspective. Several articles indicated support for "the proposition that drug problems are a symptom of failure in child-parent and child-teacher relationships."[155] The youngest suburban baby boomers, such as Tammy Simpson, described the late 1960s and early 1970s as a different time that saw some youngsters trying

> dope from the ... age of twelve. Dropping acid when we were fifteen. In high school ... things like cocaine ... I had lots of influences in the home ... that was the setting by the early 1970s that was more the norm ... We were sexually promiscuous at fifteen and sixteen. We skipped school and drove in cars when no one was licensed or insured ... A lot of kids died on motorcycles. Kids committed suicide ... died when drinking ... I wouldn't categorize us as being evil or anything like that ... This was not at all exceptional for that time.[156]

As with others, the activities within her social group were the norm. There is no evidence to suggest that all young people engaged in this kind of drug use. Most interviewees confirmed that recreational drug use was greater by the late 1960s than it had been in earlier times, yet many said that they were observers rather than participants. While young people were influenced by their peers and adults, many of them kept quite small circles of friends outside of their families, and this reality came to define their lives.

Different media can be analyzed for how these changes, both real and perceived, were traced. National Film Board (NFB) documentaries reflected these changes over time. Documentaries in the 1950s focused on community-based, adult-organized activities, featuring everything from Little League Baseball to hot rodding to majorettes; however, by the early 1970s, these documentaries were replaced by darker texts best represented by *Summer Centre* (1973), in which local property is vandalized by adolescents operating from a community recreation centre.[157] The 1950s also saw the NFB produce films on delinquency and treatment methods, but they make no mention of drugs other than alcohol.[158] This was somewhat different south of the border, where some articles focused on illegal narcotics such as heroin in major US cities and drew on discursive constructs that portrayed children as relatively innocent victims at the hands of evil-doing adult pushers, pimps, and so forth.[159]

The official reports coming from the Calgary Police Force included references to illegal substances other than alcohol and tobacco for the first time in 1970. Fourteen juveniles and ten youths were identified for glue sniffing and nail polish sniffing while twenty-three juveniles and eleven youths were identified as being involved with narcotics under the Juvenile

Delinquents Act.[160] While it is likely that other incidents had been identified prior to 1970, they were not reported in the chief of police's annual reports of the 1950s or 1960s.

Conclusion

Regardless of class, gender, race, or age, some young people exhibited a remarkable ability to resist the world around them, both in the postwar suburbs and in the wider Canadian society.[161] Young people were not isolated in hived-off suburban enclaves, oblivious to the events and issues outside of them. Their childhood and adolescent cultures emerged, in some instances, to negotiate the adult world that so influenced their lives.

The night and the darkness associated with it are often metaphors for uncertainty and danger, especially for young people. The young were part of the nighttime fabric until at least the early twentieth century; with compulsory schooling, the outlawing of child labour, curfews and so forth, being outdoors at night was no longer an accepted practice. Public spaces, particularly at night, became off limits for children and young teens.

Suburban young people participated in delinquency and petty crime, with much of it remaining unknown to the most important adults in their lives. Males were in the majority in committing crimes across Calgary and in Canada more generally. While most children and adolescents felt secure in the suburbs and in the more urban spaces of cities, for some there was always a sense that the world was not as welcoming and safe as they hoped for it to be.

Adolescents, and to a lesser degree children, resisted and rebelled in myriad ways in the postwar suburbs. Some teenagers found themselves at odds with the larger world, and experimentation with illicit drugs became increasingly common, much as it did in adult cultures by the late 1960s. Some teenagers felt no need to rebel and resist; for them, the status quo was acceptable, or there was a sense that there was not much they could do about it as a young person. On more than one occasion, oral history participants were either hesitant or unwilling to reveal illicit and delinquent activities. Their reasons were likely personal, especially for those who did not request anonymity, but demonstrate that at least some of them, quite simply, had not felt compelled to engage in these kinds of activities. It seems clear that the late 1960s were quite different than the early 1950s in terms of adolescents questioning the status quo and authority in general.

Conclusion

Calgary's postwar suburbs were vibrant spaces for young people, and there was a richness and diversity to suburban living that resists simplistic generalizing. The histories of children and adolescents are often hidden, an oversight that is addressed here directly to reveal some of what happened in a postwar Calgary suburb. Historians act like translators, as the duelling languages of the present and the past are navigated constantly. In creating histories with honesty and care, one of the biggest tensions that we inevitably deal with is in the translation work performed.[1] The children and teenagers I encountered in the archival record, and the baby boomers I engaged with in dialogue, did not agree on some things. The edges of the past remained, and it is in studying these spaces of contention that new meaning can be brought to historical work.

Researching the history of childhood is fascinating on another level, as readers can lay claim to having lived what is being re-created—something that many other historians do not have the opportunity to take advantage of in their work. Clearly, race, ethnicity, gender, and, especially, class shape both childhood and adolescence experiences to a great degree. Young people, and especially adolescents, also shaped their everyday lives through the agency they exercised throughout the postwar period. These youngsters were rarely defined by their passivity or inactivity. Children had the ability to question, subvert, and resist a postwar world influenced in many ways by adults and their ideals, values, norms, and social mores.[2] In the end, many young people had positive experiences in the postwar suburbs. Yet while postwar suburban spaces were a safe place for most young people, this was not always the case. While harm did come to some, these were nonetheless cohorts that always had a lunch, not something that can be said about all children and adolescents in Canada. These middle-class and working-class youngsters from Banff Trail were not an impoverished group, although few of them came from wealthy families either. Their relative material comfort had a profound and positive impact on everything from the organized activities they were offered, to the food they had available, to the institutions that provided them with good educations and comparatively good health care.

Suburban living has become the definitive housing choice for most North Americans since the end of the Second World War.[3] Despite some drawbacks, millions of people choose to live in suburbia, in its many forms. Additionally, by the postwar years, being young was seen as a desirable and powerful, and the number of young baby boomers was an important contributor to this representation. Children and adolescents had experiences unique to the suburban spaces in which they lived. Space and place had a profound influence on childhood experiences in the postwar suburbs, and these young people also helped shape their suburban landscapes. Focusing on Banff Trail allowed for an in-depth, detailed analysis of suburban lives, something that a multi-community study would not have provided. Important studies, from various times and based almost exclusively on experiences in central Canada, provided key comparative contexts for this research, allowing me to make linkages to other experiences and influences.

Nearly all of these postwar young people, from ages five through nineteen, went to school, played, explored, discovered, and observed in ways that were more similar than dissimilar. While there was no single experience for Canadian children during the postwar era, more was shared than was not. But nuance and care must be taken when listening to the voices of siblings who grew up in the same house and, at times, even shared a bedroom for several years. It is instructive how different the reminiscences and memories of childhood can be, even when experiences are quite similar on many levels.

This book reinforces the maxim that what defines childhood and adolescence is more a matter of human actions and choice; in other words, it is cultural rather than biological necessity.[4] While there can be no universal childhood or child, some form of childhood has marked all cultures across the globe for millennia. Adolescence is a relatively recent age category in the construction of child and adolescent development, and it varies over place and time. In fact, adolescence is not acknowledged or ritualized in many cultures around the world.[5] While adolescence is most often constructed in the West, particularly in North America, it has a biological basis as a time of emerging sexuality along with its associated physical changes.[6] It is also a time for establishing an identity and, as revealed here, a time for some to ally with peers in questioning and resisting convention.[7] There are instances when adolescence seemed to be not much more than a continuation of childhood; in other ways, there were profound changes in the lives of adolescents as they aged and matured.

Childhood memory and nostalgia are often linked to place, and for most young people the family home serves as an anchor for memories associated with these early years. Childhood spaces and places significantly

shaped the lives of children and adolescents, both individually and collectively. For most young people, where they lived was critical to developing
a sense of identity; homescapes had a profound effect on them, both at the
time and as they aged as adults. For many, suburban childhoods were
not perceived to be alienating and unfulfilling. Instead, these years were
marked by discovery, freedom, and, occasionally, danger. The postwar suburban space, especially in its infancy, offered much more than calm and
peace. Postwar suburbia has been imagined and reimagined in the decades
since, by residents, guests, casual observers, and determined critics. It has
served as a site of countless promises (realized and unfulfilled), hopes, and,
for some, fantasies.[8]

Oral histories, which provided so much information on major themes,
were related with candour. Like other oral history practitioners, I am aware
that memories likely contain multiple histories and have been reconstituted on more than one occasion. Much of what people told me was positive,
and a narrative was ultimately constructed using a snowballing technique
based on grounded theory. Most participants were enthusiastic and articu-
late, and they were proud of their childhoods, many of which were shaped
by their relatively positive experience in postwar suburbia. While some
negative and violent aspects of their everyday lives were mentioned, the
interviewees chose what they shared. They possessed a degree of agency
as research participants, even if the balance of power resided elsewhere.[9]

We must remain mindful of the fact that orality also infuses the texture
of the "official" written record.[10] Meeting minutes and first-hand accounts
of events, even when written and recorded, are inherently oral. They are
also mediated. This reinforces our importance as historians, as translators, interpreters, critics, and compilers of knowledge. In the broadest context, participants' personal stories shine a light on the collective material
culture produced by postwar young people.[11] Textual sources, particularly
those created by parents, administrators, educationists, professionals, and
volunteers, demonstrated time and time again that children and adolescents needed to be monitored, regulated, and moulded into industrious,
conscientious, efficient, positive, productive, and law-abiding citizens. Yet
the writings that young people produced, and what many interviewees
said, emphasized that they had the ability to negotiate with these important influences. While this agency should not be conflated with power, it
did result in them being much more than passive receptacles, incapable of
responding to a world dominated by adults.

It was the adults within their suburban community who had the
greatest influence on their young lives. For youngsters, a deep sense of
community, imagined or romanticized in some ways now, was rooted in

place in the postwar era. Home space was critical in that bedrooms served as an important separator between childhood and adolescence, as teenagers increasingly had their own rooms by the late 1960s,[12] whereas young children often shared bedroom spaces, even across gender lines. This was important for teens in that it helped to shape their identity as something more than a child, if not yet full adults. While they carved out their own childhood spaces meant for them exclusively, children were engaged in their community. They were aware of the adult world that they stepped into out of necessity. For some critics, this waned in later years, as increasingly sheltered young people, islanded from the adult world, experience problems in older teenagehood and afterwards.[13]

Beyond their homes, postwar students spent countless hours in schools. At times, particularly as adolescents, young people spent more of their waking hours in school than in their family homes. We have seen that the classroom experience reflected and refracted the ever-present adult threats of the 1950s and 1960s, particularly the Cold War. Clearly, not only the Cold War but also both world wars continued to influence young lives through stories, images, and representations. From the perspective of childhood and adolescence, the 1950s and 1960s were "postwar" in name only to suburban young people.

Even though young people may not have been aware of it, social class remained an important determinant in their everyday lives. While race, gender, and ethnicity cannot be discounted as important influences, class is invariably linked to health and health care, family status, education, work, and sports and recreation activities in childhood across all temporal periods.[14] Social class also shaped child-rearing practices and the amount of time that children and adolescents were able to spend with their parents. There was a degree of homogeneity that led many young people to not recognize class; class lines were blurred culturally in that middle-class and working-class young people attended the same schools, played similar sports, engaged in the same activities, and had comparatively similar homes in some suburbs. While the structural relations of class may be a social reality, how we view or interpret them, if at all as children, differs given the historical context; a certain sensibility about the importance of class may be ideologically obscured or glossed over for many reasons. Much like the focus on race should not be only on people of colour, attention to class does not simply mean focusing on working-class children. We need to understand the complex relations of class at all levels of society, both as a structural reality and how people did—or did not—interpret their relations with other classes. Ultimately, these young suburbanites lived comparatively healthy, safe, and comfortable postwar lives.

Although young people often experienced class relations with little or no conscious recognition of them, their material surroundings and class relations had a profound influence on their everyday lives. Paying attention to gender difference and power relations also highlighted that girls experienced their suburban lives quite distinctly from boys. Drawing on social-regulation conceptions of power, as something productive that yielded behaviours and events, helped to explain opportunities for resistance by children and adolescents.

Although there was increasing leisure time in the 1950s and 1960s, suburban children and adolescents also worked. While some participants were indifferent to the paid and unpaid work they did as children and adolescents, much of it at home, many of them explored how their work contributed to their changing sense of identity as adolescents. It was not a carefree childhood or adolescence, but young lives were no longer defined mainly by long working hours, regardless of place of residence.

Neither children nor adolescents seemed aware of the privilege associated with the "whiteness" that marked Banff Trail, as it did in many postwar Canadian suburbs. Race was a rare topic of conversation in the 1950s among young people, although by the late 1960s it was discussed increasingly, mainly in the context of the civil rights movement in the United States. In the 1960s, nearly 70 percent of Calgarians identified their ethnic origins as either British or German.[15]

Both class and gender helped to shape childhood and adolescence in terms of leisure, recreation, and play. While sports and recreation were important elements in the lives of countless children and adolescents, this was not the case for all. This is where an important distinction between childhood and adolescence can be made; most children had limited say in what organized activities they undertook, whereas adolescents expressed their hopes and desires to a much greater degree. Childhood play, in its many forms, remains the key way that children express themselves individually and through their childhood cultures. In the postwar period, activities were increasingly organized and formalized, despite participants discussing how much they enjoyed leisure time that they, and not adults, had organized as youngsters. Even though the postwar suburban experience was often characterized as generic and planned, most young people seemed to find both time and the space(s) to enjoy and roam their community and larger areas, both on foot, by bike, and, later, if they had the means, in cars.

Boyhood and girlhood experiences and representations were quite distinct throughout this era, reflecting idealized postwar adult gender roles that promoted women as passive, inactive, and working inside in the home. The idealized suburban father was active, worked outside the home and spent his leisure time outdoors, action-oriented, and the sole breadwinner. National polling reflected the primacy of fathers in families: a 1966 Gallup Poll saw 65 percent of Canadians agree with a statement "fathers should be top boss of the family in this country."[16] Some of this began to be challenged by people of all ages as the 1960s wore on, although these roles remained dominant throughout the period. Within the context of the advice and recommendations of influential experts, such as nurses, doctors, psychologists, and social workers, the health and wellness of young people also came into sharper focus and took greater hold of institutions such as schools and families by the early 1970s. Class mattered to the health of young people. Their health improved drastically in this period owing to numerous scientific advances, better access to physicians, vaccinations, health care, and so forth. Working- and middle-class children and adolescents in Banff Trail were obvious beneficiaries of these advancements.

Letting go of the belief that children, and especially girls, necessarily acquire greater power or autonomy and independence as they age is the key to understanding the complex and often untidy shift to adolescence in these years. By the end of the 1960s, the topic of sexual education for teenagers had entered Canadian society's mainstream flow of information, and the tone of the "official" message changed quite decidedly in terms of its frankness. A very real shift in pedagogy occurred. However, informal sexual education remained the primary way that both males and females explored emerging sexualities.

While relatively safe, suburban adolescence could also be marked by crime, delinquency, and, at times, disturbing violence. Many young suburbanites felt secure and comfortable, but for others there was a belief that the world was not the peaceful place that it was made out to be by older people. Young people resisted and rebelled in several ways in Banff Trail, as they did in the broader Canadian youth culture. The social turmoil that defined the late 1960s in Canada had a huge influence in this regard. At times adolescents were at odds with the larger world, but experimentation with alcohol, illicit recreational drugs, and so forth became increasingly common, much as it did in adult cultures by the late 1960s and early 1970s. Clearly, young people were not cocooned in isolated suburban enclaves, unaware of larger events and issues outside them. In a related vein, males were the main perpetrators in committing various crimes or acts of "juvenile delinquency" across Calgary and elsewhere in Canada. This gendered difference has been the case since record keeping began in Canada, yet there were circumstances when young females were involved in these activities.

It is fascinating to research and write about analytical categories in an era that so many people can claim at least a slice of knowledge about based on the experiences, memories, and myths they carry with them. It is exhilarating, humbling, and daunting all at the same time. My primary task has been to try to better understand postwar suburbia in Canada through the viewfinder of childhood and adolescence, to explore it critically and in a meaningful way. The children of that time have begun to grey, yet this era seems to stand still in many ways. So many of us think of it as an idyllic time when unending hope and prosperity went hand in hand for most. These oversimplifications do not capture the nuances and subtleties of these times. It was both a complicated and a complex era, enriched by the people of all ages who shaped it. In tracing what some of our youngest citizens contributed to that history, it became clear that writing history entails tremendous simplification and a compacting of what has come before. Yet even if we don't get everything "right," surely the found meanings make us better able to understand how we might continue to strive to make society more equitable today. A life without hope for better times for all, and especially for our children, is not one that any of us should wish to live.

No study is exhaustive, and there were several themes and topics that were merely raised or not explored in any great depth. An entire monograph could be devoted to children's health and wellness in this era. Mental health and bullying received cursory treatment, and those topics, in an historical context, certainly deserve much more attention from academics. Because of the obesity and inactivity epidemic that we are currently dealing with in North America, understanding what was going on in these relatively active times for young people may provide us with ideas to help ease the health problems associated with a sedentary lifestyle. Spirituality and religious beliefs remained vital in many young lives in the 1950s and 1960s, despite increasing secularization across North America. More study needs to be done on these topics through the lens of childhood and adolescence. Many of these childhood lives extended into the early 1970s, and the archival record and oral histories revealed significant shifts in childhood and adolescence by the early 1970s.[17] In the end, I was unable to explore the 1970s in any sustained way, as they fell outside the bounds of this study. That topic needs to happen in the context of a broader childhood history. Another fruitful area of study will be linking baby boomer childhoods to aging. This influential cohort has continued to grab headlines into the new millennium, and the first retirees are now approaching their early 1970s. The boomers will once again need society's help in very real ways, and understanding their life course in a more meaningful way will help all of us as we navigate our own lives. Finally, more transnational studies of suburbia and its intersections with young people are needed. While I linked the American experience to Calgary and Canada as much as I could,

Asia and Europe could provide some relevant material, as the suburbs are an important part of many young people's lives on those continents.

The influential urbanist Jane Jacobs was right in speaking about the importance of community and neighbourhood and their ability to effect positive change by resisting the worst aspects of unchecked "progress" in the 1950s and the early 1960s. National polling reflected some of Jacobs' optimism. A 1959 Gallup Poll asked Canadians to think about the world in ten years' time and "if it will be a better place to live in that it is now, not so good, or just about the same?" More than 50 percent believed it would be better while just 16 percent thought it would be "not so good."[18] Contrary to what some will try to convince us, people do care about one another, particularly when relationships are personalized and we feel we have a vested interest in one another's lives. One of the best measures of a community, of any size, is how it treats its youngest, most vulnerable members as well as the wisest members, who are among the aged. Many, if not all of us, carry a lifelong attachment to our childhood communities.

If we are not young now, we once were. This undeniable fact cannot and should not be forgotten. Young people offer hope and promise. They represent an ongoing state of becoming. We are all richer if young people are valued, respected, and consulted as important members of a compassionate and caring social group that seeks to erase the acute inequalities that continue to plague Canada in so many ways.

Appendices

Appendix 1: Interview Questions for Research Participants

1. In which community did you grow up?
2. Please describe your neighbourhood/community as you remember it from your childhood. Do you think this view has changed over time?
3. Please describe both the exterior and interior of your home.
4. Can you describe your room to me? Did you share it with any siblings?
5. Was your suburban home your first home? If not, do you remember other places of residence before? Did you move elsewhere afterwards? If yes, where?
6. Where did you attend school as a child? What do you remember the most about your years in school?
7. What school-related activities did you participate in as a child and youth?
8. When, if at all, do you remember breaking the rules in any setting, whether it was at home, in school, in the streets, or anywhere else?
9. Did your parents/guardians work outside the home? If so, what did they do?
10. How was housework handled in your home?
11. Did you do any paid work as a child or youth? What did you do with earned wages?
12. When did you start working? How did you find this work?
13. Did you travel to do this work? If yes, how did you do this?
14. What kind of work did you engage in, inside your home? Did you have regular tasks? Were they recognized or rewarded in any way?
15. Do you recall your siblings or friends working both outside and/or inside the home? What did they do?
16. Can you talk about how your family, and in particular your parents, shaped your childhood?
17. How did your friends and siblings contribute to this as well?
18. Do you feel that your parents, siblings, or friends had the most influence on your childhood or youth? How was the influence exercised?
19. What sports, recreational, and leisure activities did you, siblings, or friends engage in? Did these activities take place in your community in which you lived or elsewhere?

20. Were the roles of boys and girls a topic of discussion at home, at school, and in popular culture? When and where did you first experience sex education?

21. Do you recall discussing these topics with friends, siblings, parents, or teachers?

22. What did you enjoy doing in your spare time? Do you remember participating in any specific evening or nighttime activities?

23. Was there a diversity of "race" and "ethnicity" in your neighbourhood? How about in the larger city? As a child/youth do you remember how *race* and *ethnicity* were defined and by whom or what institutions?

24. Do you recall discussing the Great Depression as a child and/or youth? With whom and where did you have these discussions?

25. What do you recall about the Second World War and how it impacted your childhood? Do you recall discussing it during this time?

26. What did the terms *Soviet Union, A-Bomb,* and *communism* mean to you, if anything at all, as a child and/or youth?

27. Did you spend any time shopping in Calgary? Where did you do this, and who did you go with?

28. How was your health as a child? Do you recall being injured or sick? Can you remember how you felt about injury and/or sickness as a child and/or as a youth?

29. How would you describe the health of other family members, friends, and community members during your childhood?

30. Do you remember discussing health, diet, weight, and exercise as a child? Where and with whom did you discuss this?

31. Did you spend time in the streets of your community, in the parks, or in nearby spaces?

32. How did you perceive your community and other community members as a child? How would you characterize them from an adult perspective?

33. Have you ever lived in a suburban community since leaving your childhood? If you have, how would you describe your suburban home?

34. Do you recall any negative aspects of your childhood experiences? What was your favourite part of your childhood?

Appendix 2: Basic Demographic Information of Interviewees

Interviewee	Birth Date	Death Date	Sex
1	1952	N.D.	M
2	1955	N.D.	M
3	1954	N.D.	M
4	1961	N.D.	M
5	1957	N.D.	F
6	1958	N.D.	F
7	1963	N.D.	F
8	1964	N.D.	F
9	N.A.	N.D.	F
10	1953	N.D.	F
11	1949	N.D.	M
12	1960	N.D.	M
13	1946	N.D.	F
14	1959	N.D.	M
15	1960	N.D.	F
16	1960	N.D.	M
17	1962	N.D.	F
18	1961	N.D.	F

Appendix 3: Information Regarding Interview Protocols

All interviews were audio recorded digitally and transcribed later for analysis by the author, James Onusko. Interviewees were able to decline answering any questions during the interview, end the interview, or withdraw from participation while the initial writing was completed. Interviewees agreed that gathered information would be used as part of the PhD dissertation and future publications. All interviewees were given the choice to remain anonymous or to have their names used. The interviewees were all given the opportunity to review their interviews in audio format and asked to submit any changes to their responses at that time. There were no interviewees who submitted changes following review.

NOTES

INTRODUCTION

1 Canadian Gallup Poll, November 1959, no. 279, "Country Achieved Most in Decade," question 5.

2 Stephanie Coontz, *The Way We Never Were: American Families and the Nostalgia Trap* (New York: Basic Books, 2016), 22.

3 Bill Bryson, *The Life and Times of the Thunderbolt Kid* (New York: Broadway Books, 2006), 12.

4 While there has been ongoing debate about this, negative views of the suburbs continue to influence both popular and academic authors. See William M. Dobriner, *Class in Suburbia* (Englewood Cliffs, NJ: Prentice-Hall, 1963); S.D. Clark, *The Suburban Society* (Toronto: University of Toronto Press, 1966); Scott Donaldson, *The Suburban Myth* (New York: Columbia University Press, 1969); Kenneth T. Jackson, *Crabgrass Frontier: The Suburbanization of the United States* (New York: Oxford University Press, 1985); Jane Jacobs, *The Death and Life of Great American Cities,* 2nd ed. (New York: Vintage Books, 1992); Mark Clapson, *Suburban Century: Social Change and Urban Growth in England and the United States* (New York: Berg, 2003); Dolores Hayden, *Building Suburbia: Green Fields and Urban Growth, 1820–2000* (New York: Pantheon, 2003); Setha Low, *Behind the Gates: Life, Security, and the Pursuit of Happiness in Fortress America* (New York: Routledge, 2003); Richard Harris, *Creeping Conformity: How Canada Became Suburban, 1900–1960* (Toronto: University of Toronto Press, 2004); Robert M. Fogelson, *Bourgeois Nightmares: Suburbia, 1870–1930* (New Haven, CT: Yale University Press, 2005).

5 For further reading on alternative views of childhood, youth, and families in this era, see Coontz, *The Way We Never Were*; Mary Louise Adams, *The Trouble with Normal: Postwar Youth and the Making of Heterosexuality* (Toronto: University of Toronto Press, 1997); Mona Gleason, *Normalizing the Ideal: Psychology, Schooling and the Family in Postwar Canada* (Toronto: University of Toronto, 1999); Elise Chenier, *Strangers in Our Midst: Sexual Deviancy in Postwar Ontario* (Toronto: University of Toronto Press, 2008).

6 Sinclair Lewis's *Babbitt*, published in 1922, was likely the first novel to satirize the suburbs. Without question, Malvina Reynolds's song "Little Boxes" represented a popular position on suburbia in the United States for many (and, for some, in Canada) and continues to do so. It also served as the opening theme song for HBO's *Weeds,* a recent television series that explores contemporary life in the suburbs.

7 Harris, *Creeping Conformity*, 6, 15; Clapson, *Suburban Century*, 9, 10; Kevin M. Kruse and Thomas J. Sugrue, eds., *The New Suburban History* (Chicago: University of Chicago Press, 2006), 1–2.

8   Family sizes did increase during this time, and more women, in terms of percentages, were giving birth compared to the Great Depression and wartime years.

9   Doug Owram, *Born at the Right Time: A History of the Baby Boom Generation* (Toronto: University of Toronto Press, 1996). Owram argues throughout his book that this generation was and is powerful, influential, and distinct from previous generations. He also argues that, increasingly, families had much less influence than peer groups in this period. From the perspective of many pre- and early adolescents, the peer group had much less influence than siblings and families.

10 All historians of childhood in Canada are indebted to the work of preceding historians. For foundational readings, see Neil Sutherland, *Children in English-Canadian Society: Framing the Twentieth-Century Consensus* (Toronto: University of Toronto Press, 1976), and *Growing Up: Childhood in English Canada from the Great War to the Age of Television* (Toronto: University of Toronto Press, 1997); Joy Parr, ed., *Childhood and Family in Canadian History* (Toronto: McClelland and Stewart, 1982); Gleason, *Normalizing the Ideal*; Nancy Janovicek and Joy Parr, eds., *Histories of Canadian Children and Youth* (Toronto: Oxford University Press, 2003); Cynthia Comacchio, *The Dominion of Youth: Adolescence and the Making of Modern Canada* (Waterloo: Wilfrid Laurier University Press, 2006).

11 The only book to focus exclusively on this period in Calgary is Robert Stamp, *Suburban Modern: Postwar Dreams in Calgary* (Victoria: Touchwood Editions, 2004).

12 The two most cited contemporary studies related to postwar suburbs are John R. Seeley, R. Alexander Sim, and E.W. Loosley, *Crestwood Heights: A Study of the Culture of Suburban Life* (Toronto: University of Toronto Press, 1963); Clark, *The Suburban Society*.

13 Stamp, *Suburban Modern,* 85, 95, and 121; Harris, *Creeping Conformity,* 11, 168, 169; and Jackson, *Crabgrass Frontier,* 243–45, 259.

14 Not all will agree on this usage, but this is the time period I am referencing when I use the terms *modern* and *modernity* throughout this book. For further discussion, see Marshall Berman, *All That Is Solid Melts into Air: The Experience of Modernity* (Brooklyn, NY: Verso Press, 1983); Anthony Giddens, *Modernity and Self-Identity: Self and Society in the Late Modern Age* (Redwood City, CA: Stanford University Press, 1991); Keith Walden, *Becoming Modern in Toronto: The Industrial Exhibition and the Shaping of Late Victorian Toronto Culture* (Toronto: University of Toronto Press, 1997).

15 Dr. Benjamin Spock's *The Common Sense Book of Baby and Child Care* has sold millions of copies and continues to influence many parents. First published in 1946, it epitomizes the shift by many to seek expert advice in all aspects of children's lives.

16 Interestingly, as I broached the topic of the Second World War with interviewees, a surprisingly high number of them had recollections of stories about the First World War from great-grandparents and grandparents. In certain instances, both wars were mentioned, but in a few discussions it was the First World War that remained with them. For a good discussion of parenting in this period, see Mary Ann Mason, "Whose Child? Parenting and Custody in the Postwar Period," in *Reinventing Childhood After World War II*, ed. Paula S. Fass and Michael Grossberg (Philadelphia: University of Pennsylvania Press, 2012).

17 See Bryan D. Palmer, *Canada's 1960s: The Ironies of Identity in a Rebellious Era* (Toronto: University of Toronto Press, 2009).

18   For discussion of age categories, see Howard P. Chudacoff, *Children at Play: An American History* (New York: New York University Press, 2007), xv. In discussing prairie farm children, the author defines them as between the ages of four and sixteen: Sandra Rollings-Magnusson, *Heavy Burdens on Small Shoulders: The Labour of Pioneer Children on the Canadian Prairies* (Edmonton: University of Alberta Press, 2009), 11.

19   Philippe Ariès, *Centuries of Childhood* (New York: Vintage, 1962).

20   For further reading on this point, see Anthony Volk, "The Evolution of Childhood," *Journal of the History of Childhood and Youth* 4, no. 3 (Fall 2011): 470–94.

21   Robert McIntosh, "Constructing the Child: New Approaches to the History of Childhood in Canada," *Acadiensis* 28, no. 2 (Spring 1999): 127.

22   Paula S. Fass and Michael Grossberg, eds., *Reinventing Childhood after World War II* (Philadelphia: University of Pennsylvania Press, 2012), ix.

23   Sutherland, *Children in English-Canadian Society.*

24   Comacchio, *The Dominion of Youth*. For the American context, see Howard P. Chudacoff, *How Old Are You? Age Consciousness in American Culture* (Princeton, NJ: Princeton University Press, 1992).

25   Veronica Strong-Boag, "Home Dreams: Women and the Suburban Experiment in Canada, 1945–60," *Canadian Historical Review* 72, no. 4 (1991): 471–504.

26   Marta Gutman and Ning de Coninck-Smith, eds., *Designing Modern Childhoods: History, Space and the Material Culture of Childhood* (Piscataway, NJ: Rutgers University Press, 2008), 2–4.

27   Steven Mintz, *Huck's Raft: A History of American Childhood* (Cambridge, MA: Belknap Press, 2005), ix.

28   For further reading, see Joan Sangster, *Transforming Labour: Women and Work in Postwar Canada* (Toronto: University of Toronto Press, 2010), and *Earning Respect: The Lives of Working Women in Small-Town Ontario, 1920–1960* (Toronto: University of Toronto Press, 1995).

29   Cecilia Benoit, *Women, Work and Social Rights: Canada in Historical and Comparative Perspective* (Scarborough, ON: Prentice Hall Canada, 2000).

30   Rosemary Hennessy and Chrys Ingraham, *Materialist Feminism: A Reader in Class, Difference, and Women's Lives* (New York: Routledge, 1997), 1.

31   Ibid., 2.

32   Gleason, "Disciplining the Student Body," 189–215, and *Normalizing the Ideal.*

33   Donald A. Ritchie, *Doing Oral History* (Toronto: Oxford University Press, 2015), 19.

34   Lynn Abrams, *Oral History Theory* (Toronto: Routledge, 2010), 86.

35   Robert Perks and Alistair Thomson, eds., *The Oral History Reader* (New York: Routledge, 2016), 3.

36   Abrams, *Oral History Theory,* 86.

37   Alessandro Portelli, "What Makes Oral History Different?," in Perks and Thomson, *The Oral History Reader,* 53.

38   Ibid., 87.

39   For further reading on oral history scripts associated with childhood, see Sutherland, *Growing Up,* 10 and 11.

40   Abrams, *Oral History Theory,* 83.

41   Ibid.

42   Alessandro Portelli, *The Death of Luigi Trastulli and Other Stories* (Albany: State University of New York Press, 1991), 2.

43   Ibid., 5.

44   Joan Sangster, "Telling Our Stories: Feminist Debates and the Use of Oral History," *Women's History Review* 3, no. 1 (1994): 5–28.

45   For further discussion of postwar fatherhood, families, and childhood based on a series of oral histories, see Robert Rutherdale, "Just Nostalgic Family Men? Off-the-Job Family Time, Providing, and Oral Histories of Fatherhood in Postwar Canada, 1945–1975," *Oral History Forum* 29 (2009): 1–25.

46   Ibid.

47   Michael Frisch, *A Shared Authority: Essays in the Craft and Meaning of Oral and Public History* (Albany: State University of New York Press, 1990).

48   There may be no group of children who can claim more of a school's lasting impact than the Indigenous students who attended residential schools for decades. While outside the bounds of this book, for further reading, see Aimee Craft, *A Knock on the Door: The Essential History of Residential Schools from the Truth and Reconciliation Commission of Canada* (Winnipeg: University of Manitoba Press, 2015); J.R. Miller, *Shingwauk's Vision: A History of Native Residential Schools* (Toronto: University of Toronto Press, 1996); John Milloy, *A National Crime: The Canadian Government and the Residential School System, 1879–1986* (Winnipeg: University of Manitoba Press, 1999).

49   Intersections between race and labour have been examined critically by several scholars. See Kay J. Anderson, *Vancouver's Chinatown: Racial Discourse in Canada, 1875–1980* (Montreal/Kingston: McGill-Queen's University Press, 1991); and Vic Satzewich, *Racism and the Incorporation of Foreign Labour* (New York: Routledge, 1991).

CHAPTER 1: Mapping Suburbia

1   Marta Gutman, "The Physical Spaces of Childhood," in *The Routledge History of Childhood in the Western World,* ed. Paula S. Fass (New York: Routledge, 2015), 249.

2   For further discussion, see Miguel Sicart, *Play Matters* (Cambridge, MA: MIT Press, 2014), 51.

3   John R. Gillis, "Epilogue: The Islanding of Children-Reshaping the Mythical Landscapes of Childhood," in *Designing Modern Childhoods: History, Space, and the Material Culture of Children,* ed. Marta Gutman and Ning de Coninck-Smith (New Brunswick, NJ: Rutgers University Press, 2008), 319; and Simon Sleight, *Young People and the Shaping of Public Space in Melbourne, 1870–1914* (Farnham: Ashgate, 2013).

4   Gutman, "The Physical Spaces of Childhood," 249.

5   Ibid., 250.

6   Gillis, "Epilogue," 317.

7   Kenneth T. Jackson, *Crabgrass Frontier: The Suburbanization of the United States* (Toronto: Oxford University Press, 1987), 5.

8   As historical geographer Richard Harris has argued, independent political status as a marker for suburbs has not been a requisite to the same degree in Canada as it has been in the United States. For further reading on the political orientation of Canadian suburbs, see Harris, *Creeping Conformity: How Canada Became Suburban, 1900–1960* (Toronto: University of Toronto Press, 2004), 22. For an American context, see Kevin M. Kruse and Thomas J. Sugrue, eds., *The New Suburban History* (Chicago: University of Chicago Press, 2006), 6–9.

9   Harris, *Creeping Conformity*, 99–102.

10   Jackson, *Crabgrass Frontier*, 25.

11   John C. Bacher, *Keeping to the Marketplace* (Montreal/Kingston: McGill-Queen's University Press, 1993), 268.

12   There was a near universal sentiment against cities from intellectuals, and many artists took to the romanticized rural lifestyle to find meaning in life. Physical health was tied to questions of social, moral, and intellectual health. For further reading, see John Sewell, *The Shape of the City: Toronto Struggles with Modern Planning* (Toronto: University of Toronto Press, 1993), 4–5, 10.

13   Richard Harris and Michael E. Mercier, "How Healthy Were the Suburbs?," *Journal of Urban History* 31, no. 6 (September 2005): 773.

14   Ibid., 785.

15   For further reading, see Harris, *Creeping Conformity*.

16   Mark Clapson, *Suburban Century: Social Change and Urban Growth in England and the United States* (New York: Berg, 2003), 29.

17   Toronto and Montreal did develop extensive streetcar systems. To a lesser extent, so did Halifax, Hamilton, Saint John, and Winnipeg, although not concurrently. Calgary had a more modest system, but, nevertheless, it did have one. For further reading, see Colin K. Hatcher and Tom Schwarzkopf, *Calgary's Electric Transit* (Montreal: Railfare DC Books, 2009).

18   Harris, *Creeping Conformity*, 42.

19   Richard Harris, *Unplanned Suburbs: Toronto's American Tragedy, 1900 to 1950* (Baltimore, MD: Johns Hopkins University Press, 1996), 8.

20   Suzanne Morton, *Ideal Surroundings: Domestic Life in a Working-Class Suburb in the 1920s* (Toronto: University of Toronto Press, 1995), 152.

21   Ibid., 7.

22   Ibid., 154. This was not exclusive to Atlantic Canada, as these broad changes were experienced, in some form, across the country.

23   Harris, *Creeping Conformity*, 106. In Toronto specifically there were some basic housing standards implemented, and this also contributed to owner-builders choosing the suburbs, which offered little in services but lower taxes and the ability to build more or less as wished. For further reading, see Harris, *Unplanned Suburbs*, 167.

24   Max Foran, *Calgary: An Illustrated History* (Toronto: James Lorimer, 1978), 90.

25   Ibid., 98.

26   Richard A. Baine, *Calgary: An Urban Study* (Vancouver: Clarke, Irwin, 1973), 27.

27   Calgary is divided into four quadrants based on Centre Street and Centre Avenue in the downtown core. The four quadrants are northwest, northeast, southwest, and southeast. All addresses continue to carry this designation following the street address.

28   Bob Shiels, *Calgary* (Calgary: Calgary Herald, 1974), 108. The Banff Trail community fits this description well, as the city annexed a lot of land in this period, and although there was significant growth, the anticipated boom did not sustain itself for several decades.

29   Donald George Harasym, "The Planning of New Residential Areas in Calgary" (masters thesis, University of Alberta, 1975), 38.

30   "Distinguished London Engineer Talks of the City Beautiful and Deplores Narrowness of Streets," *The Albertan*, 15 April 1918.

31   Shiels, *Calgary*, 101.

32   Chris Campbell, "Parks Have Rich History," *The Calgary Herald,* 14 March 1985.

33   City of Calgary, *Calgary: Celebrating 100 Years of Parks* (Calgary: City of Calgary, 2010), 59.

34   According to the 2001 federal census, nearly half of urban dwellers lived in low-density neighbourhoods, typical of post-Second World War suburbs in Canada. See Martin Turcotte, "The City-Suburb Contrast: How Can We Measure It?," Statistics Canada, http://www.statcan.gc.ca/pub/11–008-x/2008001/article/x10459-eng.htm

35   "Population, Urban and Rural, by Province and Territory," Statistics Canada, https://www150.statcan.gc.ca/n1/pub/11-516-x/sectiona/4147436-eng.htm#1. By the 2006 census, over 80 percent of Canadians lived in urban centres, and by most estimates nearly half of these urban dwellers lived in suburbs. In the United States, this percentage was likely higher.

36   Calgary's population grew from 104,718 in 1950 to 235,428 in 1960 to 385,436 in 1970. Calgary's area in square miles grew from 39.6 in 1950 to 75.8 in 1960 to 157 in 1974. For further information, see City of Calgary, *Municipal Manual* (Calgary: City of Calgary, 1950, 1960, 1970).

37   Hugh Dempsey, *Calgary: Spirit of the West* (Calgary: Glenbow and First House, 1994), 131.

38   For a better understanding of "lived" experiences in space and the belief that geographical space can be fundamentally social, see Henri Lefebvre, *The Production of Space* (New York: Wiley-Blackwell, 1992).

39   Harris, *Creeping Conformity,* 49.

40   Carol and Elmer Haggerty, in Rose Scollard, ed., *From Prairie Grass to City Sidewalks* (Calgary: Banff Trail Community Seniors, 1999), 12.

41   Maxine L. Mills, in ibid., 13.

42   Gwen Smith, interview, n.d., "Calgary in the early 1960s," *Stories From the Archives*, Glenbow Museum Archives. The sub-section was "Calgary in the early 1960s," accessed 15 March 2018.

43   Sociologist S.D. Clark noted that in Toronto postwar immigration and the rising birthrate were the main reasons for these large increases in population, and all indicators are that this was the same in other parts of North America. For further reading, see Clark, *The Suburban Society* (Toronto: University of Toronto Press, 1966), 31.

44   Sewell, *The Shape of the City*, 80.

45   Ibid., 80–88.

46   There are a number of books focusing on Levittown and its social, economic, and cultural impacts. For further reading on Levittown from two well-written but opposing viewpoints, see David Kushner, *Levittown: Two Families, One Tycoon and the Fight for Civil Rights in America's Legendary Suburb* (New York: Walker and Company, 2009); and Herbert J. Gans, *The Levittowners: Ways of Life and Politics in a New Suburban Community* (New York: Pantheon Books, 1967).

47   Clark, *The Suburban Society*, 48.

48   Ibid., 68.

49   Gordon and Shirley Fox, in Scollard, *From Prairie Grass to City Sidewalks*, 11.

50   Richard Harris notes in several places in *Creeping Conformity* that community is typically centred on children—most of the participants for this study mentioned that their parents' choices often reflected the desire to find a good neighbourhood to raise them.

51   In suburbs outside of Toronto, for instance, the new postwar communities could
     be much more than six miles away from the downtown core and not accessible to
     younger children by foot or bicycle. By contrast, in cities such as Calgary, where
     suburban development oftentimes occurred within established annexed city lim-
     its, these suburbs, while on the edge of a smaller city, might be only two to three
     miles from the downtown core.

52   Shiels, *Calgary*, 196.

53   Harold Coward, *Calgary's Growth: Bane or Boon?* (Calgary: University of Calgary
     Institute for the Humanities, 1981), 59.

54   Harasym, "The Planning of New Residential Areas in Calgary," 3.

55   Ibid., 4.

56   For further reading, see Calgary Police Force, annual reports, 1950–70, available
     at Calgary Police Service Archives. I discuss this further in the section on street-
     scapes in Calgary.

57   Harasym, "The Planning of New Residential Areas in Calgary," 57.

58   Wayne K.D. Davies and Ivan J. Townshend, "How Do Community Associations
     Vary? The Structure of Community Associations in Calgary, Alberta," *Urban
     Studies* 31, no. 10 (1994): 1743.

59   Robert Stamp, *Suburban Modern: Postwar Dreams in Calgary* (Victoria: Touch-
     wood, 2004), 87.

60   Ibid., 132. During this early phase, they built on more than fifteen hundred lots
     and worked in other Calgary quadrants, according to Stamp's research.

61   City of Calgary, *Calgary*, 65.

62   Alberta, *Report of the Royal Commission on the Metropolitan Development of Cal-
     gary and Edmonton* (Edmonton: Province of Alberta, 1956).

63   City of Calgary, *Motel Village/Banff Trail Area Redevelopment Plan: Northwest
     LRT Alignment Evaluation Study* (Calgary: City of Calgary, 1984), 19, available
     in the City of Calgary Archives.

64   Historian Dolores Hayden also notes that industrial and commercial spaces with
     significant square footage have also defined many North American suburbs: see
     Building Suburbia: Green Fields and Urban Growth, 1820–2000 (New York: Pan-
     theon, 2003), 3.

65   Jackson, *Crabgrass Frontier*, 259.

66   Gutman, "The Physical Spaces of Childhood," 249.

67   Tim Cresswell, *Place: A Short Introduction* (Toronto: Wiley-Blackwell, 2014).

68   Ibid.

69   For one of the best representations, if somewhat exaggerated, see the main neigh-
     bourhood in *Edward Scissorhands*, directed by Tim Burton (Los Angeles: Twenti-
     eth Century Fox, 1990).

70   Stamp, *Suburban Modern*, 92.

71   Doug Cass, personal interview, Cochrane, AB, 2 June 2011.

72   Rosalynn Baxandall and Elizabeth Ewen, *Picture Windows: How the Suburbs
     Happened* (New York: Basic Books, 2000), 164.

73   Lesley Hayes, personal interview, Calgary, AB, 26 July 2011.

74   Brian Rutz, telephone interview, Peterborough, ON, 12 December 2011.

75   Elizabeth Davidson, telephone interview, Peterborough, ON, 11 November 2011.

76   Jim Farquharson, personal interview, Calgary, AB, 17 December 2011.

77   William Wright, telephone interview, Peterborough, ON, 4 November 2011.

78 Frank Edward, telephone interview, Peterborough, ON, 8 December 2011.

79 For a very good exploration of American teenage bedrooms, see Jason Reid, "'My Room, Private! Keep Out! This Means You!': Brief Overview of the Emergence of the Autonomous Teen Bedroom in Post-World War II America," *Journal of the History of Childhood and Youth* 5, no. 3 (2012): 419–39.

80 Ibid., 432.

81 Paula S. Fass, *The End of American Childhood* (Princeton, NJ: Princeton University Press, 2016), 8.

82 Baxandall and Ewen, *Picture Windows,* 164.

83 It is important to qualify this, as millions of Canadians were excluded in from postwar plenty. As historian Alvin Finkel argues, this prosperity was shared unequally by Canadians, and it would be an incomplete picture (suburban nuclear family amid plenty) if it excluded working mothers, blue-collar workers on strike, hungry schoolchildren without lunches, and the growing homeless elderly. See Alvin Finkel, *Our Lives: Canada after 1945,* 2nd ed. (Toronto: Lorimer, 2012), 6, 79.

84 For further reading, see Stamp, *Suburban Modern,* 94.

85 Jackson, *Crabgrass Frontier,* 240.

86 Irene and Garnet Rusk, in Scollard, *From Prairie Grass to City Sidewalks,* 17.

87 Howard P. Chudacoff, *Children at Play: An American History* (New York: New York University Press, 2007), 4.

88 Gillis, "Epilogue," 317.

89 Dave Flavell, *Community and the Human Spirit: Oral Histories from Montreal's Point St. Charles, Griffintown and Goose Village* (Ottawa: Petra Books, 2014), 306.

90 Bruce Wilson, personal interview, Calgary, AB, 28 July 2011.

91 Doug Cass, personal interview, Cochrane, AB, 2 June 2011. This is not to suggest that most children played exclusively in a three-block radius, but in the earliest school-age years, others indicated that they played oftentimes within earshot of their parents' (and especially mothers') calls to return home for meals, get ready for bed, and so forth.

92 The active boy and the passive girl are two childhood tropes that still hold currency with some but were not reflected in this suburban community. Girls and boys, while not always playing together, were certainly active in childhood, and some individuals, of both genders, displayed varying degrees of activity and passivity.

93 For an informed discussion on the intertwining of oral history and nostalgia, particularly some of the emotional and mythologizing aspects, see Robert Rutherdale, "Just Nostalgic Family Men? Off-the-Job Family Time, Providing, and Oral Histories of Fatherhood in Postwar Canada, 1945–1975," *Oral History Forum* 29 (2009): 1–9; and Constantine Sedikides, Tim Wildschut, Jamie Arndt, and Clay Routledge, "Nostalgia: Past, Present, and Future," *Current Directions in Psychological Science* 17, no. 5 (October 2008): 304–7.

94 Allan Matthews, personal interview, Calgary, AB, 29 July 2011.

95 Ibid.

96 Mary Baker, personal interview, Calgary, 25 July 2011.

97 Wendy Glidden, personal interview, Calgary, 2 August 2011.

98 For further reading on geography, personal landscape, and childhoods, see Neil Sutherland, *Growing Up: Childhood in English Canada from the Great War to the Age of Television* (Toronto: University of Toronto Press, 1997), 223.

99   Sarah L. Holloway and Gill Valentine, eds., *Children's Geographies* (New York: Routledge, 2000), 13. While this can be generalized, it is important to not universalize, as many young people, particularly as they moved into their teenage years, spent less and less time with their families in the home. Again, this is not exclusive to this era and has ebbed and flowed over the past hundred years throughout Canada and the United States.

100 There are dozens of examples, including "Score! Street Hockey Legal after Toronto City Council Overturns Ban," *CBC News,* 15 July 2016, https://www.cbc.ca/news/canada/toronto/street-hockey-toronto-council-1.3681162; "Basketball Complainer Moving Away," *Peterborough Examiner,* 18 December 2012, https: //www.thepeterboroughexaminer.com/news-story/8198065 -basketball-complainer-moving-away/.

101 Gillis "Epilogue," 320.

102 Jim Farquharson, personal interview, Calgary, AB, 17 October 2011.

103 Chief constable, Calgary Police Force, annual report, 1952, 45, Calgary Police Service Archives.

104 Wendy Birch, "Traffic Safety," *Aberhart Advocate* 5, no. 2 (17 December 1962): 14.

105 "Aberhart's Traffic Problem," *Aberhart* Advocate, 7. no. 2 (25 November 1964): 8.

106 Tamara Myers, "From Disciplinarian to Coach: Policing of Youth in Post-World War II Canada" (paper presented at European Social Science History Conference, Lisbon, Portugal, March 2008).

107 Barbara Grinder, *Local Colour: A Commemoration of the 75th Anniversary of the Amalgamated Transit Union Local 583* (Calgary: Amalgamated Transit Union, 1990), 52.

108 Chief of Police, Calgary Police Force, annual report, 1960, 40, Calgary Police Service Archives.

109 Ibid., 1962, 35.

110 Ibid., 1970, 22.

111 City of Calgary, "Brief of the Children's Aid Department of the City of Calgary," prepared for submission to the Royal Commission on Child Welfare (Calgary: Children's Aid Department, 1947), Social Services Department fonds, City of Calgary Archives.

112 Canadian Gallup Poll, March 1956, no. 247, "Do You Know Where Your Children Are?," question 4b.

113 Sicart, *Play Matters,* 55.

114 Jim Farquharson, personal interview, Calgary, AB, 17 October 2011.

115 Madeline and George Gablehaus, in Scollard, *From Prairie Grass to City Sidewalks,* 27.

116 We continue to learn about the importance of urban green spaces such as parks and gardens. They can affect aspects of both mental and physical health in meaningful ways. For further reading, see Tori Rodriguez, "City Parks May Mend the Mind," *Scientific American Mind,* May–June 2016, 11.

117 Chudacoff, *Children at Play,* 5. Hundreds of homes were built in this area in a few short years. With the growth being mainly north and west in this particular area, farm and ranch lands, along with comparatively open prairie, became more scarce. This trend, combined with increasing restrictions on where children were allowed to play, meant space was of the utmost importance to most if not all young children and teenagers.

118 Billy Somers, "William Aberhart High Reflects Modern Trend in Education," *Calgary Herald*, 17 December 1960, 11.

119 Harris, *Creeping Conformity*, 165. For further discussion of the centrality of suburban school spaces, see Stamp, *Suburban Modern*, 117.

120 Lucille and Ewan Lawrence, in Scollard, *From Prairie Grass to City Sidewalks*, 34.

121 Roy Farquharson, in ibid., 58.

122 William Wright, telephone interview, Peterborough, ON, 4 November 2011.

123 Chudacoff, *Children at Play*, 129.

124 Calgary crime reports were not broken down into districts in this period, although the tenor of the reports indicates that crime rates were highest in the downtown area, which makes sense given the concentration of both businesses and population, especially in the 1950s and 1960s.

125 Flavell, *Community and the Human Spirit*, 260.

126 Jim Farquharson, personal interview, Calgary, AB, 17 October 2011. Many other oral history interviewees recalled this same story. None of them had been on the scene, as Jim and his father were, as the tragic event unfolded.

127 Chief constable, Calgary Police Force, annual reports, 1950–70.

128 For further reading, see Hayden, *Building Suburbia*, 3. She also adds that the suburbs, across many time periods, have been the landscape of the imagination for many Americans. I believe this applies equally to Canadians.

129 Brian Osborne, "Landscapes, Memory, Monuments, and Commemoration: Putting Identity in Its Place," *Canadian Ethnic Studies* 33, no. 3 (2001): 39–77.

130 Margaret Atwood, *Cat's Eye* (Toronto: McClelland and Stewart, 1988), 33.

131 Ibid., 35.

132 This is a generalization and cannot be universalized when applied to the suburban childhood experience. Alternative experiences are explored in detail in the chapter on resistance, delinquency, and the night.

133 Peter Wyden, *Suburbia's Coddled Kids* (Garden City: Doubleday, 1962), 120.

134 Mavis Reimer, *Home Words: Discourses on Children's Literature in Canada* (Waterloo, ON: Wilfrid Laurier University Press, 2007), xiii.

135 Setha Low, *Behind the Gates: Life, Security, and the Pursuit of Happiness in Fortress America* (New York: Routledge, 2003), 77.

136 Baxandall and Ewen, *Picture Windows*, 167.

137 Low, *Behind the Gates*, 230. Low goes on to argue that many place-based definitions broke down as urban neighbourhoods became more heterogeneous and social groups increasingly became the basis of social and cultural identification. This was reflected in Calgary in some areas by the mid-1970s, particularly with certain "ethnic" or racial communities dominating parts of the growing city.

138 Ibid., 77.

139 Tom Martinson, *American Dreamscape: The Pursuit of Happiness in Postwar Suburbia* (New York: Carroll and Graf, 2000), xvii.

140 Bill Bryson, *The Life and Times of the Thunderbolt Kid* (New York: Broadway Books, 2006), 192.

141 Stamp, *Suburban Modern*, 111.

142 There is a lot written on Regent Park and Canada's dearth of affordable public housing. For an exploration of Regent Park, see Sean Purdy, "'Ripped Off' by the System: Housing Policy, Poverty, and Territorial Stigmatization in Regent Park Housing Project, 1951–1991," *Labour/Le Travail* 52 (2003): 45–108.

143 Baxandall and Ewen, *Picture Windows*, 93.

CHAPTER 2: Bombs, Boom, and the Classroom

1   "Editorial," *Aberhart Advocate* 11, no. 8 (6 February 1969): 3.

2   Paul Axelrod, *The Promise of Schooling: Education in Canada, 1800–1914* (Toronto: University of Toronto Press, 1997).

3   For how these activities were used to shape and discipline adolescents, see Cynthia Comacchio, *The Dominion of Youth: Adolescence and the Making of Modern Canada* (Waterloo, ON: Wilfrid Laurier University Press, 2006).

4   There may be no group of children who can claim more of a school's lasting impact than residential school students, almost none of it positive. Although outside the bounds of this book, see J.R. Miller, *Shingwauk's Vision: A History of Native Residential Schools* (Toronto: University of Toronto Press, 1996); and John Milloy, *A National Crime: The Canadian Government and the Residential School System, 1879–1986* (Winnipeg: University of Manitoba Press, 1999).

5   Kate Aitken, "Children's Art Brings Their Homelands to Life," *Globe and Mail*, 17 September 1960, A15.

6   For a great study of women's efforts, especially those of mothers, to help in Cold War battle efforts on the domestic front in Canada, see Tarah Brookfield, *Cold War Comforts: Canadian Women, Child Safety, and Global Insecurity* (Waterloo, ON: Wilfrid Laurier University Press, 2012).

7   In other words, these spaces were seen to be anticommunist and, by extension, politically conservative. See Elaine Tyler May, *Homeward Bound: American Families in the Cold War Era* (New York: Basic Books, 2008). For an overview of the Cold War, pedagogy, and American schools in the postwar period, see Andrew Hartman, *Education and the Cold War: The Battle for the American School* (New York: Palgrave Macmillan, 2008). Hartman argues that Dewey's progressivism was not perceived as stable enough to thwart the conservative tendencies of educationists in this period, at least in the United States.

8   Alvin Finkel, *Our Lives: Canada after 1945,* 2nd ed. (Toronto: Lorimer, 1997), 4.

9   While the efforts of many young activists, particularly university-aged ones, are well documented in the historical record in Canada, I would argue that the exploration of the thoughts, feelings, and nascent political leanings of pre-adolescent and early adolescent persons has been limited. For limited discussion of this younger cohort, see Doug Owram, *Born at the Right Time: A History of the Baby Boom Generation* (Toronto: University of Toronto Press, 1996). Young people and children were depicted in quite uncomplicated ways in influential television shows such as *I Love Lucy, The Ozzie and Harriet Show,* and *Father Knows Best.*

10 While there are references to the issues of young suburban children and adolescents in *Crestwood Heights,* for instance, they are confined to mental hygiene, familial concerns, and psychological maladjustment. Again, political awareness regarding communism, the bomb, and the Cold War was limited to older adolescents rather than the young peoples I focus on here.

11 For one of the best accounts of the earliest years of the Cold War in Canada, see Reg Whitaker and Gary Marcuse, *Cold War Canada: The Making of a National Insecurity State, 1945–1957* (Toronto: University of Toronto Press, 1994).

12 Ibid., 6.

13 Ibid., 364. The authors note that Canadians seemed to have embraced (not necessarily wholeheartedly, though) the bomb and the possibility of nuclear war. They

are referencing an adult perspective; however, as demonstrated throughout this chapter, young suburbanites were not necessarily supportive of the bomb and its potentialities.

14   Katie Pickles, *Female Imperialism and the National Identity: Imperial Order Daughters of Empire* (Manchester: Manchester University Press, 2009); Brian Thorn, *From Left to Right: Maternalism and Women's Political Activism in Post-war Canada* (Vancouver, UBC Press, 2016); and Gary Kinsman, D.K. Buse, and Mercedes Steedman, *Whose National Security? Canadian State Surveillance and the Creation of Enemies* (Toronto: Between the Lines, 2000).

15   For further reading, see Andrew Burtch, "Armageddon on Tour: The 'On Guard, Canada!' Civil Defence Convoy and Responsible Citizenship in the Early Cold War," *International Journal* 61, no. 3 (Summer 2006): 735–56.

16   Gleb Tsipursky, *Socialist Fun: Youth, Consumption, and State-Sponsored Popular Culture in the Soviet Union, 1945–1970* (Pittsburgh, PA: University of Pittsburgh Press, 2016).

17   "A Damp Squib," *Central Collegiate Weeper*, 1955.

18   Bruce Wilson, personal interview, Calgary, AB, 28 July 2011.

19   Ann Marie Kordas, *The Politics of Childhood in Cold War America* (Brookfield, VT: Pickering and Chatto, 2013).

20   Allan Matthews, personal interview, Calgary, AB, 29 July 2011.

21   "Air Raid Alarm System Considered for Canada," *Calgary Herald*, 23 February 1950, 1.

22   Canadian Gallup Poll, November 1959, no. 279, "In 20 Years – Atomic War?," question 8h.

23   See Hartman, *Education and the Cold War*.

24   Bruce Wilson, personal interview, Calgary, AB, 28 July 2011.

25   Ibid.

26   Banff Trail youngsters attended several schools outside of Banff Trail prior to 1960 and the building of schools to serve students of all ages in this rapidly growing area.

27   "A Boy Scout Jamboree and Canada's Capitol, 1953," *Central Collegiate Weeper*, 1955.

28   Doug Cass, personal interview, Cochrane, AB, 2 June 2011.

29   Bruce Wilson, personal interview, Calgary, AB, 28 July 2011.

30   "Chinese Fortress Falls," *Calgary Herald*, 14 June 1951, 1.

31   Mary Baker, personal interview, Calgary, AB, 25 July 2011.

32   Bruce Wilson, personal interview, Calgary, AB, 28 July 2011.

33   "Public Tends to Oppose Younger Age for Draft," *Calgary Herald*, 19 May 1951.

34   Without question, there were more recruiting advertisements in the late 1940s and early 1950s; however, it is surprising that these advertisements remained common in the late 1950s. I was even more surprised to see these advertisements still appearing in the 1960s and in high school, college, and university yearbooks and newsletters. Yearbooks from other centres— namely, Edmonton and the metropolitan Toronto area—display similar advertisements in comparable volume.

35   It is not uncommon to find imagery featuring hand-to-hand combat, rifles with bayonets, and the somewhat antiquated military dress of the two previous world wars. This was contrary to an emphasis on the modernization of Canadian military equipment and armaments characteristic of the nuclear age, entered into in the 1940s.

36   Canadian Army advertisement, *Crescent Heights Bugle,* 1952.

37   Wendy Glidden, personal interview, Calgary, AB, 2 August 2011.

38   Ibid.

39   Mary Baker, personal interview, Calgary, AB, 25 July 2011.

40   "Taps Editorial," *Aberhart Advocate* 2, no. 8 (May 1960): 6.

41   Despite some of the ongoing resistance to American hegemony that continues to get attention in academic literature in the form of George Grant's *Lament for a Nation* (Toronto: McClelland and Stewart, 1970) and the rise of the Waffle faction in left-leaning political circles, there was widespread support for the United States (including greater economic integration) across Canada by Canadians (Finkel, *Our Lives,* 27).

42   William Wright, telephone interview, Peterborough, ON, 4 November 2011.

43   For further reading and discussion, see several chapters in Amy von Heyking, *Creating Citizens: History and Identity in Alberta's Schools, 1905 to 1980* (Calgary: University of Calgary Press, 2006).

44   Sharon Johnstone, telephone interview, Peterborough, ON, 8 December 2011.

45   "Tex, 'H-Bomb,'" *Aberhart Advocate* 2, no. 9 (June 1960): 5.

46   We must remain mindful that different editors exerted varying degrees of influence on student contributors as well. While some students reported having a great deal of editorial and creative control of their work, there were suggestions that certain teachers, overseeing the student newspapers and newsletters, had significant influence over the publication's final editions.

47   "A student," "A Hope for the Future," *Aberhart Advocate* 5, no. 4 (20 March 1963): 5.

48   Editors, "Space Law," *Aberhart Advocate* 4, no. 9 (June 1962): 7.

49   Lesley Hayes, personal interview, Calgary, AB, 26 July 2011.

50   The history of childhood and adolescence is interwoven with broader cultural, social, and political events in North America. For a good discussion of this in an American context, see Steven Mintz, *Huck's Raft: A History of American Childhood* (Cambridge, MA: Belknap Press, 2004), viii.

51   Editorial, "The Tragedy of Today's Children," *The Albertan,* 25 October 1969.

52   W. McKnight, "Musical News Report," *Aberhart Advocate* 5, no. 4 (20 March 1963): 12.

53   "Editorial," *The Centralian,* 1957–58.

54   Allan Matthews, personal interview, Calgary, AB, 29 July 2011.

55   For further reading on the early Canadian and Quebec education systems and broader social change in the nineteenth century, see Axelrod, *The Promise of Schooling;* and André Dufour, *Histoire de l'éducation au Québec* (Montreal: Boreal, 1997).

56   Wendy Glidden, personal interview, Calgary, AB, 2 August 2011.

57   Neil Sutherland, *Growing Up: Childhood in English Canada from the Great War to the Age of Television* (Toronto: University of Toronto, 1997), 189.

58   Doug Cass, personal interview, Cochrane, AB, 2 June 2011.

59   Ibid.

60   Sutherland, *Growing Up,* 217.

61   Comacchio, *The Dominion of Youth,* 99.

62   Ibid., 128.

63   von Heyking, *Creating Citizens,* 92.

64   "City School Population Up by 5,000," *Calgary Herald,* 19 September 1962, 38.

65   Allan Battye, "School 'Spiral' Problem Grows," *Calgary Herald,* 3 February 1968, 1–2.

66 von Heyking, *Creating Citizens,* 95.

67 Ibid., 115.

68 For an overview of educational reforms in Canada over several decades, see Judy Lupart and Charles Webber, "Canadian Schools in Transition: Moving from Dual Education Systems to Inclusive Schools," *Exceptionality Education International* 22 (2012): 8–37.

69 Nick Kach and Kas Mazurek, *Exploring Our Educational Past: Schooling in the Northwest Territories and Alberta* (Calgary: Detselig, 1992), 204.

70 The Hall-Dennis report was the Ontario equivalent of the Cameron commission and called for sweeping educational reforms: see R.D. Gidney, *From Hope to Harris: The Reshaping of Ontario's Schools* (Toronto: University of Toronto Press, 1999).

71 In the progressive tradition, education is seen as a vehicle for limited social reform and for the broad dissemination of democratic principles and practices.

72 Lynn Speer Lemisko and Kurt W. Clausen, "Connections, Contarieties, and Convolutions: Curriculum and Pedagogic Reform in Alberta and Ontario, 1930–1955," *Canadian Journal of Education* 29, 4 (2006): 1118 and 1119.

73 "New Report Cards Show Children's 'Attitudes,'" *Calgary Herald,* 25 November 1950, 1.

74 Canadian Gallup Poll, January 1969, no. 333, "Is Area School Discipline Strict Enough?," question 9a.

75 Canadian Gallup Poll, March 1959, no. 274, "Severity of Discipline in Public School," question 1.

76 Bruce Wilson, personal interview, Calgary, AB, 28 July 2011.

77 Canadian Gallup Poll, March 1959, no. 274, "Teachers Be Allowed to Punish," question 2.

78 Bruce Wilson, personal interview, Calgary, AB, 28 July 2011. As explored throughout this book, social class (directly associated with family income) has been, and remains, a prime determiner of access to postsecondary studies.

79 Martin L. Gross, "The Three Rs and P (for Psyche)," *Life,* 21 September 1962, 11–14.

80 Mona Gleason, "Disciplining the Student Body: Schooling and the Construction of Canadian Children's Bodies, 1930 to 1960," *History of Education Quarterly* 41, no. 2 (Spring 2001): 194.

81 Frank Edward, telephone interview, Peterborough, ON, 8 December 2011.

82 Sharon Johnstone, telephone interview, Peterborough, ON, 8 December 2011.

83 William Wright, telephone interview, Peterborough, ON, 4 November 2011.

84 Tammy Simpson, telephone interview, Peterborough, ON, 24 November 2011; Elizabeth Davidson, telephone interview, Peterborough, ON, 11 November 2011; Michelle Macdonald, personal interview, Calgary, AB, 27 July 2011; and Donna McLaren, telephone interview, Peterborough, ON, 12 December 2011.

85 Jim Farquharson, personal interview, Calgary, AB, 17 October 2011.

86 Tammy Simpson, telephone interview, Peterborough, ON, 24 November 2011.

87 Sharon Johnstone, telephone interview, Peterborough, ON, 8 December 2011.

88 Lupart and Webber, "Canadian Schools in Transition," 14.

89 E.M. Borgal, "Principal's Message," *Branton Yearbook,* 1956–57, 2.

90 W.A. Branton, "Message from Mr. Branton," *Branton Yearbook,* 1956–57, 4.

91 von Heyking, *Creating Citizens,* 112; and Neil Sutherland, "The Triumph of 'Formalism': Elementary Schooling in Vancouver from the 1920s to the 1960s," *BC Studies* 69, no. 70 (1986): 175–210.

92   Frank Edward, telephone interview, Peterborough, ON, 8 December 2011.

93   Michelle Macdonald, personal interview, Calgary, AB, 27 July 2011.

94   Mary Baker, personal interview, Calgary, 25 July 2011.

95   von Heyking, *Creating Citizens,* 113.

96   Mona Gleason, *Normalizing the Ideal: Psychology, Schooling and the Family in Postwar Canada* (Toronto: University of Toronto Press, 1999), 120.

97   Sharon Johnstone, telephone interview, Peterborough, ON, 8 December 2011.

98   "Causa Belli," *Aberhart Advocate* 2, no. 9 (May 1960): 5.

99   Editor, "Is School Spirit Necessary?," *Aberhart Advocate* 6, no. 3 (January 1964): 1.

100   "Is School Spirit Necessary?," 1.

101   Katharine Rollwagen, "Classrooms for Consumer Society: Practical Education and Secondary School Reform in Post-Second World War Canada," *Historical Studies in Education* 28, no. 1 (2016): 32.

102   Laura Fowler, "Education Editorial," *Lead Balloon* 1, no. 1 (December 1970): 2. For further reading on student activism in the 1970s, see M. Des, "'Dare to Free Yourself': The Red Tide, Feminism, and High School Activism in the Early 1970s," *Journal of the History of Childhood and Youth* 7, no. 2 (2014): 295–319.

103   Elizabeth Davidson, telephone interview, Peterborough, ON, 11 November 2011.

104   D. Hunt, "Free Schools: The System of the Future?," *Aberhart Advocate* 9, no. 8 (6 February 1969): 7.

105   Sharon Johnstone, telephone interview, Peterborough, ON, 8 December 2011.

106   "School Entry Facts Outlined," *Calgary Herald,* 15 October 1955, 1, 2.

107   Daisy Dancey, "The Banff Trail Kindergarten," in Rose Scollard, ed., *From Prairie Grass to City Sidewalks* (Calgary: Banff Trail Seniors, 1999), 43, 44.

108   von Heyking, *Creating Citizens,* 96.

109   Owram, *Born at the Right Time,* 110.

110   Alvin Finkel, *The Social Credit Phenomenon* (Toronto: University of Toronto Press, 1989); and Janine Stingel, *Social Discredit: Anti-semitism, Social Credit and the Jewish Response* (Montreal/Kingston: McGill-Queen's University Press, 2000).

111   "A Mother," "Letter to the Editor," *Calgary Herald,* reprinted in *Aberhart Advocate,* 1, no. 6 (December 1968): 6.

112   Editors, "Should Religion Be Taught in School?," *Aberhart Advocate* 3, no. 4 (December 1960): 2.

113   Tina Block, "'Toilet-Seat Prayers' and Imperious Fathers: Interrogating Religion and the Family in Oral Histories of the Postwar Pacific Northwest," *Oral History Forum* 29 (2009): 19.

114   For a good overview of the intersections between families, Protestant churches, and the suburbs in postwar Calgary, see Mary Ann Shantz, "Centring the Suburb, Focusing on the Family: Calgary's Anglican and Alliance Churches, 1945–1969," *Social History* 42, no. 84 (2009): 423–46.

115   Gary Miedema, *For Canada's Sake: Public Religion, Centennial Celebrations, and the Re-making of Canada in the 1960s* (Montreal/Kingston: McGill-Queen's University Press, 2005), 4.

116   J.E. Veevers and E.M. Gee, *Religiously Unaffiliated Canadians: Demographic and Social Correlates of Secularization – Final Report,* 1988, 18.

117   "Cold War Tactics Deplored," *Globe and Mail,* 25 February 1963, 13; and "Nuclear War, Children, Spock's Latest Fight," *Globe and Mail,* 20 May 1964, 11.

118   John and Doris Watson, in Scollard, *From Prairie Grass to City Sidewalks.*

119   William Wright, telephone interview, Peterborough, ON, 4 November 2011.

120   John R. Seeley, R. Alexander Sim, and E.W. Loosley, *Crestwood Heights: A Study of the Culture of Suburban Life* (Toronto: University of Toronto Press, 1963), 146.

CHAPTER 3: Diversity Deficit and Working Days

1   Intersections between race and labour have been examined critically by several scholars: see, for instance, Kay J. Anderson, *Vancouver's Chinatown: Racial Discourse in Canada, 1875–1980* (Montreal/Kingston: McGill-Queen's University Press, 1991); and Vic Satzewich, *Racism and the Incorporation of Foreign Labour* (New York: Routledge, 1991).

2   Veronica Strong-Boag, "Home Dreams: Women and the Suburban Experiment in Canada, 1945–60," *Canadian Historical Review* 72, no. 4 (1991): 486.

3   The well-documented "white flight" from the inner cities to the suburbs in the United States has been explored and debated by many urban historians. The African Canadian population was much smaller in this period, and we don't see this same process happening in Canada. See Kevin M. Kruse, *White Flight: Atlanta and the Making of Modern Conservatism* (Princeton, NJ: Princeton University Press, 2007); and Maria Amy Kenyon, *Dreaming Suburbia: Detroit and the Production of Postwar Space and Culture* (Detroit, MI: Wayne State University Press, 2004).

4   I explore "whiteness" throughout the chapter in oral histories and some census information that supported the lack of diversity. For an excellent discussion of whiteness, including the racial status of peripheral European Canadians in the postwar period, see Noula Mina, "Taming and Training Greek 'Peasant Girls' and the Gendered Politics of Whiteness in Postwar Canada: Canadian Bureaucrats and Immigrant Domestics, 1950s–1960s," *Canadian Historical Review* 94, no. 4 (December 2013): 514–39.

5   Andrew Baldwin, Laura Cameron, and Audrey Kobayashi, eds., *Rethinking the Great White North: Race, Nature, and the Historical Geographies of Whiteness in Canada* (Vancouver: UBC Press, 2012), 2.

6   For further discussion on this prewar trend, see Bryan Palmer, *Working-Class Experience: Rethinking the History of Canadian Labour, 1800–1991*, 2nd ed. (Toronto: McClelland and Stewart, 1992).

7   Maya Pines, "Social Class, Child Development Linked," *Globe and Mail*, 10 July 1960, W3.

8   Steven Mintz, *Huck's Raft: A History of American Childhood* (Cambridge, MA: Belknap, 2004), ix.

9   "Mixture of Students for All Schools," *Globe and Mail*, 3 November 1965, 12.

10   Patrick Vitale, "A Model Suburb for Model Suburbanites: Order, Control, and Expertise in Thorncrest Village," *Urban History Review* 40, no. 1 (Fall 2011): 41–55.

11   I am defining *middle-class* as those families headed by a working professional or, in some instances, someone who operated a small business, often with a post-secondary degree or certification. These individuals, therefore, had more control over their work lives in comparison to the blue-collar or working-class families in Banff Trail.

12   It was revealed in an interviewee that he worked on a Taber sugar beet farm during one of the summers before his tenth birthday in the 1960s. His account is found later in this chapter. In general, the number of children and adolescents

who were doing both paid and unpaid work in the 1950s, 1960s, and early 1970s was surprising, as children's increasing leisure time is often emphasized as being the norm, particularly in middle-class families, by the mid-1960s.

13 Donna Kimmel, "Excitement," *Balmoral Junior High School Yearbook,* 1949–50.

14 The racialization of space is explored brilliantly in Sherene Razack, ed., *Race, Space and the Law: Unmapping a White Settler Society* (Toronto: Between the Lines, 2002).

15 Only one participant recalled an Indigenous classmate in a suburban classroom, and the dozens of yearbooks I used in researching both place and time reflected this paucity of Indigenous students in Banff Trail and other Calgary suburbs.

16 Census of Canada, 1961.

17 While few supporters of racist hierarchies remain in academe, one notable and infamous example is the recently deceased Western University professor J. Philippe Rushton. He placed humans into three main racial groupings with distinct hierarchies. For his main theoretical position, supported by a handful of racist academics into the present, see J. Philippe Rushton, *Race, Evolution and Behavior: A Life History Perspective* (Huron, MI: Charles Darwin Research Institute, 1996).

18 Anderson, *Vancouver's Chinatown,* 12.

19 Hugh Dempsey, *Calgary: Spirit of the West* (Calgary: Glenbow/Fifth House, 1999), 93–94.

20 Allan Matthews, personal interview, Calgary, AB, 29 July 2011.

21 See Moula, "Taming and Training."

22 Census of Canada, 1951.

23 Census of Canada, 1961 and 1951.

24 Doug Cass, personal interview, Cochrane, AB, 2 June 2011.

25 Wendy Glidden, personal interview, Calgary, AB, 2 August 2011.

26 Census of Canada, 1961.

27 Bruce Wilson, personal interview, Calgary, AB, 28 July 2011.

28 Lesley Hayes, personal interview, Calgary, AB, 26 July 2011.

29 Franca Iacovetta, *Gatekeepers: Reshaping Immigrant Lives in Postwar Canada* (Toronto: Between the Lines, 2006); Valerie Knowles, *Strangers at Our Gates,* rev. ed. (Toronto: Dundurn, 2007); and Ninette Kelly and Michael Trebilcock, *Making of a Mosaic: A History of Canadian Immigration Policy,* 2nd ed. (Toronto: University of Toronto Press, 2010).

30 Locating individuals who experienced racism and identified as something other than white would have helped greatly in this respect. The fact that one interviewee recalled some overt racism leads me to believe that while it may not have been rampant, it existed without question.

31 Doug Cass, personal interview, Cochrane, AB, 2 June 2011.

32 D. Bell, "Is 'Foreigner' a Dirty Word to Children?," *Maclean's,* August 1967, 4b, 68b.

33 See Constance Backhouse, *Colour-Coded: A Legal History of Racism in Canada, 1900–1950* (Toronto: University of Toronto Press, 1999); Angus McLaren, *Our Own Master Race: Eugenics in Canada, 1885–1945* (Toronto: University of Toronto Press,) 1990; and Barrington Walker, *The History of Immigration and Racism in Canada: Essential Readings* (Toronto: Canadian Scholars Press, 2008).

34 Sharon Johnstone, telephone interview, Peterborough, ON, 8 December 2011.

35 Jane Helleiner, "'The Right Kind of Children': Childhood, Gender and 'Race' in Canadian Postwar Political Discourse," *Anthropologica* 43, no. 2 (2001): 149.

36   Neil Sutherland, *Growing Up: Childhood in English Canada from the Great War to the Age of Television* (Toronto: University of Toronto Press, 1997), 250.

37   Brent Harris, telephone interview, Peterborough, ON, 9 December 2011.

38   Statistics Canada, "Proportion of Foreign-Born among the Canadian Population, 1901 to 2017," *Canadian Demographics at a Glance,* 2008, no. 91-003-XIE, 31, http: //www.statcan.gc.ca/pub/91–003-x/91–003-x2007001-eng.pdf.

39   Doug Cass, personal interview, Cochrane, AB, 2 June 2011.

40   William Wright, personal interview, Calgary, AB, 4 November 2011.

41   City of Calgary, "The Social and Human Aspects of Urban Renewal in Calgary," Social Services Department of Calgary, 1963, 16, Social Services Department fonds, City of Calgary Archives.

42   Frank Edward, telephone interview, Peterborough, ON, 8 December 2011.

43   Frankenberg's work focuses on race relations in the United States but is strikingly similar to what I have located in these memories of baby boomer suburbanites. See Ruth Frankenberg, *White Women, Race Matters: The Social Construction of Whiteness* (Minneapolis: University of Minnesota Press, 1993).

44   Mintz, *Huck's Raft,* ix. For further reading on the impact of class on both family and childhood lives, see Annette Lareau, *Unequal Childhoods: Class, Race, and Family Life* (Berkeley: University of California Press, 2003), 236.

45   Joan Sangster, *Transforming Labour: Women and Work in Postwar Canada* (Toronto: University of Toronto Press, 2010); and Leah Vosko, *Temporary Work: The Gendered Rise of a Precarious Employment Relationship* (Toronto: University of Toronto Press, 2000).

46   Strong-Boag, "Home Dreams"; and Grace MacInnis, "Bill Proposes Wages for Full-Time Mothers," *Canadian Labour* 13 (January 1968): 12.

47   For a comprehensive look at the history of daycare in Alberta, see Tom Langford, *Alberta's Daycare Controversy: From 1908 to 2009 and Beyond* (Edmonton: Athabasca University Press, 2009).

48   William Wright, telephone interview, Peterborough, ON, 4 November 2011.

49   Allan Matthews, personal interview, Calgary, AB, 29 July 2011.

50   Benjamin Schlesinger, "Multi-problem Families," *Globe and Mail,* 25 July 1963, 11.

51   Nathan E. Cohen, reported in "Proceedings of the Annual Meeting of the Vanier Institute of the Family," Vanier Institute of the Family, 1968, 30, Family Life Education Council of Calgary fonds, M6239, file 171, Glenbow Archives.

52   Doug Cass, personal interview, Cochrane, AB, 2 June 2011.

53   Frank Edward, telephone interview, Peterborough, ON, 8 December 2011.

54   Jim Farquharson, personal interview, Calgary, 17 October 2011.

55   William Whyte, *The Organization Man* (Toronto: Simon and Schuster, 1956).

56   Veronica Strong-Boag, *The New Day Recalled: Lives of Girls and Women in English Canada, 1919–1939* (Toronto: Copp Clark Pitman, 1988), 92.

57   George and Elaine Skoreyko, "The Rooster in the Garage and Other Wild Tales," in Rose Scollard, ed., *From Prairie Grass to City Sidewalks* (Calgary: Banff Trail Seniors, 1995), 75–76.

58   Richard Harris, *Unplanned Suburbs: Toronto's American Tragedy, 1900 to 1950* (Baltimore, MA: Johns Hopkins University, 1996), 16.

59   William Dobriner, *Class in Suburbia* (Englewood Cliffs, NJ: Prentice Hall), 15.

60   Skoreyko, "The Rooster in the Garage," 75–76.

61   S.D. Clark, *The Suburban Society* (Toronto: University of Toronto Press, 1966), 68.

62   Eileen Stearns, in Scollard, *From Prairie Grass to City Sidewalks,* 103.

63   Classified listings, *Calgary Herald,* 9 December 1950.

64   Stats Canada reports, used previously, "Annual Averages of Hourly Earnings of Hourly Rated Wage-Earners, Selected Industry Groups, Canada, 1945 to 1970."

65   For the two surveys of Canadian housing policy, see John C. Bacher, *Keeping to the Marketplace: The Evolution of Canadian Housing Policy* (Montreal/Kingston: McGill-Queen's University Press, 1993); and Sean Purdy, "'Ripped Off' by the System: Housing Policy, Poverty, and Territorial Stigmatization in Regent Park Housing Project, 1951–1991," *Labour/Le Travail* 52 (2003): 45–108.

66   Sutherland, *Growing Up,* 114.

67   Strong-Boag, "Home Dreams," 490.

68   Doug Cass, personal interview, Cochrane, AB, 2 June 2011.

69   William Wright, telephone interview, Peterborough, ON, 4 November 2011.

70   Brent Harris, telephone interview, Peterborough, ON, 9 December 2011.

71   Neil Sutherland, "'We Always Had Things to Do': The Paid and Unpaid Work of Anglophone Children between the 1920s and the 1960s," *Labour/Le Travail* 25 (Spring 1990): 113.

72   Ibid., 110.

73   Allan Matthews, personal interview, Calgary, AB, 29 July 2011.

74   Jim Farquharson, personal interview, Calgary, AB, 17 October 2011.

75   Michelle Macdonald, personal interview, Calgary, 27 July 2011.

76   Canadian Gallup Poll, January 1959, no. 273, "Family Members Help with Housework," question 15c.

77   Amanda Queen, "The Worm," in Scollard, *From Prairie Grass to City Sidewalks,* 50.

78   Shannon Bathall, "The Voice of the Prairies," *Aberhart Advocate* 4, no. 2 (November 1961): 3.

79   Sutherland, *Growing Up,* 139.

80   Sutherland, "We Always Had Work to Do," 135. Additionally, as Sutherland notes, family-allowance cheques for mothers helped to ease financial burdens for thousands of Canadian families.

81   Peter Baptie, *Balmoral Yearbook,* 1951–52, 7.

82   "'U' Graduates Still Jobless," *Calgary Herald,* 23 June 1950.

83   "Students Exceed Number of Jobs," *The Albertan,* 31 May 1950.

84   Beth Waters, "50% of Students Jobless – Baker," *The Gauntlet,* 23 September 1963, 4.

85   Leah F. Vosko, *Precarious Employment: Understanding Labour Market Insecurity in Canada* (Montreal/Kingston: McGill-Queen's University Press, 2005).

86   Canadian Association of Social Workers, *Social Policy Statement Booklet* (Ottawa: CASW, 1964), 1, Canadian Association of Social Workers fonds, MG 28, I 441, box 23, file 23, Library and Archives Canada.

87   Tom Elsworthy, "Student Unemployment: What Is to Be Done?," *The Gauntlet,* 11 September 1968, 4.

88   Ken Brown, "Report on University Visits," Association of Universities and Colleges of Canada, Ottawa, 1970, 3, University of Calgary Archives.

89   Sutherland, "We Always Had Work to Do," 123.

90   John R., Seeley, R. Alexander Sim, and E.W. Loosley, *Crestwood Heights: A Study of the Culture of Suburban Life* (Toronto: University of Toronto Press, 1963), 8.

91   Wendy Glidden, personal interview, 2 August 2011.

92　Miriam Forman-Brunell, *Babysitter: An American History* (New York: New York University Press, 2006).

93　This era saw babysitting courses offered by organizations such as the Red Cross, the YWCA, and St. John's Ambulance, and many of these programs continue to operate across Canada.

94　"Urges Training for 'Sitters,'" *The Albertan*, 18 July 1950.

95　Sutherland, "We Always Had Work to Do," 129.

96　"Babysitting," *Aberhart Advocate* 7, no. 3 (16 December 1964), n.p.

97　Forman-Brunell, *Babysitter*, 69.

98　Mary Baker, personal interview, Calgary, AB, 25 July 2011.

99　Lisa Blair, personal interview, Calgary, AB, 17 October 2011.

100　Tammy Simpson, telephone interview, Calgary, AB, 24 November 2011.

101　Forman-Brunell, *Babysitter*, 10.

102　Doug Cass, personal interview, Cochrane, AB, 2 June 2011.

103　Jim Farquharson, personal interview, Calgary, AB, 17 October 2011.

104　Sutherland, "We Always Had Things to Do," 126.

105　Frank Edward, telephone interview, Peterborough, ON, 8 December 2011.

106　Allan Matthews, personal interview, Calgary, AB, 29 July 2011.

107　Bruce Wilson, personal interview, Calgary, AB, 28 July 2011.

108　Frank Edward, telephone interview, Peterborough, ON, 8 December 2011.

109　William Wright, telephone interview, Peterborough, ON, 4 November 2011.

110　Sharon Johnstone, telephone interview, Peterborough, ON, 8 December 2011.

111　Jim Witte, "Child Labor in South Beet Field Charged," *The Albertan*, 16 March 1970.

112　Jim Farquharson, personal interview, Calgary, AB, 17 October 2011.

113　"For Graduates Seeking a Future," *Branton Yearbook*, 1957–58, 36.

114　Bank of Montreal advertisement, *Crescent Heights Bugle*, 1954, 72.

115　Henderson Secretarial School advertisement, *Crescent Heights Bugle*, 1952, 146.

116　Census of Canada, 1961.

117　This trend continued to the point that 337,425 people belonged to visible minorities in 2011, and they made up almost 28.1 percent of the total population: "Ethnic Diversity in Canada," *Live in Calgary*, accessed 22 March 2013, http://www.liveincalgary.com/overview/calgary-facts/demographics/ethnic-diversity.

CHAPTER 4: The Serious Business of Play

1　William Wright, telephone interview, Peterborough, ON, 4 November 2011.

2　There is no causation link to be made here, but it is certainly correlative. Church life was a part of many suburban households, although the children had varying levels of commitment to religious life. Some accepted teachings wholeheartedly while others were not interested outside of attending church as part of their familial duties.

3　Kristine Alexander, "Can the Girl Guide Speak? The Perils and Pleasures of Looking for Children's Voices in Archival Research," *Jeunesse* 4, no. 1 (2012): 132–45.

4　For further reading, see Howard P. Chudacoff, *Children at Play: An American History* (New York: New York University Press, 2007), xv. While Chudacoff's research focuses on the United States, these experiences generally seem to be mirrored across Canada.

5   Ibid., 2.

6   City of Calgary, *Calgary: Celebrating 100 Years of Parks* (Calgary: City of Calgary, 2010), 23.

7   Bob Shiels, *Calgary* (Calgary: Calgary Herald, 1974), 175.

8   Susan Herrington, "Muscle Memory: Reflections on the North American Schoolyard," in *Multiple Lenses, Multiple Images: Perspectives on the Child across Time, Space, and Disciplines,* ed. Hillel Goelman, Shiela K. Marshall, and Sally Ross (Toronto: University of Toronto Press, 2004), 101.

9   Chudacoff, *Children at Play,* 1.

10 Sharon Wall, *The Nurture of Nature: Childhood, Antimodernism, and Ontario Summer Camps, 1920–55* (Vancouver: UBC Press, 2010), 4. There is more generalized discussion of this in several pages of the book's concluding chapter.

11 Herrington "Muscle Memory," 94.

12 Ibid., 97. This is a concept that I explore in more detail in Chapter 5, which focuses on gender and sexuality.

13 Ibid., 102.

14 Robert McIntosh, "Constructing the Child: New Approaches to the History of Childhood in Canada," *Acadiensis* 28, no. 2 (Spring 1999): 135.

15 Doug Cass, personal interview, Cochrane, AB, 2 June 2011.

16 Jack W. Berryman, "From the Cradle to the Playing Field: America's Emphasis on Highly Organized Sports for Preadolescent Boys," *Journal of Sport History* 2, no. 2 (1975): 112. Berryman considers American children and teenagers, but these same processes were under way in Canada as well. While on a smaller scale, because of a much smaller population, there was much piggybacking, as there continues to be in contemporary Canada. Sharon Wall also discusses this in the Canadian context. Advice literature began to flourish in the early decades of the twentieth century—advocating rigidity and organization in childhood lives. For further reading, see Wall, *The Nature of Nurture,* 253.

17 Berryman, "From Cradle to the Playing Field," 115.

18 "Scouts Call at City Homes for Toys Worth Repairing," *Calgary Herald,* 2 December 1939, 11.

19 Jane Jacobs, *The Death and Life of Great American Cities,* 2nd ed. (New York: Vintage Books, 1992), 79.

20 On juvenile delinquency in Canada, see Joan Sangster, *Girl Trouble: Female Delinquency in English Canada* (Toronto: Between the Lines, 2002); Tamara Myers, *Caught: Montreal's Modern Girls and the Law, 1869–1945* (Toronto: University of Toronto Press, 2006); and D. Owen Carrigan, *Juvenile Delinquency in Canada: A History* (Toronto: Irwin, 1998, 1998).

21 Berryman, "From Cradle to the Playing Field," 116.

22 Art Irwin, in Rose Scollard, ed., *From Prairie Grass to City Sidewalks* (Calgary: Banff Trail Community Seniors, 1999), 51.

23 Frank Edward, telephone interview, Peterborough, ON, 8 December 2011.

24 For another perspective that emphasizes the agency and mobility of suburban adolescents in this era, see Franca Iacovetta, "Gossip, Contest, and Power in the Making of Suburban Bad Girls: Toronto, 1945–60," *Canadian Historical Review* 80, no. 4 (December 1999): 585–625.

25 Elizabeth Davidson, telephone interview, Peterborough, ON, 11 November 2011.

26 Census of Canada, 1941, 1951, and 1961.

27   Jacobs, *The Death and Life of Great American Cities,* 85–86.

28   Donna McLaren, telephone interview, Peterborough, ON, 11 December 2011.

29   Wendy Glidden, personal interview, Calgary, AB, 2 August 2011.

30   Granted, some of this may have been due to memories that can be reconstituted several times over the years, but she recalled other activities vividly, indicating to me that these other activities were not part of her or her siblings' experiences. Additionally, she was involved in several other organized activities such as the Canadian Girls in Training, so it was not that she was unable to recall *any* childhood activities.

31   For further reading, see Lynn Spigel, *Make Room for TV: Television and the Family Ideal in Postwar America* (Chicago: University of Chicago Press, 1992).

32   Neil Sutherland, *Growing Up: Childhood in English Canada from the Great War to the Age of Television* (Toronto: University of Toronto Press, 1997), x.

33   Chudacoff, *Children at Play,* 154.

34   Sutherland, *Growing Up,* x.

35   Doug Cass, personal interview, Cochrane, AB, 2 June 2011.

36   Wendy Glidden, personal interview, Calgary, AB, 2 August 2011.

37   Jim Chambers, *Recollections: A Baby Boomer's Memories of the Fabulous Fifties* (Morrisville, NC: Lulu Press, 2009), 11.

38   Bruce Wilson, personal interview, Calgary, AB, 28 July 2011.

39   Steven Mintz, *Huck's Raft: A History of American Childhood* (Cambridge, MA: Belknap Press, 2004), 298.

40   Chudacoff, *Children at Play,* 157.

41   Jim Farquharson, personal interview, Calgary, AB, 17 October 2011.

42   Sharon Johnstone, telephone interview, Peterborough, ON, 8 December 2011.

43   "T.V.—Good or Bad?," *Central Weeper,* February 1955, 1.

44   City of Calgary, Department of Youth Research Division, *Recreation in the City of Calgary: A Survey of Interests, Activities and Opportunities,* (Calgary: City of Calgary, 1966), 419, available in City of Calgary Archives.

45   Paul Rutherford, "Researching Television History: Prime Time Canada, 1952–1967," *Archivaria* 20 (Summer 1985): 91.

46   "Kids' TV: The Best and Worst," *Chatelaine,* September 1974, 39.

47   Canadian Gallup Poll, March 1956, no. 247, "Influence of TV?," question 1a; and Canadian Gallup Poll, June 1966, no. 319, "T.V. a Good Influence on Family Life?," question 11.

48   For further reading on audience reception theory specifically related to encoding and decoding, see Stuart Hall, "Encoding and Decoding in Television Discourse," CCCS Stencilled Paper 7, University of Birmingham, 1973.

49   "T.V. or Not T.V.," *Aberhart Advocate* 7, no. 2 (25 November 1964): 3.

50   One of the major themes of Chudacoff's *Children at Play,* an influential book on the history of childhood, is the increasing regulation of time for young people.

51   City of Calgary, *Recreation in the City of Calgary,* 442.

52   Calgary Boys Club, *Annual Report* (Calgary: Calgary Boys Club, 1950–51), 115, Boys and Girls Clubs of Calgary fonds, M7547, file 1, Glenbow Archives.

53   The Calgary Boys Club and its directives will be explored in greater detail in the chapter on delinquency and crime.

54   Lesley Hayes, personal interview, Calgary, AB, 26 July 2011.

55   City of Calgary, *Recreation in the City of Calgary,* 422.

56   Chambers, *Recollections,* 63.

57   Doug Cass, personal interview, Cochrane, AB, 2 June 2011.

58   "Teen Topics by Sally," *Calgary Herald,* 11 January 1950.

59   Mariah Adin, *The Brooklyn Thrill-Kill Gang and the Great Comic Book Scare of the Fifties* (Santa Barbara, CA: Praeger, 2015).

60   William Wright, telephone interview, Peterborough, ON, 4 November 2011.

61   Mary Baker, personal interview, Calgary, AB, 25 July 2011.

62   Doug Cass, personal interview, Cochrane, AB, 2 June 2011.

63   Bill Bryson, *The Life and Times of the Thunderbolt Kid* (New York: Broadway Books, 2006), 127.

64   Cynthia Comacchio, *The Dominion of Youth: Adolescence and the Making of Modern Canada* (Waterloo, ON: Wilfrid Laurier University Press, 2006), 212.

65   William Wright, telephone interview, Peterborough, ON, 4 November 2011.

66   Rosalynn Baxandall and Elizabeth Ewen, *Picture Windows: How the Suburbs Happened* (New York: Basic Books, 2000), 230.

67   David Wasserman, "Modern Music Dictionary," *Aberhart Advocate* 6, no. 4 (17 March 1964): 4, n.p.

68   The Festival Express was a train tour of some of the most popular North American musical acts of the late 1960s and early 1970s. Performances were held in Toronto, Winnipeg, and Calgary. One of the best sources for further information is a 2003 documentary that focuses on the acts, the travel, and the festival's impact on the people who went out to see the show. See Bob Smeaton, dir., *Festival Express* (New York City, NY: THINK Film, 2003).

69   Jim Farquharson, personal interview, Calgary, AB, 17 October 2011.

70   Brent Harris, telephone interview, Peterborough, ON, 9 December 2011.

71   Sharon Johnstone, telephone interview, Peterborough, ON, 8 December 2011.

72   Allan Matthews, personal interview, Calgary, AB, 29 July 2011.

73   Calgary Boys Club, *Executive Director's Report* (Calgary: Calgary Boys Club, 1960), 1, Boys and Girls Club of Calgary fonds, M7547, file 1, Glenbow Archives.

74   "Editorial," *Aberhart Advocate,* vol. 3, no. 2 (December 1960): 1.

75   "Two Guides to Canada's Rich Burgeoning Teenage Market," *Financial Post,* October 1967 [n.d.], 20.

76   Baxandall and Ewen, *Picture Windows,* 146. This was embodied in a new generation of stars such as Frank Sinatra and, to the greatest extent, Elvis Presley, who burst onto the American television scene in 1955, had dozens of chart-topping hits, and starred in a long string of movies that featured his music.

77   William Wright, telephone interview, Peterborough, ON, 4 November 2011.

78   Chudacoff, *Children at Play,* 138.

79   "Wide Variety of Toys for Children This Christmas," *Calgary Herald,* 20 December 1951.

80   Daniel Thomas Cook, *The Commodification of Childhood* (Durham, NC: Duke University Press, 2004), 6.

81   Bruce Wilson, personal interview, Calgary, AB, 28 July 2011.

82   John R. Seeley, R. Alexander Sim, and E.W. Loosley, *Crestwood Heights: A Study of the Culture of Suburban Life* (Toronto: University of Toronto Press, 1963), 103.

83   Bryson, *The Life and Times of the Thunderbolt Kid,* 21.

84   Baxandall and Ewen, *Picture Windows,* 152.

85   Wendy Glidden, personal interview, Calgary, AB, 2 August 2011.

86   Ibid.

87   Doug Owram, *Born at the Right Time: A History of the Baby Boom Generation* (Toronto: University of Toronto Press, 1996), 310.

88   W. Reynolds, "Youthful Rebels Resisting Role of the Docile Consumer," *Financial Post,* 25 January 1969, 63.

89   Wendy Glidden, personal interview, Calgary, AB, 2 August 2011.

90   Cook, *The Commodification of Childhood,* 10–11.

91   On suburban teenage mobility, see Iacovetta, "Gossip, Contest, and Power in the Making of Suburban Bad Girls," 585–624.

CHAPTER 5: Healthy Minds in Healthy Bodies

1   It would be several decades before the majority of women doing paid work outside the home, especially married women, would become commonplace in Canada. For further reading, see Joan Sangster, *Transforming Labour: Women and Work in Postwar Canada* (Toronto: University of Toronto Press, 2010).

2   Wendy Glidden, personal interview, Calgary, AB, 2 August 2011.

3   John R. Stilgoe, *Borderland: Origins of the American Suburb, 1820–1939* (New Haven, CT: Yale University Press, 1988), 16.

4   Suzanne Morton, *Ideal Surroundings: Domestic Life in a Working-Class Suburb in the 1920s* (Toronto: University of Toronto Press, 1995), 154, 155.

5   Ibid., 13.

6   Ibid., 200.

7   Veronica Strong-Boag, *The New Day Recalled: Lives of Girls and Women in English Canada, 1919–1939* (Toronto: Copp Clark Pitman, 1988), 217.

8   Ibid., 22.

9   Joseph E. Illick, *American Childhoods* (Philadelphia: University of Pennsylvania Press, 2002), 64.

10   See Lillian Faderman, *Odd Girls and Twilight Lovers: A History of Lesbian Life in Twentieth-Century America* (Toronto: Penguin Books, 1991).

11   Sharon Wall, *The Nurture of Nature: Childhood, Antimodernism, and Ontario Summer Camps, 1920–55* (Vancouver: UBC Press, 2010), 201.

12   Ibid., 8.

13   Robert McIntosh, "Constructing the Child: New Approaches to the History of Childhood in Canada," *Acadiensis* 28, no. 2 (Spring 1999): 135.

14   Steven Mintz, *Huck's Raft: A History of American Childhood* (Cambridge, MA: Belknap Press, 2006), 284. For an exploration of postwar masculinity relating mainly to adults, see Christopher Dummitt, *The Manly Modern: Masculinity in Postwar Canada* (Vancouver: UBC Press, 2007).

15   Veronica Strong-Boag, "Home Dreams: Women and the Suburban Experiment in Canada, 1945–60," *Canadian Historical Review* 72, no. 4 (1991): 471.

16   Richard Harris, *Creeping Conformity: How Canada Became Suburban, 1900–1960* (Toronto: University of Toronto Press, 2004), 38.

17   Brian Rutz, telephone interview, Peterborough, ON, 12 December 2011.

18   Neil Sutherland, "'We Always Had Things to Do': The Paid and Unpaid Work of Anglophone Children between the 1920s and the 1960s," *Labour/Le Travail* 25 (Spring 1990): 110.

19   For a history of child care in Calgary and Alberta more broadly, see Tom Langford,

Alberta's Day Care Controversy: From 1908 to 2009 and Beyond (Edmonton: Athabasca University Press, 2011).

20 Strong-Boag, "Home Dreams," 476–77.

21 For the integral roles that women and specifically mothers played in Canada in this period, see Tarah Brookfield, *Cold War Comforts: Canadian Women, Child Safety, and Global Insecurity* (Waterloo, ON: Wilfrid Laurier University Press, 2012).

22 Bruce Wilson, personal interview, 28 July 2011. For studies of the histories of education, pedagogies, and teachers in Canada, see Ruth Sandwell, *To the Past: History Education, Public Memory, and Citizenship in Canada* (Toronto: University of Toronto Press, 2006); Sara Z. Burke and Patrice Milewski, *Schooling in Transition: Readings in Canadian History of Education* (Toronto: University of Toronto Press, 2012); and Douglas O. Baldwin, *Teachers, Students and Pedagogy: Readings and Documents in the History of Canadian Education* (Markham, ON: Fitzhenry and Whiteside, 2008).

23 On boyhood during these years, see Christopher J. Greig, *Ontario Boys: Masculinity and the Idea of Boyhood in Postwar Ontario, 1945–1960* (Waterloo, ON: Wilfrid Laurier University Press, 2014).

24 L.H. Garstin, "Our Schools Are Loaded against Boys," *Maclean's*, 23 February 1963, 13–15.

25 Mary Baker, personal interview, Calgary, AB, 25 July 2011.

26 Mothers also contributed to this; most male interviewees mentioned that mothers often encouraged sons to spend time with their fathers, with a wide variance of success in it being quality time. When it was organic, it seemed to have the most meaning for most interviewees.

27 Robert Rutherdale, "Just Nostalgic Family Men? Off-the-Job Family Time, Providing, and Oral Histories of Fatherhood in Postwar Canada, 1945–1975," *Oral History Forum* 29 (2009): 5.

28 S.D. Clark, *The Suburban Society* (Toronto: University of Toronto Press, 1966).

29 William Wright, telephone interview, Peterborough, ON, 4 November 2011.

30 Susan Saegert, "Masculine Cities and Feminine Suburbs: Polarized Ideas, Contradictory Realities," *Signs* 5, no. 3 (Spring 1980): 105.

31 Sutherland, "We Always Had Things to Do," 113.

32 Boys Clubs of Canada, *Study of the City of Calgary* (Montreal: Boys Clubs of Canada, 1956), 42, Boys and Girls Clubs of Calgary fonds, M7547, file 11, Glenbow Archives.

33 For further reading on the idealized active and controlling gendered boy, see Mona Gleason, "Embodied Negotiations: Children's Bodies and Historical Change in Canada, 1930 to 1960," *Journal of Canadian Studies* 34, no. 1 (Spring 1999): 119.

34 Mary Baker, personal interview, Calgary, AB, 25 July 2011.

35 Tammy Simpson, telephone interview, Peterborough, ON, 13 December 2011.

36 Bruce Wilson, personal interview, Calgary, AB, 28 July 2011.

37 Ibid.

38 Margaret Atwood, *Cat's Eye* (Toronto: McClelland and Stewart, 1988), 30.

39 Wendy Glidden, personal interview, Calgary, AB, 2 August 2011.

40 While highly gendered, the instances of women working outside the home and doing something other than homemaking has been explored elsewhere. For some of the best works across temporal lines, see Sangster, *Transforming Labour*; Morton, *Ideal Surroundings*; and Franca Iacovetta and Mariana Valverde, eds., *Gender Conflicts: New Essays in Women's History* (Toronto: University of Toronto Press, 1992).

41   Margeurite Glow, "Equality versus Supremacy," *Central Collegiate Weeper*, February 1957, 31.

42   Wendy Glidden, personal interview, Calgary, AB, 2 August 2011.

43   "Editorial," *Aberhart Advocate* 10, no. 11 (April 1969): 3.

44   Radicalism was obviously quelled in student publications, and the interviewees for this book could never be confused with militant radicals. There were certainly individuals who experienced the stirrings of progressive views by their late teens but nothing beyond that was found in the literary culture or in oral histories.

45   Frank Edward, telephone interview, Peterborough, ON, 8 December 2011.

46   Mary Baker, personal interview, Calgary, AB, 25 July 2011.

47   It seems clear that the subject was taboo through the 1960s as well. Not one article or essay appeared in any school newspapers or newsletters in this period about teenage pregnancy and motherhood. It was not until the mid-1960s that there was serious and meaningful discussion of teenage sexuality.

48   "Teen-Age Mothers—YWCA Study," *Canadian Welfare* 40 (May–June 1964): 140–41; and "More Teen-Age Unwed Mothers," Globe and Mail, 2 March 1967, W2.

49   See Heather Dryburgh, "Teenage Pregnancy," Statistics Canada, Health Reports 12, no. 1: https://www150.statcan.gc.ca/n1/en/pub/82-003-x/2000001/article/5299-eng .pdf?st=YI8DQEHy, and on teenage pregnancy, especially from the perspective of teenagers themselves, see Robert Coles, *The Youngest Parents* (New York: W.W. Norton, 1997).

50   Allan Matthews, personal interview, Calgary, AB, 29 July 2011.

51   Donna McLaren, telephone interview, Peterborough, ON, 12 December 2011.

52   Bill Bryson, *The Life and Times of the Thunderbolt Kid* (New York: Broadway Books, 2006), 111.

53   Gleason, "Embodied Negotiations," 123.

54   Ibid., 129.

55   Valerie J. Korinek, *Roughing It in the Suburbs: Reading Chatelaine Magazine in the Fifties and Sixties* (Toronto: University of Toronto Press, 2000), 369.

56   Michelle Macdonald, personal interview, Calgary, AB, 27 July 2011.

57   Barry Matthews, telephone interview, Peterborough, ON, 31 October 2011.

58   "Early Sex Schooling Urged," *Calgary Herald*, 2 February 1962, 23.

59   Bruce Wilson, personal interview, Calgary, AB, 28 July 2011.

60   "Sex Films Approved for Grades 7, 8 and 9," *Globe and Mail*, 2 February 1967, W4.

61   Mary Louise Adams, *The Trouble with Normal: Postwar Youth and the Making of Heterosexuality* (Toronto: University of Toronto Press, 1997), 164.

62   William Wright, telephone interview, Peterborough, ON, 4 November 2011.

63   John R. Seeley, Alexander Sim, and E.W. Loosley, *Crestwood Heights: A Study of the Culture of Suburban Life* (Toronto: University of Toronto Press, 1963), 99.

64   Allan Matthews, personal interview, Calgary, AB, 29 July 2011.

65   Adams, *The Trouble with Normal*, 167.

66   Allan Matthews, personal interview, Calgary, AB, 29 July 2011.

67   Mona Gleason, "Disciplining the Student Body: Schooling and the Construction of Canadian Children's Bodies, 1930 to 1960," *History of Education Quarterly* 41, no. 2 (Spring 2001): 215.

68   Canadian Gallup Poll, August 1968, no. 331, "Should Adult Homosexual Act Be Criminal?," question 14.

69   Brian Rutz, telephone interview, Peterborough, ON, 12 December 2011.

70   For further reading, see Adams, *The Trouble with Normal*.

71   Mary Baker, personal interview, Calgary, AB, 25 July 2011.

72   Adams, *The Trouble with Normal*, 9.

73   Ibid., 167.

74   Gleason, "Embodied Negotiations," 131.

75   D. Hunt, "Andy Little," *Aberhart Advocate* 11, no. 6 (December 1969): 7.

76   Elise Chenier, *Strangers in Our Midst: Sexual Deviancy in Postwar Ontario* (Toronto: University of Toronto Press, 2008), 5.

77   See Marshall McLuhan, *Understanding Media: The Extensions of Man* (Cambridge, MA: MIT Press, 1994).

78   Family Life Education, Sex Education and Other Aspects of Family Life, Elementary Curriculum Committee (Calgary: September 1968), 6, Family Life Education Council of Calgary fonds, M6239, file 16, Glenbow Archives.

79   D. Hunt, "Sex Education and Us,"*Aberhart Advocate* 10, no. 10 (March 1969): 7.

80   Canadian Gallup Poll, February 1964, no. 306, "Approval of Sex Education in High Schools," question 13.

81   Cynthia Comacchio, *The Dominion of Youth: Adolescence and the Making of Modern Canada* (Waterloo, ON: Wilfrid Laurier University Press, 2006), 97.

82   Eleanor Burritt, "'Going Steady' System Popular in Calgary,'" *Calgary Herald*, 21 April 1950.

83   Donna McLaren, telephone interview, Peterborough, ON, 12 December 2011.

84   Ibid.

85   Mary Baker, personal interview, Calgary, AB, 25 July 2011. It is a prominent theme emphasized throughout the definitive book on the history of babysitting, Miriam Forman-Brunell's *Babysitting: An American History* (New York: New York University Press, 2009).

86   Peggy Barnsley, "This Steady Business," *Central Collegiate Institute Weeper*, June 1957, 5.

87   Canadian Gallup Poll, June 1963, no. 303, "Should High School Students 'Go Steady'?," question 13.

88   "How to Choose a Mate," *Aberhart Advocate* 5, no. 4 (20 March 1963): 6.

89   Donna McLaren, telephone interview, Peterborough, ON, 11 December 2011.

90   City of Calgary, Department of Youth Research Division, Recreation in the City of Calgary: A Survey of Interests, Activities and Opportunities (Calgary: City of Calgary, 1966), 405, available in City of Calgary Archives.

91   "Teen Topics by Sally," *Calgary Herald*, 27 February 1950; "Mrs. Thompson Advises: Girl, 16, Too Young to Be Able to Choose Husband Wisely," *Globe and Mail*, 28 October 1959, 17; and Eleanor Burritt, "Majority of 'Teeners' Approve 'Going Steady,'" *Calgary Herald*, 17 January 1950.

92   Canadian Gallup Poll, November 1960, no. 285, "Is Practice of Birth Control Wrong?," question 8.

93   Lesley Hayes, personal interview, Calgary, AB, 26 July 2011.

94   Howard P. Chudacoff, *Children at Play: An American History* (New York: New York University Press, 2007), 64.

95   Jack W. Berryman, "From the Cradle to the Playing Field: America's Emphasis on Highly Organized Sports for Preadolescent Boys," *Journal of Sport History* 2, no. 2 (1975): 116.

96   Shirley Tillotson, *The Public at Play: Gender and the Politics of Recreation in Postwar Ontario* (Toronto: University of Toronto Press, 2000). My findings reflect more of what Veronica Strong-Boag concludes in "Home Dreams," 471–504.

97   "Youngsters Have Fun as Playgrounds Open," *Calgary Herald*, 7 July 1950.

98   Barry Matthews, telephone interview, Peterborough, ON, 31 October 2011.

99   City of Calgary, Recreation in the City of Calgary, 407.

100   Korinek, *Roughing It in the Suburbs*, 25.

101   "95,613 Children Make Use of 21 Playgrounds," *The Albertan*, 28 January 1950.

102   Owram, *Born at the Right Time*, 110.

103   Jack F. Way, Camp Adventure Annual Report (Calgary: Calgary Boys Club, 1961), 1, Boys and Girls Club of Calgary fonds, M7547, file 14, Glenbow Archives.

104   "Girl Guide Ranks Increase in Canada," Calgary Herald, 2 June 1952, 7.

105   For further reading, see Margaret Prang, "'The Girl God Would Have Me Be': The Canadian Girls in Training, 1915–39," *Canadian Historical Review* 66, no. 2 (1985): 154–84; and Veronica Strong-Boag, *Janey Canuck: Women in Canada, 1919–1939* (Ottawa: Canadian Historical Association, 1994).

106   While it was not often expressed as cynicism, in the archival record it is striking how many adolescents "played" with the higher ideals of many organizations. Many of them had obviously learned what answers were required of them but did not necessarily espouse these ideals wholly.

107   Allan Matthews, personal interview, Calgary, AB, 29 July 2011.

108   Elaine Seskevich, "Guides Don't Just Push Cookies," *Calgary Herald*, 14 January 1970, 59.

109   See Neil Sutherland, *Children in English-Canadian Society: Framing the Twentieth-Century Consensus* (Waterloo, ON: Wilfrid Laurier University Press, 2000); and Mona Gleason, *Small Matters: Canadian Children in Sickness and Health, 1900–1940* (Montreal/Kingston: McGill-Queen's University Press, 2013).

110   J.D. Griffin, M.D., "Problem of Mental Health in Canada," *Social Worker* 15, no. 1 (September 1946): 5, Canadian Association of Social Workers fonds, MG 28, I 441, box 21, file 6, Library and Archives Canada.

111   "Cancer Takes Toll among Children and Teen-Agers," *Calgary Herald*, 22 February 1950, 7.

112   "Money Needed to Care for Children's Health," *Calgary Herald*, 29 November 1950, 6. This predates universal health care in Canada, which was instituted in 1966. While layers remained in the state system, this was the birth of a system with national standards. See Alvin Finkel, *Social Policy and Practice in Canada: A History* (Waterloo, ON: Wilfrid Laurier University Press, 2006).

113   For further anecdotal evidence, see Clark, *The Suburban Society*; and William Dobriner, *Class in Suburbia* (Englewood Cliffs, NJ: Prentice Hall, 1963).

114   Laura J. Miller, "Family Togetherness and the Suburban Ideal," *Sociological Forum* 10, no. 3 (September 1995): 396–97. Miller argues that there was a moral aspect to this as well, with cities proper cast as sinful and potentially able to lure people away from familial activities.

115   Harris, *Creeping Conformity*, 54.

116   Max Foran, *Calgary: An Illustrated History* (Toronto: James Lorimer, 1978), 116.

117   Richard Harris and Michael E. Mercier, "How Healthy Were the Suburbs?," *Journal of Urban History* 31, no. 6 (September 2005): 785.

118   Wayne K.D. Davies and Ivan J. Townshend, "How Do Community Associations Vary? The Structure of Community Associations in Calgary, Alberta," *Urban Studies* 31, no. 10 (1994): 1743.

119   For a history of polio, see Gareth Williams, *Paralysed with Fear: The Story of Polio* (New York: Palgrave Macmillan, 2013).

120   "Student's Long Holiday Ends," *Calgary Herald*, 22 September 1952, 1.

121   "GP or Specialist for the Children," *Financial Post*, 11 June 1960, 70.

122   "Teen Topics by Sally," *Calgary Herald*, 20 January 1951.

123   Mona Gleason, *Normalizing the Ideal: Psychology, Schooling and the Family in Postwar Canada* (Toronto: University of Toronto Press, 1999), 9.

124   "Euthanasia," *Aberhart Advocate* 4, no. 9 (June 1962): 11.

125   Letter to the editor, *Aberhart Advocate* 4, no. 5 (February 1962): 1.

126   For the cultural history of smoking in a global context, see Sander L. Gilman and Xun Zhou, eds., *Smoke: A Global History of Smoking* (London: Reaktion, 2004).

127   "Only One-Quarter of Our Teenagers Smoke," *Financial Post*, 27 February 1965, 23.

128   Bryson, *The Life and Times of the Thunderbolt Kid*, 70.

129   For a timeline of the changes, see "A Legal History of Smoking in Canada," CBC News, 29 July 2011, http: //www.cbc.ca/news/health/a-legal-history-of-smoking -in-canada-1.982213.

130   Doug Cass, personal interview, Cochrane, AB, 2 June 2011.

131   Canadian Gallup Poll, August 1963, no. 304, "Average # of Cigarettes Smoked Per Day?"

132   "Think Twice before Starting to Smoke Cigarettes," *Aberhart Advocate* 1, no. 5 (June 1959): 9.

133   "My Experience with the Habit," *Aberhart Advocate* 7, no. 6 (16 April 1965): 12.

134   Doug Cass, personal interview, Cochrane, AB, 2 June 2011.

135   Bruce Wilson, personal interview, Calgary, AB, 28 July 2011.

136   The importance of all of this cannot be overstated. These measures not only helped to prevent illness but also, in most instances, kept both children and adolescents alive. For an excellent study of young people's health in Canada in a global context, see Cynthia Comacchio, Janet Golden, and George Weiz, eds., *Healing the World's Children: Interdisciplinary Perspectives on Child Health in the Twentieth Century* (Montreal/Kingston: McGill-Queen's University Press, 2008).

137   Tammy Simpson, telephone interview, Peterborough, ON, 24 November 2011.

138   Brian Rutz, telephone interview, Peterborough, ON, 12 December 2011.

139   Owram came to a similar conclusion in *Born at the Right Time*.

140   George P. Hunt, "Two Mothers and a Brave Doctor," *Life*, 4 June 1965, 3.

141   While many would argue that this expansion did not go nearly far enough, there is no denying that there were critical improvements in health care for most Canadian citizens in this period. For further reading, see Alvin Finkel, *Social Policy and Practice*; and Dominique Marshall, *The Social Origins of the Welfare State: Quebec Families, Compulsory Education, and Family Allowances, 1940–1955* (Waterloo, ON: Wilfrid Laurier University Press, 2006).

142   R.D. Fraser, "Number of Physicians, Dentists and Nurses, Population per Physician, Dentist and Nurse, Number of Graduates of Medical and Dental Schools, Canada, 1871–1975," Statistics Canada, series B82–92, http: //www.statcan.gc.ca/ pub/11–516-x/pdf/5500093-eng.pdf.

143   R.D. Fraser, "Annual Rates of Notifiable Diseases, Canada, 1926–1975," Statistics Canada, series B517–25, http: //www.statcan.gc.ca/pub/11–516-x/pdf/5500093-eng .pdf.

144   "Junior Red Cross Hospital Formally Opened in Calgary," *Calgary Daily Herald*, 20 May 1922, 1.

145   Gayle Herchak, "Hospital Care of Yesteryear Goes on File," *Calgary Herald*, 27 June 1980.

146   Mary Baker, personal interview, Calgary, AB, 25 July 2011.

147   Brian Rutz, telephone interview, Peterborough, ON, 12 December 2011.

148   Michelle Macdonald, personal interview, Calgary, AB, 27 July 2011.

149   For histories of hospitals, see Guenter B. Risse, *Mending Bodies, Saving Souls: A History of Hospitals* (Toronto: Oxford University Press, 1999); Charles E. Rosenberg, *The Care of Strangers: The Rise of America's Hospital System* (Baltimore, MD: Hopkins Fulfillment Service, 1995); and Rosemary Stevens, *In Sickness and in Wealth: American Hospitals in the Twentieth Century* (Toronto: Harper Collins, 1990.)

150   Tammy Simpson, telephone interview, Peterborough, ON, 24 November 2011.

151   Lesley Hayes, personal interview, Calgary, AB, 26 July 2011.

152   For further reading on postwar television viewing, individualization, and increasing consumption, see Sonia Livingstone, "Half a Century of Television in the Lives of Our Children," *Annals of the American Academy of Political and Social Science* 625 (2009): 151–63.

153   Mary Baker, personal interview, Calgary, AB, 25 July 2011.

154   For an exploration of the North American fast food industry in historical context, see Eric Schlosser, *Fast Food Nation* (Boston: Houghton Mifflin, 2001). For another book detailing some of the cultural history and psychology associated with food, see Leon Rappoport, *How We Eat: Appetite, Culture, and the Psychology of Food* (Toronto: ECW Press, 2003).

155   Bruce Wilson, personal interview, Calgary, AB, 28 July 2011.

156   "Too Many Empty Calories," *Life*, 16 February 1962, 46.

157   Tammy Simpson, telephone interview, Peterborough, ON, 24 November 2011.

158   Sharon Johnstone, telephone interview, Peterborough, ON, 8 December 2011.

159   Tammy Simpson, telephone interview, Peterborough, ON, 24 November 2011.

160   There are no numbers to be found specifically in Canada, but US companies such as Swanson, which also sold dinners in Canada, were selling millions of dinners by the mid-1950s. For further reading, see Paul Farhi, "The Man Who Gave America a Taste of the Future," *Washington Post*, 22 July 2005, http://www.washingtonpost.com/wp-dyn/content/article/2005/07/21/AR2005072102249.html.

161   "Children on Good Diet Show Growth Spurts," *Globe and Mail*, 10 July 1969, W3; "Malnutrition Check of Canadians Is Ordered by Health Minister," *Globe and Mail*, 21 February 1969, 11.

162   William Wright, telephone interview, Peterborough, ON, 4 November 2011.

163   Wendy Glidden, personal interview, Calgary, AB, 2 August 2011.

164   "MD Urges Slimming for Chubby Children," *Globe and Mail*, 8 October 1968, 10; and "Fat Children Termed Lazy Rather Than Greedy," *Globe and Mail*, 26 April 1967, 10.

165   Canadian Gallup Poll, November 1959, no. 279, "What Would You Say Is the Most Urgent Problem Facing You and Your Family in 1960?," question 2.

166   For a cultural history of obesity, with some emphasis on childhood, see Sander L. Gilman, *Fat: A Cultural History of Obesity* (Cambridge: Polity, 2008).

167   Sharon Johnstone, telephone interview, Peterborough, ON, 8 December 2011.

168   Barry Matthews, telephone interview, Peterborough, ON, 31 October 2011.

169   Jim Chambers, *Recollections: A Baby Boomer's Memories of the Fabulous Fifties* (Morrisville, NC: Lulu Press, 2009), 7.

170   For a comprehensive look at the Canada Food Guide and changes to it, see

Government of Canada, "History of Canada's Food Guides from 1942 to 1972," http: //www.hc-sc.gc.ca/fn-an/food-guide-aliment/context/fg_history-histoire_ga-eng.php.

171   For a brilliant study of teenage girls, representation, and moral panic in the United States, see Shayla Thiel-Stern, *From the Dance Hall to Facebook: Teen Girls, Mass Media, and Moral Panic in the United States, 1905–2010* (Boston: University of Massachusetts Press, 2014).

172   Mary Baker, personal interview, Calgary, AB, 25 July 2011.

CHAPTER 6: Things That Go Bump in the Night

1   Margaret Atwood, *Cat's Eye* (Toronto: McClelland and Stewart, 1988), 51.

2   Pat Hagen "Child of Darkness," *Aberhart Advocate* 11, no. 9 (19 February 1969): 15.

3   Dorothy Sangster, "Why Teen-Age Girls Run from Home," *Globe and Mail*, 30 May 1963, 15.

4   J. Dingman, "How to Live with 'the Child You Don't Like,'" *Chatelaine*, January 1970, 16, 68–69.

5   Roger A. Ekirch, *At Day's Close: Night in Times Past* (New York: Norton, 2005), xxvi.

6   Michelle Macdonald, personal interview, Calgary, AB, 27 July 2011.

7   See Susan Kohl Malone, "Early to Bed, Early to Rise? An Exploration of Adolescent Sleep Hygiene Practices," *Journal of School Nursing* 27, no. 5 (October 2011): 348–54.

8   Tamara Myers, "Solution: A History of Juvenile Sundown Regulations in Canada," in *Lost Kids: Vulnerable Children and Youth in Twentieth-Century Canada and the United States*, ed. Mona Gleason, Tamara Myers, Leslie Paris, and Veronica Strong-Boag (Vancouver: UBC Press, 2010), 97–98.

9   Bryan D. Palmer, *Cultures of Darkness: Night Travels in the Histories of Transgression* (New York: Monthly Review Press, 2000), 13.

10   John David Pare, "The Night," Aberhart Opus 8 Yearbook, 1965–66, 97.

11   There were also several references to nightmares in essays, poems, and short stories.

12   Palmer, *Cultures of Darkness*, 6.

13   William Wright, telephone interview, Peterborough, ON, 4 November 2011.

14   Brent Harris, telephone interview, Peterborough, ON, 9 December 2011.

15   Ekirch, *At Day's Close*, xxvi.

16   See Betty Friedan, *The Feminine Mystique* (New York: Norton, 1963); Lewis Mumford, *The City in History: Its Origins, Its Transformations, and Its Prospects* (New York: Harcourt, Brace and World, 1961); and William H. Whyte, *The Organization Man* (Toronto: Simon and Schuster, 1956).

17   Mary Baker, personal interview, Calgary, AB, 25 July 2011.

18   Sharon Johnstone, telephone interview, Peterborough, ON, 8 December 2011.

19   Brian Rutz, telephone interview, Peterborough, ON, 12 December 2011.

20   Myers, "Solution," 108 and 109. With online luring, stalking, and generalized issues around child pornography, many parents today are concerned when young people are in the privacy of their rooms and have access to the internet at their fingertips. These "safe" places are no longer viewed as havens for older children and teens, as many high-profile cases have clearly demonstrated. One of the more infamous cases in Canada is teenager Amanda Todd's experience in British Columbia, which ended in her tragic suicide at age fifteen, in 2012.

21　The term juvenile has not been used in discussions of teenage crime since the implementation of the Young Offenders Act in 1994, which was repealed and replaced with the Youth Criminal Justice Act in 2003. The original legislation was the 1908 Juvenile Delinquents Act.

22　Jason van Rassel, "Majority of Teen Crimes Occur in Daytime," *Calgary Herald*, 11 March 2008.

23　The car allowed adolescents to expand their horizons both literally and metaphorically over the course of the twentieth century. For further reading on how it affected adolescent mobility in the postwar period, see Franca Iacovetta, "Gossip, Contest and Power in the Making of Suburban Bad Girls: Toronto, 1945–60," *Canadian Historical Review* 80, no. 4 (December 1999): 585–624.

24　Gordon Selkirk, "Editorial," *Aberhart Advocate* 5, no. 3 (12 February 1963): 4.

25　Barry Matthews, telephone interview, Peterborough, ON, 31 October 2011.

26　Allan Matthews, personal interview, Calgary, AB, 29 July 2011.

27　Ron Fenerty, "I Won't Be Back," *Central Weeper*, June 1957, 17.

28　Jim Farquharson, personal interview, Calgary, AB, 17 October 2011.

29　Sharyn Bennett, "The Night," *Opus 8 Yearbook*, 1965–66, 100.

30　See James A. Clapp, "Growing Up Urban: The City, the Cinema and American Youth," *Journal of Popular Culture* 40, no. 4 (2007): 601–29; and Steven Cohan, *Masked Men: Masculinity and the Movies in the Fifties* (Bloomington: Indiana University Press, 1997).

31　Bill Bryson, *The Life and Times of the Thunderbolt Kid* (New York: Broadway Books, 2006), 196.

32　William Wright, telephone interview, Peterborough, ON, 4 November 2011.

33　Wendy Glidden, personal interview, Calgary, AB, 2 August 2011.

34　Brent Harris, telephone interview, Peterborough, ON, 9 December 2011.

35　Neil Sutherland, "'We Always Had Things to Do': The Paid and Unpaid Work of Anglophone Children between the 1920s and the 1960s," *Labour/Le Travail* 25 (Spring 1990): 105–41.

36　Myers, "Solution," 109.

37　Jim Farquharson, personal interview, Calgary, AB, 17 October 2011.

38　"Night-Riding Telegraph Boys Now 'Illuminated,'" *Calgary Herald*, 28 March 1950.

39　This was anecdotal but mentioned by several interviewees. The census reveals that roughly one in five (21.1 percent) of young Canadians aged fifteen to twenty-four were employed on a part-time basis in Canada. This number dramatically increased to nearly half (47.3 percent) by 2012. See Statistics Canada, "Work Employment Rate," Indicators of Well-Being in Canada, accessed 1 December 2018, http://www4.hrsdc.gc.ca/.3ndic.1t.4r-eng.jsp? iid=13.

40　Tammy Simpson, telephone interview, Peterborough, ON, 24 November 2011.

41　Jim Farquharson, personal interview, Calgary, AB, 17 October 2011.

42　See Iacovetta, "Gossip, Contest, and Power," 585–625.

43　Joan Sangster, *Girl Trouble: Female Delinquency in English Canada* (Toronto: Between the Lines, 2002), 9.

44　In precontact North America, Indigenous societies had their own practices of social control for young people that often emphasized mediation, restitution, or ostracism versus direct incarceration. These methodologies and practices would be viewed by some today as being lax in punitive and remedial qualities. See Marta Tienda and William Julius Wilson, eds., *Youth in Cities: A Cross-national Perspective* (New York: Cambridge University Press, 2002), 145.

45 This is often done within the broader discourse of youth in peril or the loss of values in the younger generation. By the late nineteenth century in Canada, what was constructed as juvenile delinquency was, first of all, property crimes in cities, committed mostly by young, working-class children and teenagers against wealthy upper-class adults. This was gendered criminal activity in that it was performed by normally unsupervised boys who were particularly problematic in roaming urban streets and sometimes working as bootblacks or newsboys. However, these boys were also exposed to more serious crime and adult habits such as gambling and drinking. See Joan Sangster, *Girl Trouble; and Julian Tanner, Teenage Troubles: Youth and Deviance in Canada*, 3rd ed. (Toronto: Oxford University Press, 2010), 27.

46 For a history of social work in twentieth-century Canada, see Therese Jennissen and Colleen Lundy, *One Hundred Years of Social Work: A History of the Profession in Canada, 1900–2000* (Waterloo, ON: Wilfrid Laurier University Press, 2011).

47 Ibid., 31.

48 Sangster, *Girl Trouble*, 5.

49 Ibid., 6.

50 Tamara Myers, *Caught: Montreal's Modern Girls and the Law, 1869–1945* (Toronto: University of Toronto Press, 2006), 9.

51 Ibid., 4.

52 Tamara Myers and Mary Anne Poutanen, "Cadets, Curfews and Compulsory Schooling: Mobilizing Anglo Children in WW II Montreal," *Social History* 38, no. 76 (2005): 389.

53 Ibid., 369. These efforts to create good citizens span across the entire postwar period and continue into the present day.

54 Sangster, *Girl Trouble*, 13.

55 Ibid.

56 Chief Constable, Calgary Police Force, annual report, 1952, 20, Calgary Police Service Archives.

57 Ibid., 1955, 17.

58 Ibid., 1968, 16.

59 City of Calgary, Children's Aid Department, Annual Report (Calgary: Children's Aid Department, 1965), 3–9, Social Services Department fonds, City of Calgary Archives; and Canadian Conference on Social Welfare, annual reports, 1964–66, Canadian Council on Social Development fonds, M 28, I 10, box 362, file 4, Library and Archives Canada.

60 "Alberta Stops Babying Delinquents," *Calgary Herald*, 2 November 1951.

61 Tanner, *Teenage Troubles*, 3.

62 "Lowering the Boom on Juvenile Crime," *Calgary Herald*, 28 May 1951.

63 S.M. Katz, "Truth about Teen-Age Drinking," *Maclean's*, 21 June 1958, 13–15, 51–54; and D.L. Stein, "'Have' Delinquents: Why Do They Go Wrong?," *Maclean's*, 25 January 1965, 22–23.

64 "What to Do about Juvenile Crime," *Life*, 15 March 1954, 24.

65 Angelo Patri, "Woodshed Treatment No Help to Delinquent," *Globe and Mail*, 13 June 1956, 15.

66 Maxine H. Wray, "A Study of the Operation of the Specialized Juvenile Investigative Force," City of Calgary Police Force, 26 March 1976, 1, City of Calgary Archives.

67 "New Attitude toward Police by Teenagers," *Calgary Herald*, 22 January 1952.

68 This line of argument can be traced back to the nineteenth century and is found easily in many recent articles regarding delinquency and crime committed by young people.

69 Graham Pike, "Youth Dept. Is Farce," *The Albertan*, June 1961.

70 Calgary's population increased from 129,060 in 1951 to 403,319 by 1971. Canada Census, 1951 and 1971.

71 See D. Owen Carrigan, *Juvenile Delinquency in Canada: A History* (Toronto: Irwin), 1998..

72 "Executive Director's Report," Calgary Boys Club annual report, 1954–55, 2, Calgary Boys and Girls Clubs of Calgary fonds, M7547, file 1, Glenbow Archives.

73 City of Calgary, Children's Aid Department, annual report, 1962, 8.

74 Southern Alberta Branch, Canadian Association of Social Workers, executive meeting minutes, March 1962 and February 1962, Canadian Association of Social Workers fonds, MG 28, I 441, box 25, file 6, Library and Archives Canada; and Joy Maines, "Through the Years in C.A.S.W.," 1959, 1, Canadian Association of Social Workers fonds, MG 28, I 441, box 1, file 1, Library and Archives Canada.

75 "Youth Scarred after Beating by Teen Gang," *Calgary Herald*, 9 January 1951, 1.

76 "City Juveniles Defiant after Police Warning," *The Albertan*, 9 January 1951, 1.

77 Canadian Gallup Poll, March 1960, no. 281, "Opinion of Parent's Strictness," question 5.

78 Tanner, *Teenage Troubles*, 6.

79 Chief Constable, City of Calgary Police Force, annual report, 1950, 23.

80 Ibid., 24.

81 Ibid., 34–35.

82 R. Erlam, "Getting to the Heart of the Matter: War on Juvenile Delinquency in Whitehorse," *North* 14 (July–August 1967): 2–5.

83 It is difficult to assess the why here, but without question some of it might have been a justification for employment and to establish the need to address the issue in a multitude of ways within a larger discourse of wanting to protect and aid yet punish, if needed, the troubled adolescent.

84 "Juvenile Delinquency Lowest in 20 Years," *Calgary Herald*, 14 April 1951.

85 Sangster, *Girl Trouble*, 6.

86 Canadian Gallup Poll, January 1961, no. 286, "Juvenile Delinquency – Important Problem," question 13a.

87 Atwood, *Cat's Eye*, 51.

88 Mary Baker, personal interview, Calgary, AB, 25 July 2011.

89 Neil Sutherland, *Growing Up: Childhood in English Canada from the Great War to the Age of Television* (Toronto: University of Toronto, 1997), 90.

90 Elise Chenier, *Strangers in Our Midst: Sexual Deviancy in Postwar Ontario* (Toronto: University of Toronto Press, 2008), 3–4.

91 Iacovetta, "Gossip, Contest, and Power," 594.

92 Wendy Glidden, personal interview, Calgary, AB, 2 August 2011.

93 J.C. Spencer, "Work with Hard-to-Reach Youth," *Canadian Welfare* 36 (15 July 1960): 165–70.

94 Iacovetta, "Gossip, Contest and Power," 586–87.

95 City of Calgary, Children's Aid Department, annual report, 9.

96 Canadian Gallup Poll, January 1965, no. 10, "To Reduce Juvenile Delinquency It Has Been Suggested That If a Child under 18 Breaks the Law, One of the Parents

Must Pay the Fine and/or Serve the Child's Jail Sentence, Would You Approve or Disapprove of Such a Plan in Your Community?," question 4.

97   Calgary Boys Club, Executive Director's Report (Calgary: Calgary Boys Club, 1957), 6, Boys and Girls Clubs of Calgary fonds, M7547, file 1, Glenbow Archives.

98   While there can be no doubt that efforts were made to expand the social welfare state in the postwar period, ultimately, the welfare state peaked in the late 1960s with the creation of a universal Medicare system in Canada but no permanent national housing strategy or national child care system. See Alvin Finkel, *Social Policy and Practice in Canada: A History* (Waterloo, ON: Wilfrid Laurier University Press, 2006).

99   The Alberta Association of Social Workers, "Brief to the Government of Alberta, Recommending the Use of Cash Payments in the Social Allowance and Social Assistance Programmes," 1966, 7, Canadian Association of Social Workers fonds, MG 28, I 441, box 25, file 1, Library and Archives Canada.

100   Alberta Association of Social Workers, "Brief for the Patterson Committee on Adoptions," April 1965, Canadian Association of Social Workers fonds, MG 28, I 441, box 25, file 1, Library and Archives Canada.

101   Ibid.

102   Family Life Education Council, "Brief on Family and Community Living," 1969, 3, Family Life Education Council of Calgary fonds, M6239, box 15, Glenbow Archives.

103   City of Calgary, Children's Aid Department, "Brief of the Children's Aid Department of the City of Calgary," 1947, 18, Social Services Department fonds, City of Calgary Archives.

104   Ann Landers, "Justified Gripes against Parents," *Life*, 18 August 1961, 86.

105   Jim Farquharson, personal interview, Calgary, AB, 17 October 2011.

106   City of Calgary, Children's Aid Department, "Brief of the Children's Aid Department of the City of Calgary," 1965, 5, Social Services Department fonds, City of Calgary Archives.

107   Howard P. Chudacoff, *Children at Play: An American History* (New York: New York University Press, 2007), 149.

108   William Wright, telephone interview, Peterborough, ON, 4 November 2011.

109   Further research could and needs to be done on bullying in this period, as the acts themselves did seem to occur, without all of the attendant technology of today. Those who did mention it felt it was often brief and simply a part of their childhood or adolescence experiences. In contrast, it has been viewed as, quite possibly, the major issue of childhood and adolescence in the past ten years in North America.

110   Wayne Bill, "City Youth Charged with Murder," *The Albertan*, 20 August 1968.

111   There are brief reports about juvenile delinquency in each chief constable annual report from this era. Usually there is a table that details the offences for that year.

112   Faye Esler Hall, "Branton Junior High School," in Rose Scollard, ed., *From Prairie Grass to City Sidewalks* (Calgary: Banff Trail Community Seniors, 1999), 48.

113   Brent Harris, telephone interview, Peterborough, ON, 9 December 2011.

114   "Teen-Agers Protest Poor Publicity," Calgary Herald, 17 April 1952.

115   Sangster, *Girl Trouble*, 171.

116   Canadian Gallup Poll, November 1963, no. 305, "Would You Say There Is More Juvenile Delinquency in This Community Today, Than There Was, Say Ten Years Ago?," question 2.

117   Dr. Colettte Carisse, "The New Families in Modern Society," part of a paper pre-
      pared for the 1968 Annual Meeting of the Vanier Institute of the Family, M6239,
      file 3, Glenbow Archives.
118   Sangster, *Girl Trouble*, 176.
119   Iacovetta, "Gossip, Contest, and Power," 623.
120   Owen D. Carrigan, *Juvenile Delinquency in Canada: A History* (Toronto: Irwin,
      1998); and H. Litsky, "Cult of the Juvenile Court," *Canadian Welfare* 46 (July–
      August 1970): 8, 15.
121   Brent Harris, telephone interview, Peterborough, ON, 9 December 2011. This
      questioning of faith and religion fits in well with broader currents that saw the
      influence of the churches waning by the late 1960s and early 1970s in Canada.
      See Magda Fahrni and Robert Rutherdale, eds., *Creating Postwar Canada: Com-
      munity, Diversity and Dissent, 1945–75* (Vancouver: UBC Press, 2007).
122   "Parents Accentuate Rebellion, MD Says," *Globe and Mail*, 23 November 1967, W6.
123   Bruce West, "What Gap?," *Globe and Mail*, 1 August 1969, 23.
124   Tanner, *Teenage Troubles*, 27–28.
125   Michael Zuckerman, "The Paradox of American Adolescence," *Journal of the His-
      tory of Childhood and Youth* 4, no. 1 (Winter 2011): 14. However, this area does
      need to be explored more, along with the forms and expressions of childhood and
      adolescent rebellion.
126   Ibid., 42. I think the distinction between left-wing politics and radical movements
      should be made, as left-wing politics are often interested in making the Can-
      adian political framework better for working-class people while radical move-
      ments often promote different political and economic systems or major changes
      to existing structures, at the very least.
127   Roy Farquharson, in Scollard, *From Prairie Grass to City Sidewalks*, 58.
128   Dennis and Ruth Hunt, in ibid., 23.
129   Leon Kuczynski, ed., *Handbook of Dynamics in Parent-Child Relations* (Toronto:
      Sage, 2002), 21.
130   "More Complex Decisions: Social Worker in Favor of the Generation Gap and
      Wishes It Were Bigger," *Globe and Mail*, 18 April 1969, 10.
131   Dominic Wyse and Angela Hawtin, eds., *Children: A Multi-professional Perspec-
      tive* (London: Arnold Publishers, 2000), 61.
132   Mona Gleason, "Disciplining the Student Body: Schooling and the Construction
      of Canadian Children's Bodies, 1930–1960," *History of Education Quarterly* 41,
      no. 2 (Spring 2001): 196.
133   Michelle Macdonald, personal interview, Calgary, AB, 27 July 2011.
134   Allan Matthews, personal interview, Calgary, AB, 29 July 2011.
135   Donna McLaren, telephone interview, Peterborough, ON, 12 December 2011.
136   "Discipline," *Aberhart Advocate* 10, no. 11 (3 April 1969): 8–10.
137   Bryan D. Palmer, *Canada's 1960s: The Ironies of Identity in a Rebellious Era*
      (Toronto: University of Toronto Press, 2009).
138   "School Grads Raise Doubts on Education's Value," *Calgary Herald*, 4 July 1966,
      22.
139   "The Advocate Opens a Grievance Bureau," *Aberhart Advocate* 10, no. 11 (3 April
      1969): 1.
140   Zuckerman, "The Paradox of American Adolescence," 17.

141   There are some excellent books on the 1968 student uprisings. For a small sample, see Mitchell Abidor, *May Made Me: An Oral History of the 1968 Uprising in France* (Chico, CA: AK Press, 2018); and Ronald Fraser, *1968: A Student Generation in Revolt* (New York: Pantheon, 1988).

142   Holly V. Scott, *Younger Than That Now: The Politics of Age in the 1960s* (Amherst: University of Massachusetts Press, 2016).

143   "Students Are Revolting," *Aberhart Advocate* 11, no. 3 (1 November 1968): 7.

144   V. Del Buono, "Youth in Revolt," *World Affairs* 35 (March 1970): 5–6.

145   Canadian Gallup Poll, October 1968, no. 332, "Do You Think That Students Should or Should Not Have a Greater Say in the Running of University Affairs?," question 6.

146   "Student's Revolutionary Council," *Aberhart Advocate* 7, no. 2 (25 November 1964): 4.

147   Doug Owram, *Born at the Right Time: A History of the Baby Boom Generation* (Toronto: University of Toronto Press, 1996), 215.

148   Ibid., 217; and J. Ruddy, "Stop the World—They Want to Get Off," *Maclean's*, 1 November 1965, 20–22, 47.

149   "Press Club Letter," William Aberhart High School, 17 March 1970, William Aberhart Archives.

150   Bruce Wilson, personal interview, Calgary, AB, 28 July 2011.

151   Dr. James L. Goddard, "Should It Be Legalized? 'Soon We Will Know,'" *Life*, 31 October 1969, 34.

152   Marcel Martel, "Law versus Medicine: The Debate over Drug Use in the 1960s," in Fahrni and Rutherdale, *Creating Postwar Canada*, 315-333.

153   "Use of LSD among Average Teens Likely to Grow, Parents Warned," *Globe and Mail*, 4 January 1968, W4; Peter Whelan, "A Subculture of Users in High School: Girl, 16, Tells of 3 Tabs of Acid, Suicide Run, 18 Months in Drug World," *Globe and Mail*, 18 November 1969, 1; and Richard J. Needham, "Give Us This Day Our Daily Drug," *Globe and Mail*, 31 October 1969, 6.

154   For a three-part series based on Gallup data, see Jennifer Robison, "Decades of Drug Use: Data from the '60s and '70s," Gallup, accessed 2 December 2013, http://www.gallup.com/poll/6331/decades-drug-use-data-from-60s-70s.aspx.

155   "The Drug Problem," *Calgary Herald*, 2 October 1971, 4.

156   Tammy Simpson, telephone interview, Peterborough, ON, 24 November 2011.

157   Brian J. Low, *NFB Kids: Portrayals of Children by the National Film Board of Canada, 1939-1989* (Waterloo, ON: Wilfrid Laurier University Press, 2002), 222.

158   For a good documentary example, see Fergus McDonell, dir., *Borderline* (Ottawa: National Film Board of Canada, 1956).

159   There were also solutions offered based on new modern technologies in medicine to treat addicts, particularly young ones. For further reading, see Herbert Brean, "Children in Peril: 'Pushers' Are Selling Narcotics to Thousands of Teenagers," *Life*, 11 June 1951, 116–26.

160   "Juvenile Delinquency Detail Report for Year 1970," Chief of Police, Calgary Police Force, annual report, 1970, Calgary Police Service Archives.

161   Richard J. Needham, "Beards, Beatniks and Bare Feet," *Globe and Mail*, 8 August 1966, 6; and Bryan Wilson, "The Here and Now of Hippy Escapism," *Globe and Mail*, 31 March 1967, 7.

CONCLUSION ·

1   Paul A. Cohen, *History in Three Keys* (New York: Columbia University Press, 1998), 297.

2   While children and adolescents possess agency, we know that forces and influences operate on their lives and that many of these forces, be they state, institutional, familial, cultural, or social, were beyond young people's control.

3   Richard Harris, *Creeping Conformity: How Canada Became Suburban, 1900–1960* (Toronto: University of Toronto Press, 2004), 6, 15; Mark Clapson, *Suburban Century: Social Change and Urban Growth in England and the United States* (New York: Berg, 2003), 9, 10; and Kevin M. Kruse and Thomas J. Sugrue, *The New Suburban History* (Chicago: University of Chicago Press, 2006), 1–2.

4   Joy Parr, ed., *Childhood and Family in Canadian History* (Toronto: McClelland and Stewart, 1982), 7–8; Neil Sutherland, *Growing Up: Childhood in English Canada from the Great War to the Age of Television* (Toronto: University of Toronto Press, 1997), x; Steven Mintz, *Huck's Raft: A History of American Childhood* (Cambridge, MA: Belknap Press, 2004), 2; Joseph E. Illick, *American Childhoods* (Philadelphia: University of Pennsylvania Press, 2002), ix-x; Cynthia Comacchio, *The Dominion of Youth: Adolescence and the Making of Modern Canada* (Waterloo, ON: Wilfrid Laurier University Press, 2006), 211–12; Peter N. Stearns, *Childhood in World History* (New York: Routledge, 2006), 1–4; and Howard P. Chudacoff, *Children at Play: An American History* (New York: New York University Press, 2007), 18, 69.

5   Michael Zuckerman, "The Paradox of American Adolescence," *Journal of the History of Childhood and Youth* 4, no. 1 (Winter 2011): 13.

6   The timeframe for these physical changes is not static, though, as puberty, especially among girls, has been arriving three or four years earlier in recent years, relative to just a few decades ago.

7   Zuckerman, "The Paradox of American Adolescence," 13. For further reading, see Comacchio, *The Dominion of Youth*, 1–5.

8   See Dolores Hayden, *Building Suburbia: Green Fields and Urban Growth, 1820–2000* (New York: Pantheon, 2003), 3. She also adds that the suburbs across many time periods have been the landscape of the imagination for many Americans, and this applies equally to Canadians.

9   Valerie Raleigh Yow, *Recording Oral History: A Guide for the Humanities and Social Sciences,* 2nd ed. (Walnut Creek: Altamira, 2005); Studs Terkel, *Working: People Talk about What They Do All Day and How They Feel about What They Do* (New York: New Press, 1997); Joan Sangster, "Telling Our Stories: Feminist Debates and the Use of Oral History," *Women's History Review* 3, no. 1 (1994): 5–28; and Michael Frisch, *A Shared Authority: Essays on the Craft and Meaning of Oral and Public History* (Albany: State University of New York, 1990).

10   Alessandro Portelli, *The Death of Luigi Trastulli and Other Stories* (New York: State University of New York Press, 1991), 5.

11   For further reading on the use of oral history in a similar context, see Joan Sangster, "Telling Our Stories: Feminist Debates and the Use of Oral History," *Women's History Review* 3, no. 1 (1994): 5–28.

12   For a very good exploration of teenage bedrooms in the postwar era in an American context, see Jason Reid, "'My Room, Private! Keep Out! This Means You!':

Brief Overview of the Emergence of the Autonomous Teen Bedroom in Post-World War II America," *Journal of the History of Childhood and Youth* 5, no. 3 (2012): 419–39.

13   John R. Gillis, "Epilogue: The Islanding of Children-Reshaping the Mythical Landscapes of Childhood," in *Designing Modern Childhoods: History, Space, and the Material Culture of Children,* ed. Marta Gutman and Ning de Coninck-Smith (New Brunswick, NJ: Rutgers University Press, 2008), 328.

14   Mintz, *Huck's Raft,* ix.

15   Census of Canada, 1961.

16   Canadian Gallup Poll, June 1966, no. 319, "Someone Has Said That Fathers Should Be Top Boss of the Family in This Country: Do You Agree or Disagree with This?," question 11.

17   Doris Anderson, "If the Family's So Great, Help It," *Chatelaine,* February 1970.

18   Canadian Gallup Poll, November 1959, no. 279, "World Be Better, Worse in 10 Years?," question 6.

Bibliography

Archival Records
City of Calgary Archives
Children's Aid Department fonds
Social Services Department fonds

Glenbow Archives
Boys and Girls Clubs of Calgary fonds
Family Life Education Council of Calgary fonds
Social Service fonds
Vanier Institute of the Family fonds

Library and Archives Canada
Canadian Association of Social Workers fonds.
Canadian Council on Social Development fonds.

Newspapers and Magazines
The Albertan
Calgary Herald
Canadian Labour
Canadian Welfare
Chatelaine
Financial Post
The Gauntlet
Globe and Mail
Life
Maclean's
Scientific American Mind
Washington Post

School Newspaper and Yearbook Collections
Aberhart Advocate
Balmoral Junior High School Yearbooks
The Centralian
Central Collegiate Weeper
Crescent Heights Bugle
Lead Balloon

Oral Histories

*Baker, Mary. Personal Interview. Calgary, AB. 25 July 2011.
*Blair, Lisa. Personal Interview. Calgary, AB. 17 October 2011.
Cass, Doug. Personal Interview. Cochrane, AB. 2 June 2011.
*Davidson, Elizabeth. Telephone Interview. Peterborough, ON. 11 November 2011.
*Edward, Frank. Telephone Interview. Peterborough, ON. 8 December 2011.
Farquharson, Jim. Personal Interview. Calgary, AB. 17 October 2011.
Glidden, Wendy. Personal Interview. Calgary, AB. 2 August 2011.
Harris, Brent. Telephone Interview. Peterborough, ON. 9 December 2011.
Hayes, Lesley. Personal Interview. Calgary, AB. 26 July 2011.
*Johnstone, Sharon. Telephone Interview. Peterborough, ON. 8 December 2011.
*Macdonald, Michelle. Personal Interview. Calgary, AB. 27 July 2011.
Matthews, Allan. Personal Interview. Calgary, AB. 29 July 2011.
Matthews, Barry. Telephone Interview. Peterborough, ON. 31 October 2011.
McLaren, Donna. Telephone Interview. Peterborough, ON. 12 December 2011.
Rutz, Brian. Telephone Interview. Peterborough, ON. 12 December 2011.
*Simpson, Tammy. Telephone Interview. Peterborough, ON. 24 November 2011.
Wilson, Bruce. Personal Interview. Calgary, AB. 28 July 2011.
*Wright, William. Telephone Interview. Peterborough, ON. 4 November 2011.

* Pseudonym used for anonymity

Other Sources

Abidor, Mitchell. *May Made Me: An Oral History of the 1968 Uprising in France.* Chico, CA: AK Press, 2018.

Abrams, Lynn. *Oral History Theory.* Toronto: Routledge, 2010.

Adams, Mary Louise. *The Trouble with Normal: Postwar Youth and the Making of Heterosexuality.* Toronto: University of Toronto Press, 1997.

Adin, Mariah. *The Brooklyn Thrill-Kill Gang and the Great Comic Book Scare of the Fifties.* Santa Barbara, CA: Praeger, 2015.

Alberta. *Report of the Royal Commission on the Metropolitan Development of Calgary and Edmonton.* Edmonton: Province of Alberta, 1956.

Alexander, Kristine. "Can the Girl Guide Speak? The Perils and Pleasures of Looking for Children's Voices in Archival Research." *Jeunesse* 4, no. 1 (2012): 132–45.

Anderson, Kay. *Vancouver's Chinatown: Racial Discourse in Canada, 1875–1980.* Montreal/Kingston: McGill-Queen's University Press, 2006.

Ariès, Philippe. *Centuries of Childhood.* New York: Vintage, 1962.

Atwood, Margaret. *Cat's Eye.* Toronto: McClelland and Stewart, 1998.

Axelrod, Paul. *The Promise of Schooling: Education in Canada, 1800–1914.* Toronto: University of Toronto Press, 1997.

Bacher, John C. *Keeping to the Marketplace: The Evolution of Canadian Housing Policy.* Montreal/Kingston: McGill-Queen's University Press, 1993.

Backhouse, Constance. *Colour-Coded: A Legal History of Racism in Canada, 1900–1950.* Toronto: University of Toronto Press, 1999.

Baine, Richard A. *Calgary: An Urban Study.* Vancouver: Clarke, Irwin, 1973.

Baldwin, Andrew, Laura Cameron, and Audrey Kobayashi, eds. *Rethinking the Great White North: Race, Nature, and the Historical Geographies of Whiteness in Canada.* Vancouver: UBC Press, 2011.

Baldwin, Douglas O. *Teachers, Students and Pedagogy: Readings and Documents in the History of Canadian Education.* Markham, ON: Fitzhenry and Whiteside, 2008.

Baxandall, Rosalynn, and Elizabeth Ewen. *Picture Windows: How the Suburbs Happened.* New York: Basic Books, 2000.

Benoit, Cecilia. *Women, Work and Social Rights: Canada in Historical and Comparative Perspective.* Scarborough, ON: Prentice Hall Canada, 2000.

Berman, Marshall. *All That Is Solid Melts into Air: The Experience of Modernity.* Brooklyn, NY: Verso Press, 1983.

Berryman, Jack W. "From the Cradle to the Playing Field: America's Emphasis on Highly Organized Sports for Preadolescent Boys." *Journal of Sport History* 2, no. 2 (1975): 112–31.

Block, Tina. "'Toilet-Seat Prayers' and Imperious Fathers: Interrogating Religion and the Family in Oral Histories of the Postwar Pacific Northwest." *Oral History Forum* 29 (2009): 1–27.

Brookfield, Tarah. *Cold War Comforts: Canadian Women, Child Safety, and Global Insecurity.* Waterloo, ON: Wilfrid Laurier University Press, 2012.

Bryson, Bill. *The Life and Times of the Thunderbolt Kid.* New York: Broadway Books, 2006.

Burke, Sara Z., and Patrice Milewski. *Schooling in Transition: Readings in Canadian History of Education.* Toronto: University of Toronto Press, 2012.

Burtch, Andrew. "Armageddon on Tour: The 'On Guard, Canada!' Civil Defence Convoy and Responsible Citizenship in the Early Cold War." *International Journal* 61, no. 3 (Summer 2006): 735–56.

Canada. "History of Canada's Food Guides from 1942 to 1972." http: //www.hc-sc.gc.ca/fn-an/food-guide-aliment/context/fg_history-histoire_ga-eng.php.

Carrigan, D. Owen. Juvenile Delinquency in Canada: A History. Toronto: Irwin, 1998.

Chambers, Jim. *Recollections: A Baby Boomer's Memories of the Fabulous Fifties.* Morrisville, NC: Lulu Press, 2009.

Chenier, Elise. *Strangers in Our Midst: Sexual Deviancy in Postwar Ontario.* Toronto: University of Toronto Press, 2008.

Chudacoff, Howard P. *Children at Play: An American History.* New York: New York University Press, 2007.

———. *How Old Are You? Age Consciousness in American Culture.* Princeton, NJ: Princeton University Press, 1992.

City of Calgary. *Calgary: Celebrating 100 Years of Parks.* Calgary: City of Calgary, 2010.

———. *Motel Village/Banff Trail Area Redevelopment Plan – Northwest LRT Alignment Evaluation Study.* Calgary: City of Calgary, 1984.

———. *Municipal Manual.* Calgary: City of Calgary, 1950, 1960, 1970.

———. Department of Youth Research Division. *Recreation in the City of Calgary: A Survey of Interests, Activities and Opportunities.* Calgary: City of Calgary, 1966.

Clapp, James A. "Growing Up Urban: The City, the Cinema and American Youth." *Journal of Popular Culture* 40, no. 4 (2007): 601–29.

Clapson, Mark. *Suburban Century: Social Change and Urban Growth in England and the United States.* New York: Berg, 2003.

Clark, S.D. *The Suburban Society.* Toronto: University of Toronto Press, 1966.

Cohan, Steven. *Masked Men: Masculinity and the Movies in the Fifties.* Bloomington: Indiana University Press, 1997.

Cohen, Paul A. *History in Three Keys.* New York: Columbia University Press, 1998.

Coles, Robert. *The Youngest Parents.* New York: W.W. Norton, 1997.

Comacchio, Cynthia. *The Dominion of Youth: Adolescence and the Making of Modern Canada.* Waterloo, ON: Wilfrid Laurier University Press, 2006.

Comacchio, Cynthia, Janet Golden, and George Weisz, eds. *Healing the World's Children: Interdisciplinary Perspectives on Child Health in the Twentieth Century.* Montreal/Kingston: McGill-Queen's University Press, 2008

Cook, Daniel Thomas. *The Commodification of Childhood: The Children's Clothing Industry and the Rise of the Child Consumer.* Durham, NC: Duke University Press, 2004.

Coontz, Stephanie. *The Way We Never Were: American Families and the Nostalgia Trap.* New York: Basic Books, 2016.

Coward, Harold. *Calgary's Growth: Bane or Boon?* Calgary: University of Calgary Institute for the Humanities, 1981.

Craft, Aimee. *A Knock on the Door: The Essential History of Residential Schools from the Truth and Reconciliation Commission of Canada.* Winnipeg: University of Manitoba Press, 2015.

Cresswell, Tim. *Place: A Short Introduction.* Toronto: Wiley-Blackwell, 2014.

Dancey, Daisy. "The Banff Trail Kindergarten." In *From Prairie Grass to City Sidewalks* edited by Rose Scollard, 43-44. Calgary: Banff Trail Seniors, 1999.Davies, Wayne K.D., and Ivan J. Townshend. "How Do Community Associations Vary? The Structure of Community Associations in Calgary, Alberta." *Urban Studies* 31, no. 10 (1994): 1737–61.

Dempsey, Hugh. *Calgary: Spirit of the West.* Calgary: Glenbow/Fifth House, 1994.

Des, M. "'Dare to Free Yourself': The Red Tide, Feminism, and High School Activism in the Early 1970s." *Journal of the History of Childhood and Youth* 7, no. 2 (2014): 295–319.

Dobriner, William M. *Class in Suburbia.* Englewood Cliffs, NJ: Prentice Hall, 1963.

Donaldson, Scott. *The Suburban Myth.* New York: Columbia University Press, 1969.

Dufour, Andre. *Histoire de l'éducation au Québec.* Montreal: Boreal, 1997.

Dummitt, Christopher. *The Manly Modern: Masculinity in Postwar Canada.* Vancouver: UBC Press, 2007.

Ekirch, Roger A. *At Day's Close: Night in Times Past.* New York: Norton, 2005.

Elkin, Frederick. *The Family in Canada.* Ottawa: Vanier Institute of the Family, 1964.

Faderman, Lillian. *Odd Girls and Twilight Lovers: A History of Lesbian Life in Twentieth-Century America.* Toronto: Penguin Books, 1991.

Fahrni, Magda, and Robert Rutherdale, eds. *Creating Postwar Canada: Community, Diversity and Dissent, 1945–75.* Vancouver: UBC Press, 2008.

Fass, Paula S. *The End of American Childhood.* Princeton, NJ: Princeton University Press, 2016.

Fass, Paula S., and Michael Grossberg, eds. *Reinventing Childhood after World War II.* Philadelphia: University of Pennsylvania Press, 2012.

Fass, Paula S., and Mary Mason, eds. *Childhood in America.* New York: New York University Press, 2000.

Finkel, Alvin. *Our Lives: Canada after 1945.* 2nd ed. Toronto: Lorimer, 1997.

———. *The Social Credit Phenomenon.* Toronto: University of Toronto Press, 1989.

———. *Social Policy and Practice in Canada: A History.* Waterloo, ON: Wilfrid Laurier University Press, 2006.

Flavell, Dave. *Community and the Human Spirit: Oral Histories from Montreal's Point St. Charles, Griffintown and Goose Village.* Ottawa: Petra Books, 2014.

Fogelson, Robert M. *Bourgeois Nightmares: Suburbia, 1870–1930*. New Haven, CT: Yale University Press, 2005.

Foran, Max. *Calgary: An Illustrated History*. Toronto: James Lorimer, 1978.

Forman-Brunell, Miriam. *Babysitting: An American History*. New York: New York University Press, 2009.

Frankenberg, Ruth. *White Women, Race Matters: The Social Construction of Whiteness*. Minneapolis: University of Minnesota Press, 1993.

Fraser, Ronald. *1968: A Student Generation in Revolt*. New York: Pantheon, 1988.

Friedan, Betty. *The Feminine Mystique*. New York: Norton, 1963.

Frisch, Michael. *A Shared Authority: Essays on the Craft and Meaning of Oral and Public History*. Albany: State University of New York Press, 1990.

Gans, Herbert J. *The Levittowners: Ways of Life and Politics in a New Suburban Community*. New York: Pantheon Books, 1967.

Giddens, Anthony. *Modernity and Self-Identity: Self and Society in the Late Modern Age*. Redwood City, CA: Stanford University Press, 1991.

Gidney, R.D. *From Hope to Harris:The Reshaping of Ontario's Schools*. Toronto: University of Toronto Press, 1999.

Gillis, John R. "Epilogue: The Islanding of Children-Reshaping the Mythical Landscapes of Childhood." In *Designing Modern Childhoods: History, Space, and the Material Culture of Children*, edited by Marta Gutman and Ning de Coninck-Smith, 316–330. New Brunswick, NJ: Rutgers University Press, 2008.

Gilman, Sander. *Fat: A Cultural History of Obesity*. Cambridge: Polity, 2008.

Gilman, Sander L., and Xun Zhou, eds. *Smoke: A Global History of Smoking*. London: Reaktion, 2004.

Gleason, Mona. "Disciplining the Student Body: Schooling and the Construction of Canadian Children's Bodies, 1930 to 1960." *History of Education Quarterly* 41, no. 2 (Spring 2001): 189–215.

———. "Embodied Negotiations: Children's Bodies and Historical Change in Canada, 1930–1960." *Journal of Canadian Studies* 34, no. 1 (1999): 112–38.

———. *Normalizing the Ideal: Psychology, Schooling and the Family in Postwar Canada*. Toronto: University of Toronto Press, 1999.

———. *Small Matters: Canadian Children in Sickness and Health, 1900–1940*. Montreal/Kingston: McGill-Queen's University Press, 2013.

Grant, George. *Lament for a Nation*. Toronto: McClelland and Stewart, 1970.

Greig, Christopher J. *Ontario Boys: Masculinity and the Idea of Boyhood in Postwar Ontario, 1945–1960*. Waterloo, ON: Wilfrid Laurier University Press, 2014.

Grinder, Barbara. *Local Colour: A Commemoration of the 75th Anniversary of the Amalgamated Transit Union Local 583*. Calgary: Amalgamated Transit Union, 1990).

Gutman, Marta. "The Physical Spaces of Childhood." In *The Routledge History of Childhood in the Western World*, edited by Paula S. Fass, 249–266. New York: Routledge, 2015.

Gutman, Marta, and Ning de Coninck-Smith, eds. *Designing Modern Childhoods: History, Space and the Material Culture of Childhood*. Piscataway, NJ: Rutgers University Press, 2008.

Hall, Stuart. "Encoding and Decoding in Television Discourse." CCCS Stencilled Paper 7, University of Birmingham, 1973.

Harasym, Donald George. "The Planning of New Residential Areas in Calgary." Master's thesis. University of Alberta, 1975.

Harris, Richard. *Creeping Conformity: How Canada Became Suburban, 1900–1960.* Toronto: University of Toronto Press, 2004.

———. *Unplanned Suburbs: Toronto's American Tragedy, 1900 to 1950.* Baltimore, MD: Johns Hopkins University Press, 1996.

Harris, Richard, and Michael E. Mercier. "How Healthy Were the Suburbs?" *Journal of Urban History* 31, no. 6 (September 2005): 767–98.

Hartman, Andrew. *Education and the Cold War: The Battle for the American School.* New York: Palgrave Macmillan, 2008.

Hatcher, Colin K., and Tom Schwarzkopf. *Calgary's Electric Transit.* Montreal: Railfare DC Books, 2009.

Hayden, Dolores. *Building Suburbia: Green Fields and Urban Growth, 1820–2000.* New York: Pantheon, 2003.

Helleiner, Jane. "'The Right Kind of Children': Childhood, Gender and 'Race' in Canadian Postwar Political Discourse." *Anthropologica* 43, no. 2 (2001): 143–52.

Hennessy, Rosemary, and Chrys Ingraham. *Materialist Feminism: A Reader in Class, Difference, and Women's Lives.* New York: Routledge, 1997.

Herrington, Susan. "Muscle Memory: Reflections on the North American Schoolyard." In *Multiple Lenses, Multiple Images: Perspectives on the Child across Time, Space, and Disciplines,* edited by Hillel Goelman, Sheila K. Marshall, and Sally Ross, 91–108. Toronto: University of Toronto Press, 2004.

Holloway, Sarah L., and Gill Valentine, eds. *Children's Geographies.* New York: Routledge, 2000.

Iacovetta, Franca. *Gatekeepers: Reshaping Immigrant Lives in Postwar Canada.* Toronto: Between the Lines, 2006.

———. "Gossip, Contest, and Power in the Making of Suburban Bad Girls: Toronto, 1945–60." *Canadian Historical Review* 80, no. 4 (December 1999): 585–625.

Iacovetta, Franca, and Mariana Valverde, eds. *Gender Conflicts: New Essays in Women's History.* Toronto: University of Toronto Press, 1992.

Illick, Joseph E. *American Childhoods.* Philadelphia: University of Pennsylvania Press, 2002.

Jackson, Kenneth T. *Crabgrass Frontier: The Suburbanization of the United States.* Toronto: Oxford University Press, 1985.

Jacobs, Jane. *The Death and Life of Great American Cities.* 2nd ed. New York: Vintage, 1992.

Janovicek, Nancy, and Joy Parr, eds. *Histories of Canadian Children and Youth.* Toronto: Oxford University Press, 2003.

Jennissen, Therese, and Colleen Lundy. *One Hundred Years of Social Work: A History of the Profession in Canada, 1900–2000.* Waterloo, ON: Wilfrid Laurier University Press, 2011.

Kach, Nick, and Kas Mazurek. *Exploring Our Educational Past: Schooling in the Northwest Territories and Alberta.* Calgary: Detselig, 1992.

Kelly, Ninette, and Michael Trebilcock. *Making of a Mosaic: A History of Canadian Immigration Policy.* 2nd ed. Toronto: University of Toronto Press, 2010.

Kenyon, Maria Amy. *Dreaming Suburbia: Detroit and the Production of Postwar Space and Culture.* Detroit, MI: Wayne State University Press, 2004.

Kinsman, Gary, D.K. Buse, and Mercedes Steedman. *Whose National Security? Canadian State Surveillance and the Creation of Enemies.* Toronto: Between the Lines, 2000.

Knowles, Valerie. *Strangers at Our Gates*. Rev. ed. Toronto: Dundurn, 2007.

Kordas, Ann Marie. *The Politics of Childhood in Cold War America*. Brookfield, VT: Pickering and Chatto, 2013.

Korinek, Valerie J. *Roughing It in the Suburbs: Reading Chatelaine Magazine in the Fifties and Sixties*. Toronto: University of Toronto Press, 2000.

Kruse, Kevin M. *White Flight: Atlanta and the Making of Modern Conservatism*. Princeton, NJ: Princeton University Press, 2007.

Kruse, Kevin M., and Thomas J. Sugrue, eds. *The New Suburban History*. Chicago: University of Chicago Press, 2006.

Kuczynski, Leon, ed. *Handbook of Dynamics in Parent-Child Relations*. Toronto: Sage, 2002.

Kushner, David. *Levittown: Two Families, One Tycoon and the Fight for Civil Rights in America's Legendary Suburb*. New York: Walker and Company, 2009.

Langford, Tom. *Alberta's Day Care Controversy: From 1908 to 2009 and Beyond*. Edmonton: Athabasca University Press, 2011.

Lareau, Annette. *Unequal Childhoods: Class, Race, and Family Life*. Berkeley: University of California Press, 2003.

Lefebvre, Henri. *The Production of Space*. New York: Wiley-Blackwell, 1992.

Livingstone, Sonia. "Half a Century of Television in the Lives of Our Children." *Annals of the American Academy of Political and Social Science* 625 (2009): 151–63.

Low, Brian J. *NFB Kids: Portrayals of Children by the National Film Board of Canada, 1939–89*. Waterloo, ON: Wilfrid Laurier University Press, 2002.

Low, Setha. *Behind the Gates: Life, Security, and the Pursuit of Happiness in Fortress America*. New York: Routledge, 2003.

Lupart, Judy, and Charles Webber, "Canadian Schools in Transition: Moving from Dual Education Systems to Inclusive Schools." *Exceptionality Education International* 22 (2012): 8–37.

Malone, Susan Kohl. "Early to Bed, Early to Rise? An Exploration of Adolescent Sleep Hygiene Practices." *Journal of School Nursing* 27, no. 5 (October 2011): 348–54.

Marshall, Dominique. *The Social Origins of the Welfare State*. Waterloo, ON: Wilfrid Laurier University Press, 2006.

Martel, Marcel. "Law versus Medicine: The Debate over Drug Use in the 1960s." In *Creating Postwar Canada: Community, Diversity and Dissent, 1945–75*, edited by Magda Fahrni and Robert Rutherdale, 315–333. Vancouver: UBC Press, 2008

Martinson, Tom. *American Dreamscape: The Pursuit of Happiness in Postwar Suburbia*. New York: Carroll and Graf, 2000.

Mason, Mary Ann. "Whose Child? Parenting and Custody in the Postwar Period." In *Reinventing Childhood after World War II*, edited by Paula S. Fass and Michael Grossberg, 68–83. Philadelphia: University of Pennsylvania Press, 2012.

May, Elaine Tyler. *Homeward Bound: American Families in the Cold War Era*. New York: Basic Books, 2008.

McDonell, Fergus, dir. *Borderline*. Ottawa: National Film Board of Canada, 1956.

McIntosh, Robert. "Constructing the Child: New Approaches to the History of Childhood in Canada." *Acadiensis* 28, no. 2 (Spring 1999): 126–40.

McLaren, Angus. *Our Own Master Race: Eugenics in Canada, 1885–1945*. Toronto: University of Toronto Press, 1990.

McLuhan, Marshall. *Understanding Media: The Extensions of Man*. Cambridge, MA: MIT Press, 1994.

Miedema, Gary. *For Canada's Sake: Public Religion, Centennial Celebrations, and the Re-making of Canada in the 1960s.* Montreal/Kingston: McGill-Queen's University Press, 2005.

Miller, J.R. *Shingwauk's Vision: A History of Native Residential Schools.* Toronto: University of Toronto Press, 1996.

Miller, Laura J. "Family Togetherness and the Suburban Ideal." *Sociological Forum* 10, no. 3 (1995): 393–418.

Milloy, John S. *A National Crime: The Canadian Government and the Residential School System, 1879–1986.* Winnipeg: University of Manitoba Press, 1999.

Mina, Noula. "Taming and Training Greek 'Peasant Girls' and the Gendered Politics of Whiteness in Postwar Canada: Canadian Bureaucrats and Immigrant Domestics, 1950s–1960s." *Canadian Historical Review* 94, no. 4 (December 2013): 514–39.

Mintz, Steven. *Huck's Raft: A History of American Childhood.* Cambridge, MA: Belknap Press, 2005.

Morton, Suzanne. *Ideal Surroundings: Domestic Life in a Working-Class Suburb in the 1920s.* Toronto: University of Toronto Press, 1995.

Mumford, Lewis. *The City in History: Its Origins, Its Transformations, and Its Prospects.* New York: Harcourt, Brace and World, 1961.

Myers, Tamara. *Caught: Montreal's Modern Girls and the Law, 1869–1945.* Toronto: University of Toronto Press, 2006.

———. "From Disciplinarian to Coach: Policing of Youth in Post-World War II Canada." Paper presented at European Social Science History Conference, Lisbon, Portugal, March 2008.

———. "Nocturnal Disorder and the Curfew Solution: A History of Juvenile Sundown Regulations in Canada." In *Lost Kids: Vulnerable Children and Youth in Twentieth-Century Canada and the United States,* edited by Mona Gleason, Tamara Myers, Leslie Paris, and Veronica Strong-Boag, 95–114. Vancouver: UBC Press, 2010.

Myers, Tamara, and Mary Anne Poutanen. "Cadets, Curfews, and Compulsory Schooling: Mobilizing Anglophone Children in WW II Montreal." *Social History* 38, no. 76 (October 2005): 367–97.

Osborne, Brian. "Landscapes, Memory, Monuments, and Commemoration: Putting Identity in its Place." *Canadian Ethnic Studies* 33, no. 3 (2001): 39–77.

Owram, Doug. *Born at the Right Time: A History of the Baby Boom Generation.* Toronto: University of Toronto Press, 1996.

Palmer, Bryan D. *Canada's 1960s: The Ironies of Identity in a Rebellious Era.* Toronto: University of Toronto Press, 2009.

———. *Cultures of Darkness: Night Travels in the Histories of Transgression.* New York: Monthly Review Press, 2000.

———. *Working-Class Experience: Rethinking the History of Canadian Labour, 1800–1991.* 2nd ed. Toronto: McClelland and Stewart, 1992.

Parr, Joy, ed. *Childhood and Family in Canadian History.* Toronto: McClelland and Stewart, 1982.

Perks, Robert, and Alistair Thomson, eds. *The Oral History Reader.* New York: Routledge, 2016.

Pickles, Katie. *Female Imperialism and the National Identity: Imperial Order Daughters of Empire.* Manchester: Manchester University Press, 2009.

Portelli, Allessandro. *The Death of Luigi Trastulli and Other Stories: Form and Meaning in Oral History.* Albany: State University of New York Press, 1991.

———. "What Makes Oral History Different?" In *The Oral History Reader,* edited by Robert Perks and Alistair Thomson, 48–58. New York: Routledge, 2016.

Prang, Margaret. "'The Girl God Would Have Me Be': The Canadian Girls in Training, 1915–39." *Canadian Historical Review* 66, no. 2 (1985): 154–84.

Purdy, Sean. "'Ripped Off' by the System: Housing Policy, Poverty, and Territorial Stigmatization in Regent Park Housing Project, 1951–1991." *Labour/Le Travail* 52 (2003): 45–108.

Queen, Amanda. "The Worm." In *From Prairie Grass to City Sidewalks,* edited by Rose Scollard, 50. Calgary: Banff Trail Seniors, 1995.

Rappoport, Leon. *How We Eat: Appetite, Culture, and the Psychology of Food.* Toronto: ECW Press, 2003.

Razack, Sherene, ed. *Race, Space and the Law: Unmapping a White Settler Society.* Toronto: Between the Lines, 2002.

Reid, Jason. "'My Room, Private! Keep Out! This Means You!': Brief Overview of the Emergence of the Autonomous Teen Bedroom in Post-World War II America." *Journal of the History of Childhood and Youth* 5, no. 3 (2012): 419–39.

Reimer, Mavis. *Home Words: Discourses on Children's Literature in Canada.* Waterloo, ON: Wilfrid Laurier University Press, 2007.

Risse, Guenter. *Mending Bodies, Saving Souls: A History of Hospitals.* Toronto: Oxford University Press, 1999.

Ritchie, Donald A. *Doing Oral History.* Toronto: Oxford University Press, 2015.

Rollings-Magnusson, Sandra. *Heavy Burdens on Small Shoulders: The Labour of Pioneer Children on the Canadian Prairies.* Edmonton: University of Alberta Press, 2009.

Rollwagen, Katharine. "Classrooms for Consumer Society: Practical Education and Secondary School Reform in Post-Second World War Canada." *Historical Studies in Education* 28, no. 1 (2016): 32–52.

Rosenberg, Charles E. *The Care of Strangers: The Rise of America's Hospital System.* Baltimore, MD: Hopkins Fulfillment Service, 1995.

Rushton, J. Philippe. *Race, Evolution and Behavior: A Life History Perspective.* Huron, MI: Charles Darwin Research Institute, 1996.

Rutherdale, Robert. "Just Nostalgic Family Men? Off-the-Job Family Time, Providing, and Oral Histories of Fatherhood in Postwar Canada, 1945–1975." *Oral History Forum* 29 (2009): 1–19.

Rutherford, Paul. "Researching Television History: Prime Time Canada, 1952–1967." *Archivaria* 20 (Summer 1985): 79–93.

Saegert, Susan. "Masculine Cities and Feminine Suburbs: Polarized Ideas, Contradictory Realities." *Signs* 5, no. 3 (Spring 1980): 96–111.

Sandwell, Ruth. *To the Past: History Education, Public Memory, and Citizenship in Canada.* Toronto: University of Toronto Press, 2006.

Sangster, Joan. *Earning Respect: The Lives of Working Women in Small-Town Ontario, 1920–1960.* Toronto: University of Toronto Press, 1995.

———. *Girl Trouble: Female Delinquency in English Canada.* Toronto: Between the Lines, 2002.

———. "Telling Our Stories: Feminist Debates and the Use of Oral History." *Women's History Review* 3, no. 1 (1994): 5–28.

———. *Transforming Labour: Women and Work in Postwar Canada.* Toronto: University of Toronto Press, 2010.

Satzewich, Vic. *Racism and the Incorporation of Foreign Labour.* New York: Routledge, 1991.

Schlosser, Eric. *Fast Food Nation*. Boston: Houghton Mifflin, 2001.

Scollard, Rose, ed. *From Prairie Grass to City Sidewalks*. Calgary: Banff Trail Seniors, 1999.

Scott, Holly V. *Younger Than That Now: The Politics of Age in the 1960s*. Amherst: University of Massachusetts Press, 2016.

Sedikides, Constantine, Tim Wildschut, Jamie Arndt, and Clay Routledge. "Nostalgia: Past, Present, and Future." *Current Directions in Psychological Science* 17, no. 5 (October 2008): 304–7.

Seeley, John R., R. Alexander Sim, and E.W. Loosley. *Crestwood Heights: A Study of the Culture of Suburban Life*. Toronto: University of Toronto Press, 1963.

Sewell, John. *The Shape of the City: Toronto Struggles with Modern Planning*. Toronto: University of Toronto Press, 1993.

Shantz, Mary Ann. "Centring the Suburb, Focusing on the Family: Calgary's Anglican and Alliance Churches, 1945–1969." *Social History* 42, no. 84 (2009): 423–46.

Shiels, Bob. *Calgary*. Calgary: Calgary Herald, 1974.

Sicart, Miguel. *Play Matters*. Cambridge, MA: MIT Press, 2014.

Skoreyko, George and Elaine. "The Rooster in the Garage and Other Wild Tales. In *From Prairie Grass to City Sidewalks,* edited by Rose Scollard, 75-76. Calgary: Banff Trail Seniors, 1995.

Sleight, Simon. *Young People and the Shaping of Public Space in Melbourne, 1870–1914*. Farnham: Ashgate, 2013.

Smeaton, Bob, dir. *Festival Express*. New York City, NY: THINK Film, 2003.

Speer Lemisko, Lynn, and Kurt W. Clausen. "Connections, Contarieties, and Convolutions: Curriculum and Pedagogic Reform in Alberta and Ontario, 1930–1955." *Canadian Journal of Education* 29, 4 (2006): 1097–1126.

Spigel, Lynn. *Make Room for TV: Television and the Family Ideal in Postwar America*. Chicago: University of Chicago Press, 1992.

Stamp, Robert. *Suburban Modern: Postwar Dreams in Calgary*. Victoria: Touchwood, 2004.

Stearns, Peter N. *Childhood in World History*. New York: Routledge, 2006.

Stevens, Rosemary. *In Sickness and in Wealth: American Hospitals in the Twentieth Century*. Toronto: Harper Collins, 1990.

Stilgoe, John R. *Borderland: Origins of the American Suburb, 1820–1939*. New Haven, CT: Yale University Press, 1988.

Stingel, Janine. *Social Discredit: Anti-semitism, Social Credit and the Jewish Response*. Montreal/Kingston: McGill-Queen's University Press, 2000.

Strong-Boag, Veronica. "Home Dreams: Women and the Suburban Experiment in Canada, 1945–60." *Canadian Historical Review* 72, no. 4 (1991): 471–504.

———. *Janey Canuck: Women in Canada, 1919–1939*. Ottawa: Canadian Historical Association, 1994.

———. *The New Day Recalled: Lives of Girls and Women in English Canada, 1919–1939*. Toronto: Copp Clark Pitman, 1988.

Sutherland, Neil. *Children in English-Canadian Society: Framing the Twentieth-Century Consensus*. Toronto: University of Toronto Press, 1976.

———. *Growing Up: Childhood in English Canada from the Great War to the Age of Television*. Toronto: University of Toronto Press, 1997.

———. "The Triumph of 'Formalism': Elementary Schooling in Vancouver from the 1920s to the 1960s." *BC Studies* 69, no. 70 (1986): 175–210.

———. "'We Always Had Things to Do': The Paid and Unpaid Work of Anglophone Children between the 1920s and the 1960s." *Labour/Le Travail* 25 (Spring 1990): 105–41.

Tanner, Julian. *Teenage Troubles: Youth and Deviance in Canada*. 3rd ed. Toronto: Oxford University Press, 2010.

Terkel, Studs. *Working: People Talk about What They Do All Day and How They Feel about What They Do*. New York: New Press, 1997.

Thiel-Stern, Shayla. *From the Dance Hall to Facebook: Teen Girls, Mass Media, and Moral Panic in the United States, 1905–2010*. Boston: University of Massachusetts Press, 2014.

Thorn, Brian. *From Left to Right: Maternalism and Women's Political Activism in Postwar Canada*. Vancouver: UBC Press, 2016.

Tienda, Marta, and William Julius Wilson, eds. *Youth in Cities: A Cross-national Perspective*. New York: Cambridge University Press, 2002.

Tillotson, Shirley. *The Public at Play: Gender and the Politics of Recreation in Postwar Ontario*. Toronto: University of Toronto Press, 2000.

Tsipursky, Gleb. *Socialist Fun: Youth, Consumption, and State-Sponsored Popular Culture in the Soviet Union, 1945–1970*. Pittsburgh, PA: University of Pittsburgh Press, 2016.

Veevers, J.E., and E.M. Gee. *Religiously Unaffiliated Canadians: Demographic and Social Correlates of Secularization – Final Report*. n.p.: 1988.

Vitale, Patrick. "A Model Suburb for Model Suburbanites: Order, Control, and Expertise in Thorncrest Village." *Urban History Review* 40, no. 1 (Fall 2011): 41–55.

Volk, Anthony. "The Evolution of Childhood." *Journal of the History of Childhood and Youth* 4, no. 3 (Fall 2011): 470–94.

von Heyking, Amy. Creating Citizens: *History and Identity in Alberta's Schools, 1905 to 1980*. Calgary: University of Calgary Press, 2006.

Vosko, Leah F. *Precarious Employment: Understanding Labour Market Insecurity in Canada*. Montreal/Kingston: McGill-Queen's University Press, 2005.

———. *Temporary Work: The Gendered Rise of a Precarious Employment Relationship*. Toronto: University of Toronto Press, 2000.

Walden, Keith. *Becoming Modern in Toronto: The Industrial Exhibition and the Shaping of Late Victorian Toronto Culture*. Toronto: University of Toronto Press, 1997.

Walker, Barrington. *The History of Immigration and Racism in Canada: Essential Readings*. Toronto: Canadian Scholars Press, 2008.

Wall, Sharon. *The Nurture of Nature: Childhood, Antimodernism, and Ontario Summer Camps, 1920–55*. Vancouver: UBC Press, 2010.

Whitaker, Reg, and Gary Marcuse. *Cold War Canada: The Making of a National Insecurity State, 1945–1957*. Toronto: University of Toronto Press, 1994.

Whyte, William. *The Organization Man*. Toronto: Simon and Schuster, 1956.

Wyden, Peter. *Suburbia's Coddled Kids*. Garden City, NY: Doubleday, 1962.

Wyse, Dominic, and Angela Hawtin, eds. *Children: A Multi-professional Perspective*. London: Arnold, 2000.

Yow, Valerie. *Recording Oral History: A Guide for the Humanities and Social Sciences*. 2nd ed. Walnut Creek, CA: Altamira, 2005.

Zuckerman, Michael. "The Paradox of American Adolescence." *Journal of the History of Childhood and Youth* 4, no. 1 (Winter 2011): 13–25.

Index

Books in the Studies in Childhood and Family in Canada Series
Published by Wilfrid Laurier University Press

Making Do: Women, Family, and Home in Montreal during the Great Depression by Denyse Baillargeon, translated by Yvonne Klein • 1999 • xii + 232 pp. • ISBN 978-0-88920-326-6

Children in English-Canadian Society: Framing the Twentieth-Century Consensus by Neil Sutherland with a new foreword by Cynthia Comacchio • 2000 • xxiv + 336 pp. • illus. • ISBN 978-0-88920-351-8

Love Strong as Death: Lucy Peel's Canadian Journal, 1833–1836 edited by J.I. Little • 2001 • x + 229 pp. • illus. • ISBN 978-0-88920-389-1

The Challenge of Children's Rights for Canada by Katherine Covell and R. Brian Howe • 2001 • viii + 244 pp. • ISBN 978-0-88920-380-8

NFB Kids: Portrayals of Children by the National Film Board of Canada, 1939–1989 by Brian J. Low • 2002 • vi + 288 pp. • illus. • ISBN 978-0-88920-386-0

Something to Cry About: An Argument against Corporal Punishment of Children in Canada by Susan M. Turner • 2002 • xx + 318 pp. • ISBN 978-0-88920-382-2

Freedom to Play: We Made Our Own Fun edited by Norah L. Lewis • 2002 • xiv + 210 pp. • ISBN 978-0-88920-406-5

The Dominion of Youth: Adolescence and the Making of Modern Canada, 1920–1950 by Cynthia Comacchio • 2006 • x + 302 pp. • illus. • ISBN-13: 978-0-88920-488-1

Evangelical Balance Sheet: Character, Family, and Business in Mid-Victorian Nova Scotia by B. Anne Wood • 2006 • xxx + 198 pp. • illus. • ISBN 978-0-88920-500-0

The Social Origins of the Welfare State by Dominique Marshall, translated by Nicola Doone Danby • 2006 • xx + 278 pp. • ISBN 978-0-88920-452-2

A Question of Commitment: Children's Rights in Canada edited by R. Brian Howe and Katherine Covell • 2007 • xiv + 442 pp. • ISBN 978-1-55458-003-3

Taking Responsibility for Children edited by Samantha Brennan and Robert Noggle • 2007 • xxii + 188 pp. • ISBN 978-1-55458-015-6

Home Words: Discourses of Children's Literature in Canada edited by Mavis Reimer • 2008 • xx + 280 pp. • illus. • ISBN 978-1-55458-016-3

Depicting Canada's Children edited by Loren Lerner • 2009 • xxvi + 442 pp. • illus. • ISBN 978-1-55458-050-7

Babies for the Nation: The Medicalization of Motherhood in Quebec, 1910–1970 by Denyse Baillargeon, translated by W. Donald Wilson • 2009 • xiv + 328 pp. • illus. • ISBN 978-1-5548-058-3

The One Best Way? Breastfeeding History, Politics, and Policy in Canada by Tasnim Nathoo and Aleck Ostry • 2009 • xvi + 262 pp. • illus. • ISBN 978-1-55458-147-4

Fostering Nation? Canada Confronts Its History of Childhood Disadvantage by Veronica Strong-Boag • 2011 • x + 302 pp. • ISBN 978-1-55458-337-9

Cold War Comforts: Maternalism, Child Safety, and Global Insecurity, 1945–1975 by Tarah Brookfield • 2012 • xiv + 292 pp. • illus. • ISBN 978-1-55458-623-3

Ontario Boys: Masculinity and the Idea of Boyhood in Postwar Ontario, 1945–1960 by Christopher Greig • 2014 • xxviii + 184 pp. • ISBN 978-1-55458-900-5

A Brief History of Women in Quebec by Denyse Baillargeon, translated by W. Donald Wilson • 2014 • xii + 272 pp. • ISBN 978-1-55458-950-0

With Children and Youth: Emerging Theories and Practices in Child and Youth Care Work edited by Kiaras Gharabaghi, Hans A. Skott-Myhre, and Mark Krueger • 2014 • xiv + 222 pp. • ISBN 978-1-55458-966-1

Abuse or Punishment? Violence Towards Children in Quebec Families, 1850–1969 by Marie-Aimée Cliche, translated by W. Donald Wilson • 2014 • xii + 396 pp. • ISBN 978-1-77712-063-0

Girls, Texts, Cultures edited by Clare Bradford and Mavis Reimer • 2015 • x + 334 pp. • ISBN 978-1-77112-020-3

Engendering Transnational Voices: Studies in Families, Work and Identities edited by Guida Man and Rina Cohen • 2015 • xii + 344 pp. • ISBN 978-1-77112-112-5

Growing Up in Armyville: Canada's Military Families during the Afghanistan Mission by Deborah Harrison and Patrizia Albanese • 2016 • xii + 250 pp. • ISBN 978-1-77112-234-4

The Challenge of Children's Rights for Canada, Second Edition by Katherine Covell, R. Brian Howe, and J.C. Blokhuis • 2018 • x + 248 pp. • ISBN 978-1-77112-355-6

A Question of Commitment: The Status of Children in Canada, Second Edition edited by Thomas Waldock • 2020 • xiv + 364 pp. • ISBN 978-1-177112-405-8

Boom Kids: Growing Up in the Calgary Suburbs, 1950–70 by James A. Onusko • 2021 • viii + 250 pp. • ISBN 978-1-77112-498-0